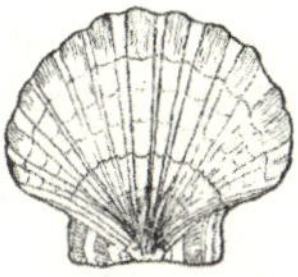

The Prayer

If it could truly breathe in the loneliness, the light
The music and the heartbeats
The highlights and the shadows
The miracles and fiery splendour
And the blandness and the songs and sorrow
Perhaps the symphony would not curdle
Perhaps the crowded clouds would clap and cry.
If it could gently understand and blend itself
And safely weave for me my rain-bowed textured patterned life
Having been shown
I would be resting there.
Fear might take to the wing
Rise and fall from storm clouds
As a sweetened rain
Sustaining my soul, greening my heart.
And the arid gaping crevices, freed
Would burst into song.
Doubt would have flown
And the sun would rise in me each morning
And the winds of change would boldly blow.
And as dewdrops nestle in cupped leaves
So would my tears of joy moisten my lover's limbs.
And as the spider spins her risky web
So would I accept the delicate beauty that is mine
Believing each footstep only as the truth
As each living morsel haphazardly awaits the moment
Of too strong a wind.

Extract from *The Journey of Trust* by Miranda Amapola

First published March 2024
By Sweet Painted Lady Books, Isle of Wight
Printed by Amazon

ISBN 978-1-3999-7608-4

Front cover photograph by Paul Orssich

MY NAME IS NOT

MATILDA

Miranda's Memoirs

MIRANDA AMAPOLA SYMINGTON

FOR MY GRANDCHILDREN
Sonny, Jude and Max

FOR MY SONS
Orion and Sky

FOR MY MOTHER

and

FOR MY FATHER
who died too young

For all those strangers who I never knew by name. Who I fleetingly glimpsed in the distance, who crossed my path, who touched my heart, and many of whom inspired a little story or poem.

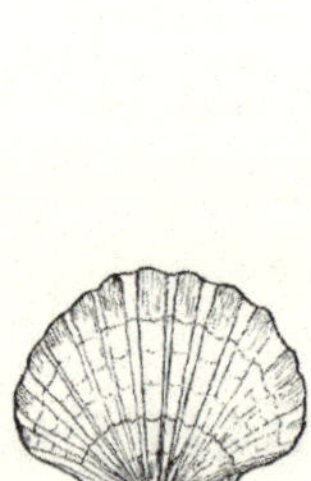

Contents

Chapter 1

Just for starters

Commissioned found object art work made in 2012

I have always been fascinated and surprised at the variety of odd things one can come across when going into a lavatory. The tiniest room in the house, the bathroom, the loo, the john, the privy or the bog can often house unexpected and unusual treasures.

I once found a little money box with penny coins stuck all over it; a sign beside it read 'please spend all your pennies here'. In another I discovered a collection of china, all 1953 Coronation memorabilia – quite valuable, I would imagine, especially now that our dear Queen Elizabeth has passed away. The pieces were arranged in a mahogany corner cupboard with a pretty etched-glass, bow-front door.

I remember a framed collection of those 40s-style rude seaside postcards, which you might send home to your auntie in the hope of shocking her, just for a bit of fun when you were away on holiday in Torquay. A collection of miniature china cats collected from around the world were lined up on a rustic shelf; several had lost their heads and paws. The shelf was precariously tied up with two pieces of string attached to two hooks – no wonder some of the poor little creatures had got damaged.

Then there is always the cascading pile of dusty, out-of-date *Homes & Gardens* magazines, or old newspapers, for those who like to do that strange thing of sitting on the loo and spending hours reading. (I've heard tell that it's the only place where some people can escape whatever it is they need to get away from.)

There are family photos, crossword wallpaper with pen conveniently placed for those brainboxes who suddenly get inspired and fill in 6 across and 12 down ... The chipped china vase filled with very tired-looking blue-silk flowers, once possibly an effective 'iris fragrance' air freshener... A glass skull with fairy lights twined around it... A picture of Jesus... The random lavatorial arrangements or the interior design if you can call it that, so amusing, and never dull, often reveal something interesting about the residents.

But the thing that intrigued me most was a quote from Goethe which I found attached by rusty drawing pins to the back of a friend's lavatory door. Struck by what I read, and not having seen it before, I copied it down. Since that day I have carried these words with me – written on scraps of paper and tucked into my purse, scrawled on an envelope and stuffed into the back pocket of my rucksack, incorporated into an artwork, written in a Christmas card and sent to friends on the other side of the world, or printed out in beautiful handwritten calligraphy, framed and hung on a wall. It feels as if I have never been without them:

Whatever you can do or dream you can, begin it.
Boldness has genius, power, and magic in it.
Begin it now.

There have been other quotes too: sayings, teachings that I have fortuitously come across and which I have used in my work. Words from the Bible which I remembered so vividly from childhood, or from Shakespeare, poets, philosophers... a few significant words I have recalled without necessarily knowing the source, perhaps a random thought spoken by a friend or even a passing stranger. My children and grandchildren, too, suddenly come out with a delightfully humorous and innocent comment. Many of these unexpectedly come to mind from time to time for no apparent reason.

But not wanting them to escape me, I wrote down many of the words on the wall going up the staircase in my family home in Mark's Corner on the Isle of Wight. I would pause, read one or two when heading up the wooden hill to bed. When that house was sold more than thirty-five years ago, a dear friend very thoughtfully wrote all those sayings down for me in a little red book. She was worried lest I might forget them during the massive upheaval of moving house. With a touch more flourish I have re-written these words on the walls of the staircase in my tiny Gurnard cottage home on the island where I still live; I add to them day by day as life jogs along.

Strive for excellence, not perfection

Leave everything a little better than you found it

The heart has reasons that reason cannot know

Remember, compliment three people every day

The only failure is the failure to try – and success is measured by how well you manage disappointment

Think big thoughts, but relish small pleasures

In God we live and move and have our being

The job of the artist is to deepen the mystery

For any speculation which at first looks crazy there is hope

Every blade of grass has its own angel that stands over it and whispers: "Grow, grow."

I am not bound to win, but I am bound to be true;
I am not bound to succeed, but I am bound to live up to what light I have

If you don't break some of the rules you miss out on some of the fun

Courage: the capacity to move ahead in spite of despair

All bad behaviours are an unmet need

Experience is what you gain when you don't get what you want

But the sayings I love the best are the family ones I recall from my childhood. They are up there on the wall too; they may make little sense to you now but, if you read on, quite possibly, they might.

Over the hills and far away

Look at the picture rail

Cabbage on the toad

Head up, bust well forward, marching, marching we will go

Get up you lazy sluggards, lying in bed all day

I'm just going to the lavatory

The witch is at home

There were many more too but, like a ghost, those particular words of Goethe have always haunted me… like an unavoidable and necessary reminder, apparently, that there was still something very important that I had to do with my life.

Whatever you can do or dream you can, begin it

And so, I have – I have at least begun trying to write this book. And yet I do not know how I am going to find my way out of this maze. I have muddled about for so long with handwritten bits and bobs, filed them, refiled them, reread them, cried upon them, ripped them up, given up, written them off, been pissed off, then forgotten about them, and finally begun again.

I have searched through years of incomprehensible random, scrappy pieces of paper which all ended up in tattered files with their labels peeling off. From 'Possible book', to 'Don't give up!', 'Mum's book' and even 'Poetry to do one day'. It's as though I have been pondering over all these pudding basins full of my jottings (not flour), but I have not had that vital ingredient, the yeast to enable the whole thing to rise.

One day I mentioned to a friend that I might like to give writing a go.

So, we spent an evening together. I read from one of the many scraps of paper. She wasn't very encouraging. 'Well, you seem to have lots to say about not very much.' I could not let that one lie and replied, 'Well, true perhaps but I think I have had an amazing life. I have had a few triumphs, several disasters, loves, laughs, some deep friendships and some wild experiences. I mean I never imagined that I would end up on a catwalk or go on an adventure across the Atlantic Ocean.' My dear friend banged on: 'But descriptive writing is so boring. If you are reading a book, something has to happen!'

I agreed, but I felt very frustrated by my friend's comments and reiterated that I thought many interesting things *had* happened to me. Well, so I liked to believe.

She went on: 'Well what's the title, anyway?'

I said I thought *Lost for Words* would be good.

Was I writing about being lost? If so, *Lost the Plot* might be a more appropriate title.

Anyway, the conversation was ridiculous, and I was not only losing the plot but seriously losing heart. We had a laugh and ended up deciding that if I ever had the nerve to approach a publisher the rejection slips would be piling up and it would be wiser to get back smartish to the day job. (I had plenty of those, so that wouldn't be a problem). But I seem to have discovered in life that whatever I resist, persists. So off I went again, still wondering. Should I? Can I? Dare I?

But what the hell is it *exactly* that I wish to write about? Is it the grieving for a long-lost love, or the ridiculous longing for some fantasy Adonis to enter my world and transform it overnight into a love-ever-after, hunky-dory little romantic story. All that knight-in-shining-armour stuff. Or might I risk it and get a little more serious. But I don't think I have the gift to be able to articulate all the things I ponder, the thought provoking stuff, so where do I even start? Perhaps just the snippets, the short stories in bite sized chunks, little cameos of life that have intrigued me, might, with time, merge and form themselves into some kind of a story about my life. I don't know. But I do have a hunch that I might regret it if I did not try to capture it in words for my grandchildren.

I have not flown to the moon, or made millions and lost it all, been shipwrecked and lived on algae for nine months, or very fortunately suffered any terrible tragedy, decided I would learn Italian backwards, or won the lottery and had my world tipped chaotically upside down overnight. No, none of these.

The pages are still blank, but something tells me that the words are there, written invisibly. They seem restless, jostling for my attention. It is this feeling that spurs me on. I will write about my family, my friends, my work, and perhaps about some of the ordinary moments. I will share tales of my adventures, and maybe describe a few of the rather more surprising ones too.

Yes, I have decided I must be bold. I will begin it now.

Chapter 2

Before my time

My parents' wedding day. Andrew and Antoinette in Oswestry June 1941. Despite the austerity of wartime they arranged a beautiful Midsummer's Day wedding. I would love to have seen my mother's spectacular bouquet and unique home made floral headdress

Granny, as we always called her, my father's mother, Mary Downer Symington, was a dear little lady always dressed in black. She was the only grandparent I ever knew, since the others had passed away before I came along. I do not know if she had a special name for Antoinette, who became my mother, the beautiful woman who her youngest son, Andrew, was desperate to make his wife. But Antoinette described herself as 'the woman who is good for nothing but painting pictures and arranging flowers'.

On the other hand, it is said that Antoinette's mother, Nellie Gordon George, did have a name for the very good-looking man whom her daughter could not make up her mind whether or not to marry. She called him 'the penniless one leg'. Hmm, not very kind – a little cruel from someone who was apparently a rotund and jovial woman who used to make everyone laugh. Yet in a way I can understand it.

At the time of my parents' meeting in 1934 my father was indeed penniless; he had few prospects and only one leg. Nine years previously, at the age of twenty-one, he had suffered the most terrible motorbike accident. As a result, he had compound fractures of his right arm and leg, a broken nose, and had undergone nine operations in an attempt to put him back together again. It was considered that he was fortunate to be alive. His right leg had to be amputated and it was thought at the time that he would have very restricted use of his right arm.

He made a very slow and painful recovery in Barts hospital, no doubt with some very kind nurses caring for him, but in those days I imagine there would have been little additional support to address the psychological trauma of such a horrific accident. So not only was he having to adjust to his very compromised physical state, he must also have been trying his best to fight off depression and feelings of despair about what his future might possibly be.

My father had an elder brother and three sisters. Dear Granny, whose married life had mostly been one of uncertainty and financial struggle, was finally abandoned by her husband and was left to cope with bringing up her large family on her own. Granny had two sisters, Bessie and Letty, and a brother, Richard, all of whom were kind and helped her as much as they could. They seemed to be forever moving from house to house trying to settle and make some sort of a home for themselves. At the time of my father's accident the family were all lodging with their Uncle Richard, who was the vicar of the church in Gedney, a small village in the middle of the flat fens on the border of Lincolnshire and Norfolk. My father was working on the land and fancied trying to carve out some sort of a living for himself by learning about farming and the ways of the countryside that he loved.

Another move then took them to the pilgrimage village of Walsingham in north Norfolk where my father, one of his sisters, his mother and aunt all lived in the old friary. It was at this juncture that my father took himself off to the Norwich School of Art, which was approximately twenty-seven miles away. (I guess he had a car, and perhaps sometimes he would travel by train.) This was all part of his recovery. Working with the arts, sculpture, writing – they were all means by which he could express himself and possibly even talk to tutors and teachers, who hopefully understood his predicament and valued the therapeutic benefits of working in this way.

It was here that he very fortuitously met my mother. She was twenty-one years old, and he was immediately transfixed by her. Would this be the beginning of a new life for him? There is no doubt he had fallen madly in love.

As for my mother, she had one sister who was ten years older than her.

A sketch of mine of the doorway of the Norwich School of Art where my parents met in 1934

She felt almost like an only child, so she once told me. By the time she was ten her sister, Eve, who would have been twenty, was gallivanting about having rather wild, disastrous affairs, so Antoinette did not have the experience of having a little playmate. Her parents seemed to me to be a rather ill-matched couple. I imagine their temperaments to have been rather different, her mother genial and good natured and her bespectacled father rather dour and gloomy in appearance. She often described her father as a strange man who had beautiful legs. I always thought that a rather odd detail to have shared.

My mother's upbringing had been different from my father's. She had been cosseted, enjoying the pleasures of a well-to-do family. They had a chauffeur, went grouse shooting in Scotland and to Europe on the Grand Cultural Tour, and my mother was taught by a private governess at home. As a young girl she would write, read, paint and study philosophy. She was deeply reflective and quiet, and she was intrigued by all the mysteries and magic of the natural world.

Her mother, although always jolly and cheerful, suffered from asthma, so they moved temporarily from Devon during the war, taking the doctor's advice that the clean and bracing Norfolk air might help her condition. 'Seamere', the house with its beautiful mere in which my mother used to swim, was a few miles from Norwich. It was during this period of living in Norfolk that my mother attended the Norwich School of Art, her path crossing with my father's.

Their romantic days at the art school, however, were short lived as my mother and her family then moved to Shropshire where my mother cared for her ailing mother. Seven years followed before their marriage in 1941. Seven years of deliberation I imagine, as to how, why, or when they might settle down together. Seven years of letters exchanged, poems shared, occasional visits, comings and goings, excitement, disappointment, hopes, fears, inevitable expectations and no doubt dreams of what might be possible one day for both of them, individually and together . . .

My mother had a passion for walking. She must have been wondering, naturally, how this might work out, while contemplating marrying this man who had only one leg. I remember on our holidays she would get out of the car when we were on our return journey from wherever we had been, and my father would chant, 'Head up, bust well forward, marching, marching we will go,' as he watched her disappear, walking the last two miles or so back to wherever we were staying. I always wondered how he must have felt. He used to warn her if it looked like rain, but she always used to say if there was a little patch of blue sky large enough to make a pair of sailor's trousers it would be fine weather. And off she would pace.

My father loved clouds, the natural world, Old Master seascapes. Brought up first in London and then in Sussex, he had experienced emotional hardship and knew what hard work was all about. Within his family there was a strong Christian faith, and when the family fell on difficult times I imagine that it was their faith which kept them all going.

His heart must have leapt when he met my mother. Suddenly there was hope that at least he was not completely written off and destined for a life of isolation and misery. The bleak picture might fade, there might be light at the end of the tunnel. Although their backgrounds were different, I don't think that he allowed this to deter him for a moment.

They no doubt discussed their history and shared all the fascinating stories of their ancestry.

My father's grandfather, Richard Gales, born in 1826, was an imposing gentleman with a huge beard, captain of the three-masted tall ship the *Chepica*, which he sailed to Australia. I have a model of the ship, carefully preserved in a glass case. If only one could hear the details of all the stories. There must have been so many treacherous voyages that he undertook circling the world, before he finally returned to shore and settled down to family life. There was an uncle who designed the Hardinge Bridge in what is now Bangladesh, and several other uncles who had leanings towards the church, which took them into the ministry to spread the Gospel.

My sister has painstakingly documented the family history and has managed to fit together a complicated jigsaw puzzle. All family histories are fascinating, especially when the information is drawn from authentic diaries, letters, journals and photographs, which ours has been. All the characters and personalities and traits that one can recognise in one's own family today link one to the past – the comings and goings, achievements, the successes, the worries, failures, love affairs, dramas and mysterious unresolved riddles. There seem to be plenty of such tales in our family.

It seems there is no clear evidence to indicate which direction my father might have taken had he not been halted in his tracks at such an early age by the accident. There are no suggestions that he might have followed in the footsteps of any of his illustrious forebears in engineering, seafaring or the Church. His own father had died in the very same year of his accident.

As children we never heard a word spoken about his own wayward father. It is apparent that he had not provided a stable role model for his children. So the history of family turmoil and emotional instability must have haunted him. I imagine he prayed that history would not repeat itself. Above all I would like to think that he hoped one day he would find himself enjoying the security of a loving relationship, through which he could create a happier environment than the one he had experienced himself as a child. One in which he felt he could safely bring up a family.

While he had still been at the art school and living with his mother in Walsingham, his brother, Lawrence, had married the daughter of a landowner in King's Lynn. Through this landed gentleman, Henry Thompson, my father was able to take his next gigantic step. He was offered the opportunity to take on the 500 acre farm High Barn, Stanhoe, as a tenant farmer. As years went by, he went on to employ two tractor drivers and a foreman.

Taking on the farm must have been a huge decision but one he could not turn down. Apparently the land had previously been thought virtually unfarmable owing to the large amount of flint on all the fields. Nothing much would grow in abundance. Flint is the primary building material of the traditional Norfolk farmhouses and cottages, and as a child I remember seeing huge piles of these glinting stones on all the headlands of the fields. In fact, we used to heave them off the fields when the tractors had unearthed them. It was one of our jobs.

And so it came to pass that my father moved to the isolated farmhouse in the fields, outside the village of Stanhoe: determined to make a go of it, determined to learn on the hoof the complexities of running a small farm, determined to make some kind of a living out of it and determined that perhaps one day the beautiful woman, my mother Antoinette, would join him there.

My mother's ancestors seemed to bask in more fortunate circumstances, with more money and opportunity for interesting travel, expeditions, cultural stimulation and a life of certain sociability. The background of my mother's family, the Fryers, seems one more associated with and rooted in the arts and culture. They all seemed to be intellectual and artistic people and pursued a life which one might describe in a slightly derogatory manner as that of privileged dilettantes.

A lovely little story my mother shared was one about her grandmother. She would request that one of the maids of the household present her with a little black velvet cushion on which were displayed the 'afternoon rings'. She would choose which she would like to wear that afternoon. No doubt her choice would be appropriate and in accordance with whoever had been invited to tea on that day. As I write I am wearing one of those rings. It has three beautiful rainbow opals set in gold along with four tiny diamonds. I love it. Fascinating to think that all those years ago it was on the finger of my great grandmother.

My understanding, from a few stories that I recall from my mother, is that she felt a little uncomfortable with some aspect of her genteel life. She loved the 'real people' as she used to call them, the salt of the earth, ordinary folk. Those who did not have to hide behind the precarious facades of their upstanding position in the social hierarchy. She always told the story of how she used to giggle with the maids as they were standing waiting at table for everyone to finish their meal. They stood with their hands behind their backs, uniformed, with neat aprons tied, politely 'serving'. If she caught the eye of a maid, they would then have to try to hide their urge to laugh at what they must both have perceived as a rather ridiculous and amusing situation.

So, coming from these rather different backgrounds it's not surprising that my mother might have wondered quite how she could adjust and fit in with the 'penniless one-legged farmer'. She was also of course ten years younger than him. But at the heart of it they were both artistic, poetical, romantic, philosophers, they were both remarkable and inspirational. They recognised these qualities in each other, and despite the one leg they were a perfect fit. They loved each other and nothing would hold them back.

When war was declared in 1939, mass evacuations took place. About three million schoolchildren were sent to safer places in the country from cities that were at risk of being bombed. One of these was Oswestry, a small town in Shropshire, near the borders of Wales.

Shropshire is still known to this day as 'the lost county', so way back then I imagine it was a quiet, undiscovered backwater. Records show that 3,300 children and 900 mothers were sent there from Liverpool at the outbreak of war.

Following their lengthy courtship, of which two years were during wartime, finally on Midsummer's Day, 21 June 1941, my mother and father, Antoinette and Andrew, were married in Oswestry.

The photograph of their wedding day is one of my favourites. I think my father is so good looking and my mother with her classical, natural elegance is a film star in the making. Here are the married couple, my mother and father and a few friends and family gathered round. The rationing system was still very much in operation, which would have meant that choice when shopping was extremely limited, especially if one had any wish to buy a smart outfit, let alone a hat, for one's wedding. But my mother obviously overcame this and managed to find a suit, a neatly pleated calf-length skirt and a matching jacket with those typical, slightly puffy leg-of-mutton sleeves with the bold wartime-look shoulder pads. Her choice of hairstyle for the big day was one of the most stylish of the times. Her long tresses, which would usually have been loosely plaited, would be more tightly plaited and then coiled and secured over her ears – hence the popular name 'earphones style'.

The hat and bouquet provide the pièce de résistance. She, being very creative of course, had somehow scrunched together some mesh wire netting into a shape that would sit presumably reasonably comfortably on her head. Through the holes of the wire netting she had poked various flowers, creating an unusual but very effective adornment for her head. A hat – or perhaps in these modern times that terrible description of a 'fascinator'.

Her bouquet is a cornucopia of flowers and foliage. A spray of lupins leaps out from among other wildflowers which had been gathered no doubt that morning from the hedgerows. It is a romantic, artistic array, tumbling and trembling from her hand which clasps it. I love it. We are left to imagine what the colours of the bouquet were, since the only photograph is in black-and-white. I fancy the lupins were that pale bluey-mauve colour with some yellows in there somewhere. Peaceful, soothing colours. It was indeed a larger-than-life bouquet, one that made a clear statement that, yes, she would always love her wildflowers, would love to arrange them, would love their scents and would always care about where they grew, and would always appreciate the miracle of such natural artworks. These are the flowers which she loved to gather and paint. Unlike the skirt, there was nothing neat about her wedding bouquet.

My father is very proudly standing beside her. I can almost read his mind: 'Look at her, my wife at last, we are together and together we shall be for ever more.' He had patiently waited so long for her to make up her mind, for this time when his bride, his wife, would return with him to what had been the lonely farmhouse in the fields. And he knew so much more about her than the few friends and family who were gathered round.

He knew she was an interesting and mysterious woman, one who knew she had seen a fairy dancing on a watering can in her garden when she was a little girl, with a spirit which embraced his spirit. A woman born out of her own time whom he longed to discover more about and be closer to. He knew that nobody would ever love her as he did and that he would be with her for ever.

The honeymoon was spent, as planned, in Wales. One of my father's favourite stories was the 'honeymoon bluebottle fly'. He always strived for perfection, but on this occasion he had to forgo that admirable attribute. He had no choice. They needed to find some provisions to take with them on their first honeymooning day of adventure. There were only a few shops open in the sleepy little town of Oswestry, limited provisions perched on virtually empty shelves, groceries were not in abundance. So, they scoured the town for whatever they could find. They eventually came across a butcher's shop, in the window of which was one solitary, sad-looking pork pie.

A huge bluebottle was buzzing madly round it, settling on it every so often, gorging itself, possibly just like them having homed in on whatever tasty morsel could be found. What were they to do? They did not like the look of the bluebottle with its noisy buzzing, nor the pie, really. But there was nothing else in the shop to buy. They stood looking at each other, wondering, but in the end bought the pie. 'If there is nothing else for our picnic, we had better not worry about a poor hungry bluebottle.'

My mother always finished the story: 'Yes, we bought the pie and then we set off to climb Snowdon.'

Snowdon is the second highest mountain in the British Isles. It is four miles to the top and 3,560 feet above sea level at the summit. Having walked it myself I have a sense of the stamina required, particularly as one approaches the top. The colder temperature breaks the rock down into a mass of tiny pieces of shaley slipperiness, and it's difficult to keep a good grip underfoot at times. But my father, never to be beaten by anything, made it all the way to the top.

In those days an artificial limb was heavy and cumbersome. The stump of his thigh fitted into the hollow metal cavity of the artificial leg. There was one plus. When on holiday abroad, usually France, he would secrete the jewellery which he had brought for my mother in the cavernous hollow of his metal limb.

The artificial leg was held in place by a wide leather strap that went around his waist and over his shoulder. He always walked with a stick, but his gait was awkward, and he had to kind of heave his leg up and over as he took each step. It was as though it were too long. It obviously made manoeuvring about a wearisome business.

To have climbed Snowdon was an astonishing achievement. What a wonderful way to mark the beginning of their adventure of married life together.

They returned together to High Barn, and it was not long before there was the pitter-patter of pittering-pattering tiny feet.

Chapter 3

Early Childhood

Babe in arms 1946. My father Richard Andrew Symington looking dapper in his trilby and me in his arms aged six months at our High Barn home in Stanhoe, Norfolk

I was born in April 1946. My sister Anabel was born in October 1944 and Antonia was born in March 1949. Anabel and I were born at our High Barn home and Antonia was born in a nursing home while alterations were being made to the house. I believe my mother had a miscarriage after the birth of Antonia; perhaps a fourth attempt was in the hope of producing a boy.

Antoinette, Andrew, Anabel, Antonia . . . but Miranda April. All A's except me. I always wondered why. But since I was born in April, I kind of accepted that April was an obvious second name. For some reason I never liked it. I asked my mother one day why my first Christian name did not begin with an 'A' like all the rest of the family. Her answer – 'Well, you were meant to be a boy and you were going to be called Adam' – helped me finally make sense of it. So, I was not the longed-for son, which I can well understand my father might have liked. Despite the possible disappointment I know he adored his three little girls.

I was sandwiched between my two sisters. Anabel led the way, as the firstborn so often does, and I think I felt intimidated at times by all that she could do and all that I felt I could not. As we grew up it seemed to me that she excelled at most things, and I always felt I was running to catch up. Antonia, being my younger sister, I always wanted to protect and care for. She was the precious little one.

Home births were commonplace in those days. Intervention was kept to a minimum and was considered unnecessary unless there had been warning signs of any complications earlier on in the pregnancy. My father would not have been present when I came into the world.

The fashion of the day was that it was best to leave the baby to cry, feed it on the dot of the four-hourly feed, after which you would push it out in the pram for a good blast of fresh air, Florence Nightingale style, baby having been tucked up very snugly in lots of blankets.

A great deal of time must have been spent dealing with the nappies. Poor mother. There were no such things as handy Huggies, these disposable nappies so convenient for today's busy mums. Terry towelling cotton nappies had to be soaked in buckets, then washed and pinned out on the line to dry in the sunshine. They had to be carefully folded into a certain shape which was comfortable for the baby, and secured with a large safety pin, usually a pink one for a girl and a blue one for a boy. All very different from today, but it was into this era that I and my two sisters were born.

Babe in mother's arms. My mother Antoinette Symington and me

I compensated for my slight feeling of inadequacy around my elder sister by pouring attention on my little sister. I adored her and, although I could not read at the time, the story goes (and I do vaguely remember it) that I was found having seated my two-and-a-half-year-old sister down in a comfy chair, reading to her in my very own made-up language. 'A-ras-a-par-a-dee-a, toot-a-toot-a adee, a-ras-a-par-a-dee-a, toot-a-toot-a adee,' I repeated this over and over while showing her pictures in the book from which I was pretending to read.

What privileged children we were to be growing up in the beautiful environment of High Barn. The nearest house was half a mile away across the fields. Mr and Mrs Brown lived there. It was a rather boring looking red-brick house around which Mr Brown had planted dark fir trees, which over the years grew and grew very tall, completely obscuring it from view from the main road – and presumably cutting out any light into the house itself. Mrs Brown was a friendly woman, and Mother used to walk across the fields sometimes to have tea in her gloomy kitchen. She called the house 'Castle Glower'.

The village of Stanhoe was a mile beyond Castle Glower, and we would often walk there along the farm track. The village had two public houses, a blacksmith, a post office and general store, a cobbler, a butcher's shop, a grocery shop, a school, a village hall, a chapel and a church. We used to take our shoes to be mended by the cobbler, Mr Curzon, and our pony, Topsy, to have her shoes mended at Algie's the blacksmith.

It is a sad village now. Nothing remains of those golden, olden days except the church, which is probably attended by only a very dwindling congregation. Many of the houses are owned by Londoners, second home owners, and most of the farm workers' cottages have been converted into bijou holiday lets. The one remaining pub is so expensive – and on the one occasion that I went there I felt uncomfortable stepping over its rather pretentious threshold.

We had a menagerie. Oscar was our first horse. I remember when he died; I witnessed the horrific sight of him being dragged by a tractor through the meadow and loaded onto a trailer to be taken away and disposed of. Then there were the two ponies, Madam and Topsy, numerous dogs, rabbits, guinea pigs, hamsters, budgerigars, a tortoise called Buttercup, cats, mice, stick insects, 100 fantail pigeons including Falra, the tame one, and last but not least Jackie, the tame jackdaw which had been rescued having fallen out of its nest. No pet rats, snakes, parrots, camels or elephants! All our animals needed constant care one way or another, sometimes being given a little more attention than I felt I was getting myself; but, of course, we loved them all. My favourites were the cats, Tigerlilly, Fifi, and Blanche.

The winters were freezing since there was no such thing as central heating. So we would all huddle round and bag the warmest place to sit right beside the fireplace. Our winter evenings were often spent listening to classical music. Our father made us sit very quietly and listen 'properly' to symphonies, operas and carols.

We were so lucky to be taken every summer to the King's Lynn Festival, which still runs today. It was founded by Lady Fermoy, one of the Queen's ladies-in-waiting. I remember hearing Yehudi Menuhin, master of the violin, and Evelyn Rothwell playing the oboe. Rothwell's husband, that extraordinary conductor Sir John Barbirolli, fascinated me as a child. I thought he resembled a little wizened shrew.

Sandringham, the Royal Family's Norfolk stately home, is very close by to Stanhoe, and Prince Charles, Princess Anne, the Queen and the Queen Mother would often be seen at the concerts. The original concert hall was very small and intimate. I remember the Queen Mother coming down the side aisle to take her seat in the front row – when she spotted us she suddenly paused and said, 'What three dear little girls!' I remember her being so poised and graceful. We were so excited she had spoken to us; we kind of thought we were now famous, and talked about it all the way home.

After the concerts, on the homeward journey if we had been good, there might be a treat. Dad would stop at the fish shop and buy 'Chiff and Fipps' as he used to call it. I loved Dad.

We did not have a television. My father considered it would be the beginning of the end, and I think he was right. Instead, we amused ourselves in the evenings with every sort of game imaginable. My favourite was so brilliant. We had a huge, illustrated book containing all the famous portraits and paintings of the great masters. One of us had to choose which one we were going to mime while the others had to guess which we were. I cannot imagine a better way of introducing children to the arts and to nurture their creative thinking. It reminds me, I must introduce this game to my grandchildren.

The other favourite was, and still is, 'Head, Body and Legs'. I'm sure you will know it but, in case not, you draw a head, fold the paper down, hand it to the next person who draws the body, folds it down, hands it to the next person who draws the legs, folds it down and has fun opening it up. My grandchildren love that one.

We'd do puzzles, play cards, and sit and draw. Paper was still in short supply, so our mother would tear the front pages out of books (since there were usually a few blank ones) and we would use that for drawing paper. In the winter, chestnuts would be roasting on the fire, and if we were lucky we might have marshmallows too.

At Christmas time Granny and Auntie Bessie would come for the day and we would sing carols around the tree. I can still envisage the delicate, lit candles held in place on the branches by those sweet little clip-on gold metal candle holders. No such thing in those days as strings of electric or battery-operated Christmas tree lights, risk assessment, plastic trees, or spray-on pine essence.

After Christmas every year we would have the magical treat of going to London. We travelled on the train from King's Lynn to Liverpool Street, where a porter would meet us and trolley our suitcases to the taxi rank. From there we would be whisked off to our smart hotel in Knightsbridge. The Normandy, I think, was the name of one of them. Beside this hotel was a little alleyway with a sweet shop where I bought my favourite liquorice raspberry jelly sweets, which were popped into a neat little white paper bag.

I vividly remember on one of our winter trips to London witnessing the terrible smog. This was caused by the reliance on coal-fired power for heating and keeping the numerous fireplaces aglow. If there was no wind, the severely polluted air did not become dispersed. The dense, yellowy-green-blackish smog hung low and brought all traffic to a complete standstill. I remember my father trying to hail a taxi, but they were all refusing to take passengers and so we walked the short distance back home to our hotel. By some estimates the worst smog, in 1952, resulted in the deaths of 12,000 people.

On our Christmas trips we sometimes used to spend a few nights in Worcester Park staying with my father's elder sister, Auntie Biddy. 'Millfield' was an imposing house in The Avenue and I always remember the clock in the hall which used to 'bong' out the chimes of Big Ben on the hour. Our aunt told us stories about the war, and how during the air raids they used to take shelter and hide underneath the dining room table. Bombs were falling all around them, but fortunately they and their house escaped damage.

Biddy seemed to be a bit of a drama queen, a hypochondriac we thought. Poor woman. She had a vast quantity of pills which she stashed behind the cushions on her sofa, and she would make a great song and a dance when her heart was having a little flutter. Her husband, Oliver, would rush round attending to her every need. He used to call her 'Ducky'.

She was not the best of cooks. The dingy, untidy kitchen smelt of gas and stale cabbage, and the cupboards were jammed with an assortment of pre-war chutneys, jams, marmalades and pickled onions, all with rather tired-looking rusty lids. At breakfast time, as we all waited in the lofty dining room, my aunt would eventually appear with plates laden with grey heaps of very unappealing devilled kidneys. My father would pull one of his funny faces, kick us under the table and we desperately had to try to contain our laughter. He was always very hot on table manners, but on these 'devilled kidney mornings' manners seemed to go out of the window. When my aunt disappeared into the kitchen to top up the teapot my mother, having been prompted by my father, would skilfully scoop some of the kidneys into her serviette and quickly secrete them in her bag, which she had cleverly hidden under the table for just such a moment of desperation.

We would always go to the famous Hamleys toy shop, and Harrods to look at the animals. I always thought that it seemed very weird and cruel, all these poor animals in cages in Harrods.

We would see a show, spend our Christmas money at the London sales and be dressed very smartly for the big city in our 'pork-pie hats'. These were strange little hats that our mother had knitted: they did look just like pork pies. Mine was pink, Anabel's was blue, and Antonia's was apricot coloured. They had tiny little pearl beads sewn around the edge, each with matching gloves. Mother had made us felt skirts which we would wear to the theatre. Just a circle of felt with a hole cut in it – very out-of-the-box and original! Same colour as the hats for each child.

One Christmas we went to see the Moscow State Circus. It was incredible, especially the tight-rope walkers balancing with their long red-and-gold poles: six men high on each other's shoulders performing their balancing tricks. My father had forgotten his cine camera which he usually took everywhere with him, so he returned to King's Lynn on the train, went back to High Barn, collected the camera, and travelled back to London having booked another ticket for the circus so that he could film it. Aren't we lucky to have a record of that historic Circus.

We went to Covent Garden to see Rudolf Nureyev and Margot Fonteyn dancing. That I shall never ever, ever, ever, ever, ever forget. Nureyev appeared from the wings and flew across the stage. Margot and he were in love in their way – they had to be. They could not have danced together with such passion had they not been.

We had many wonderful holidays, we were so lucky: the Lake District, Paris, Cornwall, France to see the Palace of Versailles and the Châteaux of the Loire valley. I think at the time maybe I felt I was being dragged round yet another boring castle, cathedral city or historic monument and would rather have been somewhere else, although at that age of course I could not quite imagine where I would rather have been.

But of course, looking back, all of this was the foundation of my introduction to the arts, culture, theatre and music, for which I am now so grateful. To have been introduced to all this at such an impressionable early age, too. It was balanced with growing up in the very natural environment of High Barn, a working farm, enjoying the more simple pleasures of the countryside and taking in the beauty of the wide open Norfolk landscape.

Our summer holidays were full of activity. We used to make what we called 'contraptions'. This was a system in which we would join together with rope all our various little trikes and pedal cars, trolleys and anything we could find which had wheels, so that we could toe them along. There were occasional accidents when one of them tipped over; it was then grazed knees and tears, rushing indoors for plaster and sympathy. But I remember it clearly being such fun.

Summer evenings were sometimes spent at the beach, especially at high tide when the sea would cover the approach road that led down to the beach at Brancaster and we would have to wait, sometimes until after dark, before we could safely return home. We would have an evening picnic, sitting up in the sand dunes.

Dad would hop down to the water's edge on his one leg. He would splash around in the shallows pretending to be a crab and try to catch us and bite our toes. What a courageous man. He always tried to make us laugh and keep his sense of humour, putting on a brave face, I guess, which must have been so difficult.

He liked to play practical jokes. He had his special plastic chocolates hidden away which he would quickly pop into a box of Black Magic and offer to his mother, aunt or a visiting guest, hoping they would choose the pretend one. He would always try to find a way of amusing us. I remember he sometimes used to tickle me at bedtime until I was nearly in tears. I didn't like that. I remember pleading with him to stop.

I enjoyed going with him to King's Lynn's market day on a Tuesday. Norfolk does have a reputation of being a flat and dull county. When you say you come from Norfolk, that's what people often say: 'I have never been there, but it is flat, isn't it?' I usually don't bother to explain.

Yes, it's not mountainous or even hilly, but (for instance) there was one drive I always loved, and it was on the way to King's Lynn where the winding road swept down to the village of Hillington. There was often a misty view, a vista to the west, and my father would always say, 'Over the hills and far away,' as we wove our way around the corners and down the hill.

We drove along in our pale green Humber Super Snipe. It was always exciting to be going into town. Even going with my mother down to the village of Stanhoe to buy half a pound of butter or to post a letter I regarded as a fun outing. King's Lynn on a Tuesday was teeming with life, a typical busy traditional market, with no imports from India or Thailand in those days. There was the odd antique and bric-à-brac stall, but mostly fruit and vegetables in abundance. We would go in summer to the bustling Corn Hall where all the farmers and seed merchants would have congregated. My father would take a sample of his freshly harvested wheat, a few grains in a little brown bag which would then be tested for their moisture content. There was this intriguing handheld device into which he placed the grains of wheat. He would shake it and the grains would fall through the holes and they would then be cut in half by pushing a lever across, thus exposing the cut surface of the grains. From this, the precise quality of the wheat would be assessed and the appropriate price for it agreed upon. Woe betide the day when the result was not a favourable one.

We would often go to Ladyman's for tea and a toasted tea cake. We would pass Woolworth's on the way, where nothing was priced over a shilling. Those were the days when we still handled money. Twenty shillings made a pound and there were twelve pennies in a shilling – halfpennies and farthings too.

I remember pinching a little packet of something from one of the open display cases in Woolworth's. I didn't know what it was. I insisted on sitting in the back of the car on the way home so that I could open the packet without my father seeing. I was so disappointed. It was a packet of hairpins. Not kirby grips, the sort I might have been able to use to hold back my hair, but the ones the older ladies used to keep their neat buns in place. I never stole anything ever again.

At Ladyman's when you bought something from the grocery store, if change was required, the lady serving would put your money into a sealed brass cylinder and attach it to an overhead kind of railway system. The cylinder would be whisked away by suction or some complex process which made a whooshing noise as it disappeared. It would arrive by this fantastical system on the upper floor gallery where another lady was sitting in a little cubicle about the size of a telephone box. She would undo the cylinder, place the correct change back into it, and send it back to the customer waiting down below. I truly thought it was magic and still do, since I understand nothing at all of a technical nature.

I mean, how do aeroplanes stay up in the sky? My very clever son of course says, 'Oh mum, for goodness sake, it's the basic law of aerodynamics which anybody can understand.' Well, I know things like this can be explained, but one of my points is that some very, very, very clever person has been able to determine exactly what is necessary in order for an aeroplane to be able stay up there in the sky. Yes, so such things can be calculated and explained if one has that kind of a brain – and thank goodness these very clever people mostly always get their sums right.

But nothing will ever convince me that you can explain the many mysteries of nature: the formation of a snowflake, every single one an intricate different pattern; the life cycle of a butterfly which turns from liquid into a stunning delicate artwork all by itself. Within ten to fifteen days a fully grown larva transforms itself into a pupa or chrysalis and safely cocooned inside, the caterpillar's body breaks down turning itself into a kind of soup. Then having reorganised itself an adult butterfly emerges in all its glory. Well, is that not utterly miraculous ?

Then there's the poor, misunderstood little ant, who can bite you if it gets in your pants but whose citadel has the most sophisticated cooling system ever. The dandelion is considered a weed, but its petalled symmetry is remarkable. Spiders at night get busy in the dark, spinning their webs, lacing my garden in the most delicate crochet art for me to marvel at in the morning. I always thank them, and the flowers for being so beautiful, because I think it is sad that they don't know what pleasure they give. But I like to think perhaps, maybe, they do know.

Nobody with a clever brain invented any of these things. That's why I believe in God or a power greater than ourselves. (There are lots of other reasons too why I believe in God.) 'The God of My Understanding', that is. But it's hard to explain 'The Great Spirit.' I think it would be arrogant to think one could explain everything anyway, but some people seem to think they can.

I was so lucky that I grew up with all these wonders of nature and was surrounded by them. I noticed them and loved them, as we lived together as a family at High Barn. We were little tomboys really, always outdoors playing, climbing trees, making dens and tree houses and tending to the growing menagerie.

We used to go to gymkhanas. I lost my nerve completely and never really regained confidence around horses following a horrible incident when Black Beauty, the horse I was riding, was startled by something and careered out of the ring. The cars were all parked close to the arena, and in those days they had big, bold chrome bumpers at the front. My black beast of a horse in its frightened state got its hoof trapped behind one of the bumpers. I was thrown off and became completely pinned underneath his huge heaving body. I could have been killed, I always think. What a lucky escape!

The summers were long. They seemed hotter than today, maybe just because we were children, but it is true that as spring approached the winter clothes were put away and the summer clothes were unearthed from their slumber. I always longed for a mauve summer dress. But my mother said mauve was a cheap colour and I could not have one.

As each summer drew towards its close we gathered all the fruit and vegetables which were then either bottled, pickled, dried or frozen, and eventually eaten. We would ride in the back of the lorries at harvest time down to the Grange, which was another barn in the village where the corn was processed, weighed up, bagged up and stored. The summers buzzed with all these activities.

The winters had their own demands: gathering sticks from the various coppices as kindling for the fires; chopping and stacking up the wood; and if we complained that we were cold, mother would get us to help clean the brass. 'That will get your blood going,' she used to say, and it usually did, for a while anyway. If we complained that it was raining, and we couldn't go out, the day would turn into a toffee-making afternoon. We would stand by the Aga and stir the huge pan of sugary water till it was bubbling and frothing and had turned to a rich, golden-brown colour. Then we would pour it into a well-used shallow baking tray, adding a very thin slice or two of lemon peel. This gave it a little tang. We had to be patient and wait until it had set. It always seemed a long wait, but it was worth it as we bit into the brittle sugary shards. I would run into Dad's office and give him a piece. He always loved it.

Daw, as we called her – Doreen being her proper name – was a young girl who lived in the village and came to help my mother in the kitchen. She taught my mother a little more about cooking. Her own mother had taught her, and she was a dab hand at all the traditional things like steak and kidney pudding, flaky pastry, dumplings and all sorts of pies and cakes. There was the one famous time when she was serving up steak and kidney pudding from the kitchen, tripped up on the step and went flying, pudding and all. My father was having a business lunch. I am not sure what happened next or what we ate. Was it all scooped up off the floor, I wonder?

The owner of the farm would arrive from King's Lynn driven by his chauffeur. The chauffeur would sit outside the dining room window in his smart Daimler car eating his sandwiches while the landlord was being wined and dined by my mother and father. After the meal the ladies – my mother and the three of us girls – would 'withdraw' to another room or rush off out somewhere, slightly relieved to be able to escape the formalities, and leave the men to business talk and to the passing of the port. Oh, goodness! How times have changed.

At bedtime we would always snuggle down in our little truckle beds. Mother would sit on the bed, and we would choose a hymn to sing together before we went to sleep.

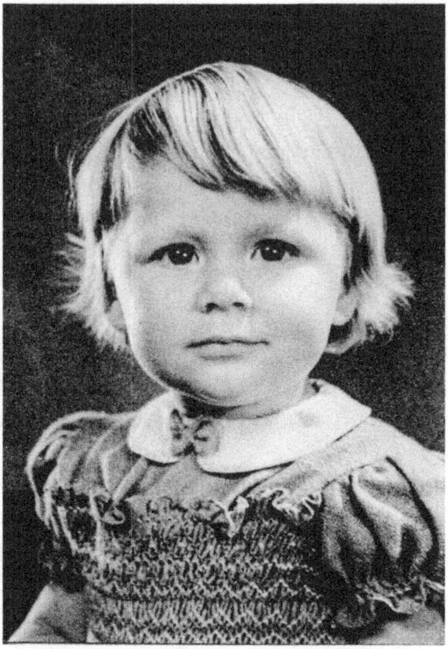

A studio snap. Me aged four, wearing a dress typical of this era, made by my mother I think with a smocking stitch bodice and neat white collar

If we were ever ill, the doctor might be summoned. He would arrive with his small brown leather case in which he kept his stethoscope. He would sit on the bed, take our temperatures, check our chests, have a chat and tell us that he thought we would soon be better. Mother would bring us up little individual trays with things to keep us occupied and to take our minds off our ailments – puzzles, colouring books, dainty morsels to eat and always a little arrangement of flowers in a wee Shippam's shrimp paste pot. She was wonderful, always paying great attention to the detail.

Once after weeks of a very sore throat the doctor advised that I should have my tonsils removed. I had to go to hospital while all the rest of the family went off to have fun at the King's Lynn fair. That really upset me.

When we were better, we might have a treat day out and go to Castle

Acre, or the valley in Ringstead, which was an old chalk pit with steep sides which we had fun climbing up and down. And in spring we would take a picnic to the bluebell woods a few miles from home.

A particular holiday I remember after we had all been ill was spent in the Lake District. I can smell it now: that earthy, damp, boggy Lake-Districty smell. I sat by a stream and diligently made a little woven basket out of the dark green spiky grasses that were growing in clumps at the edge of the water. As we walked back to the car, I filled it with little treasures which I gathered along the way: a feather, some stones, berries and flowers.

Mrs Wright was the village post lady. She had a small, whiskery face and grey hair and would bicycle a mile from the village every day, in all weathers, to deliver our post. She would come up the long drive along which there was a beautiful beech hedge which had apparently been planted by Italian prisoners of war. She probably biked about ten miles a day as she went all round the village to the other outlying farmhouses. She always gave us a little present at Christmas time, and cards. I don't know where she lived. She came on her big old 'sit-up-and-beg' bicycle which had a huge basket on the front into which all the post was stuffed into an old grey post office bag. We always looked out for her through the window when we were having our breakfast in the dining room.

Mr Kleeneze came too, once a month in his little van laden with cleaning products. My mother would always go out and greet him and buy something even if she didn't need it – a new mop head, or shoe-cleaning brushes, bright yellow dusters, or some furniture polish. His van smelt clean . . . of polish. He liked to stand and chat for a while with the doors of his van open, hoping perhaps that, as the chat continued, we'd purchase a few more goodies.

Mr Ayres delivered the coal. He lived in the village and had a thriving business. The fishmonger came once a week, always a treat when he had some delicious fresh catch driven down from Grimsby overnight. All these door-to-door services, in those days … served always with a smile.

Our birthday parties were marathons – well, they must have been for our mother, who would lay out a long, decorated table in the kitchen, laden with food. All our favourites were carefully arranged, sandwiches, cakes, jellies, ice-cream, enough for about sixteen-or-so children. Once I remember I had been to the dentist in the morning to have a plate fitted to try and correct my crooked front teeth. It was a horrible great pink thing, a plastic disc filling the roof of my mouth, with wires attached round my back teeth. And on that day of my birthday party it was so uncomfortable that I couldn't even talk. I had a kind of lisp. I asked if I could take it out. But no, I had to keep it in. I didn't think that was very good timing, to have to go to the dentist and have a plate fitted on the day of my party.

After the birthday teas we would always play all sorts of games. Tail on the donkey, musical chairs, pass the parcel, sucking up peas with a straw … Guessing the contents of things that were in little frilly paper cup-cake holders: flour, sugar, cocoa powder, salt, baking powder, semolina. We were only allowed to smell, not taste. Then there was always sardines, and we would finish with hide-and-seek. We would all disappear into the various cupboards and corners of the house, which was quite fun for our friends who did not know the house as well as we did.

Once when my best friend, Gina, had hidden under our parents' bed she was so surprised and a little uncertain when she found she was lying next to what seemed to be a leg. It was my father's spare artificial limb which he used to keep underneath the bed! Raucous shrieks from Gina. That's still one of her favourite stories that I love. I remember hiding on the top shelf of the airing cupboard in the bathroom – it seemed ages before I was found. What fun we had, and my father would always record the parties on his cine camera.

One very special outing was in February, Valentine's Day, when 'the Mart' would begin in the market square of King's Lynn. This is an ancient fair which was established more than 800 years ago and was granted a Royal Charter by Henry VIII in 1537. It marks the start of the travelling season for fairground families, many of whom have worked at the Mart for generations. Nothing like the fairs of today.

Thinking back, it was extraordinary. It is obviously very politically incorrect to describe what I am about to but, since it is a remarkable piece of history, I hope you will forgive me.

It was the viewing of 'The Midgets'. There was a scene set up in a trailer, a perfect little domestic setting, but everything was in miniature except for a huge, very fluffy sleepy marmalade cat which was sitting on a chair in the foreground. Beside the cat was a small table and a dear little lady pottering about beside it. She had a wizened face, but her body was perfectly proportioned. She was only about three feet tall, dressed in black. There was a gentleman too, not quite so miniature. The crowds were gathered round peering at them. Along the top of the trailer in red and gold lettering was a sign proclaiming:

'THE MIDGETS. To view 2/-'

What can they have been feeling or thinking? Perhaps they were pleased to be able to make some money.

Then there were the performing fleas. A table was set out, a bit like a small billiard table. The fleas (apparently) had tiny coaches attached to them, and were supposed to be having a race. You could bet on which one you thought was going to win. Doesn't this sound completely bonkers? Well, it was, but the memories are as vivid as though I was watching them right now.

Sundays were special. Simply because Sundays were Sundays. The day of rest. Shops were closed. Families got together. People went to church. We nearly always visited Granny on a Sunday. She lived in Hunstanton, which was about ten miles from Stanhoe. I stayed over for a night once and was excited as I found it was different sleeping in a house which was in a street with other houses next door and across the road. It was different from being on our farm in the middle of nowhere. What was most unfamiliar were the sounds. In the morning, instead of hearing the dawn chorus, there was the clip clop, clip clop sound of the horse-drawn milk cart coming up the road. I peered out of the window and watched him as he disappeared off to make further deliveries.

We would sometimes go to morning church, and then we always had Sunday lunch at the Lodge Hotel. It had quite extensive gardens in which we would go out and play, and very low-cut box hedges which had that very particular box hedge smell which I liked. Lunch was delicious, especially the famous jugged hare (I've still not been able to emulate that deliciously rich gravy or the dish itself – must keep searching for a recipe). Once at pudding time I was crunching away like mad on something and Dad asked me why I was I making such a noise. We noticed that the sundae dish in which the ice cream was served had a huge chip out of it, and it seemed I had been busily crunching away on the glass! Luckily it didn't seem to do me any harm.

After lunch it was off to Sunday School in Old Hunstanton Church. We sat on little chairs at the back of the church and listened to Bible stories; we sang hymns and said our prayers. I always liked Sunday School.

My godmother had given me a beautiful unique bracelet, golden, made out of twisted metal in an ornate swirly design with a simple clasp. She had bought it back from Ethiopia where she and her husband had lived for several years. Her husband was the British Consulate there when Haile Selassie was emperor. I adored this bracelet and always wore it on Sundays; that was when one wore one's Sunday best. Once when we were at church, we walked back to Granny's house, about half a mile, and halfway back I realised I had lost my bracelet. I was heartbroken. Several weeks later we were at church again. As I knelt down to pray, I looked round and noticed the woman in the pew behind us. She was leaning on the back of our pew, her hands clasped in the prayer position. Her wrists were exposed and there, upon her wrist, was my bracelet! I had to contain myself, but after a few minutes as we moved on to singing the next hymn, I nudged my mother. Oh, my goodness, I was so excited, but what were we to do?

When church had finished, we decided we would follow her and see where she lived. She sidled into one of the little cottages close by. We decided we had to brave it and knock on her door. She came to the door, bracelet and all, and very politely my mother asked how she had come by the beautiful item she was wearing on her wrist. She told us she had found it lying on the pavement a few weeks earlier. Very politely again, we told her it was we who had lost it, and would she mind very much allowing us to have it back, since it was a very special gift from my godmother. Of course she understood, took it off, and said she was so pleased to be able to return it to its rightful owner. I still have the bracelet today, having lost it twice since then while gardening!

Afternoons on Sundays at Granny's were spent having tea, being very good and polite. If we were especially well behaved we would be offered a peppermint sweet from the silver sugar bowl which was kept in a bow-fronted corner cupboard.

A visit next door to Mr and Mrs Hunter's to watch television was the ultimate treat, since we had no TV. Bill and Ben, the Flowerpot Men, Muffin the Mule and Andy Pandy were our favourites.

On the journey home we would pass a little thatched cottage standing at the edge of open fields. My father always called it the witch's cottage, and he would always get us to look across the field. If smoke was rising from the chimney, we would know that 'the witch was at home'.

From around the age of four we would wait at the bottom of the drive in the mornings, with our satchels, to get the bus to our small school at Burnham Overy, which was four miles down the hill beyond Burnham Market. It was called Mrs Hattersley's. It was a low wooden building with a veranda and long garden at the front. There were two simple schoolrooms in which we did our lessons sitting at little wooden double desks – about thirty children, and among them my best friend Gina. There was a boy I liked, and he showed me one day what the difference between me and him was. Yes, he proudly showed me his willy. Being just the three of us girls, I had no idea about such things; but when I asked if I could see it again, since it was pretty fascinating to me, alas he wouldn't show me.

I enjoyed going to that little school. We basked in the surroundings of High Barn, cosseted to some degree, but were innocent children just being children. I will treasure forever all these early childhood memories, from an era which seems to have slipped through our fingers so quickly.

When I was seven years old, in 1953, I went away to my first boarding school.

Chapter 4

Hethersett

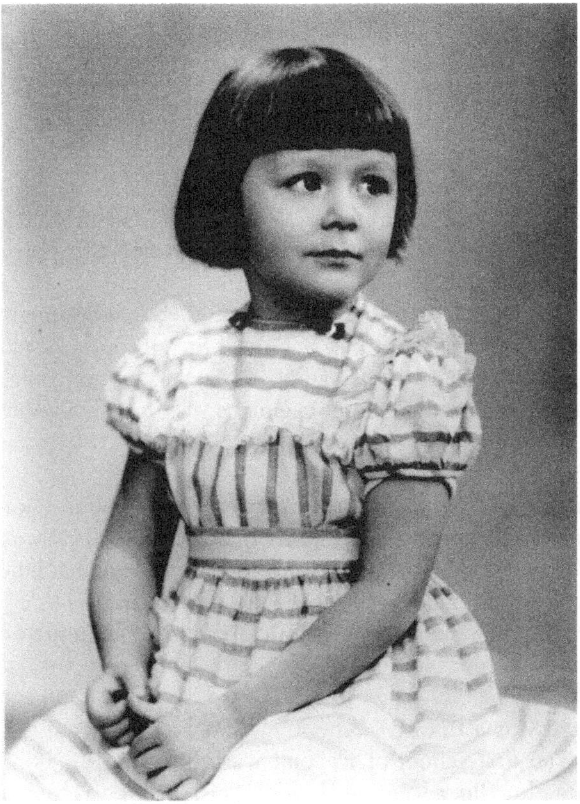

An early photo of me wearing one of my favourite dresses. I don't think my hair has ever been so neat and shiny

I am, I can, I ought, I will. We always chanted this school motto following the morning's assembly and hymn singing, before heading off into our chilly classrooms for lessons.

I thought the name of my headmistress at Hethersett School was a pretty one. I would not have minded being called Christabel myself. But her pretty name did not in my opinion quite suit her. Her grey hair was scraped back off her forehead into a tight bun, a common style for ladies of that age at that time. She must have been in her late fifties when I went to school at the age of seven. She had unfortunate teeth. Funny how such random things can make such a lasting impression on a young child.

I remember a friend's daughter once telling me she did not like her headmistress. When I asked her why that was, she said it was because she had horrible legs. I kind of understood. It was not that I did not like our headmistress, but the fact that I did not find her looks comforting to me did not help me to engender any feelings of warmth towards her. I would have preferred that, I think.

Hethersett was a P.N.E.U. school, i.e., Parents' National Educational Union. The first school of its kind was opened in London 1892 by Henrietta Franklin, a wealthy philanthropist, and it was founded on the philosophy of the education reformer Charlotte Mason (1842–1923). The basic theory and intentions were that school life should be based upon the understanding that a child is born a person. Their personality should not be encroached upon, whether by fear or love, suggestion, or influence. There was obviously a need for authority, but it was clearly understood that this should never be to the detriment of the child. It was intended that by accepting these ideas those in authority would be freeing the child from any possible emotional stress, providing a sense of security, with freedom in which to grow and with the assurance that each child would be treated individually with an appreciation of his or her specific talents, ability and needs.

There was a particular emphasis on the importance of the child's creative development, and ample scope for creative work in prose, poetry, art and handicrafts. Plenty of time was allowed for outdoor activities, nature study, physical exercise, games and study of the Bible.

It was implied that the staff should develop a 'nurturing friendship' with the children rather than present themselves as forbidding authority figures. They should always be at hand if needed, an encouraging presence, and ready to learn and discover themselves alongside the children.

In Charlotte Mason's own words, 'We should allow no separation to grow up between the intellectual and spiritual life of children but should teach them that the divine spirit has constant access to their spirits, and is their continued helper in all the interests, duties and joys of life.' She was obviously a progressive thinker who devoted her life to children, their education and their emotional wellbeing.

I believe there is some truth in the idea that any philosophy or theory is only as good as those who deliver it. There is no doubt that all the teachers at my school were all perfectly kind and perhaps very committed people, but they must themselves have been traumatised to a greater or lesser degree. The war had ended, but they had lived through it. What on earth might their tragic stories have been? Many had lost their loved ones, boyfriends, fiancés, husbands, parents, aunts and uncles, friends, siblings; their homes might have been razed to the ground; they experienced mass evacuation, and constant uncertainty. So I imagine that most, if not all of our teachers had borne the weight of horrific experiences, were harbouring desperate memories and to some extent surely must have been struggling emotionally.

So here were all our teachers picking themselves up, trying to start all over again in peacetime. Pleased no doubt to have found employment, they had maybe decided to care for little children in a way they themselves had perhaps not been cared for during wartime. They were, however, an odd bunch. I can now understand that this was not at all surprising. They were doing the very best they were capable of at the time.

Our parents had sent us to this boarding school with the very best intentions too. The ethos of the school matched their creative approach to life. It was a way of giving us a head start, one which my father certainly had not experienced himself as a young boy. My mother's education had been very different: a succession of governesses had taught her at home. We touched on this once in a conversation, how the governesses came and went rather too frequently. My mother had always wondered why. I think she suspected that perhaps her father fancied them, one after the other.

It was certainly a privilege to be attending this private, fee-paying school. What else was it? For me it was a peculiar experience which at the time I could not make head or tail of. I could not understand it because most of the time I seemed to be feeling humiliated, shameful, ridiculed, guilty, stupid, inadequate, untrustworthy and sad – whereas I thought I was supposed to be happy to be learning all sorts of facts, figures and useful and interesting things that I'd be so proud to tell people all about. But there I was.

It is only now, as a grown woman, a parent, a mother and a grandmother, that I am able to think about it from this different perspective. I observe my grandchildren. It's perfectly clear that first and foremost a child of seven needs to feel secure, know they are loved, with their parents never far away.

In later life I started to wonder whether I could truly have been only seven years old when I went to Hethersett. It did seem very young. I needed to confirm that this was not all in my imagination. So one day when I was at High Barn, I rummaged through the contents of the old oak chest in which all the family memorabilia were kept. There, along with the lace christening robe, the photos, babies' shoes, wartime magazines and much more, I found some dusty, faded brown envelopes filled with letters. Some were neatly labelled, some randomly shoved together in no order.

I found an envelope marked 'children's school letters', and one with my name on it. My mother had written in her flamboyant handwriting my name, MIRANDA 1953, and in brackets 'age 7'. So, it was confirmed.

At the end of the holidays at High Barn, I always dreaded loading up the car with our huge trunks. The school was about forty miles from our home, just outside the village of Hethersett, near Norwich and about a mile from the church. The main schoolhouse was elegant, Queen Anne-style architecture, painted white with a pretty, ornate, semi-circular front doorway with two pillars. Quite imposing. All set in beautiful grounds with a huge copper beech tree and a mulberry tree, an outdoor raised theatre area where we used to perform our plays, and further extensive gardens and woods. A sweeping driveway led off the main road. It was always when we turned in to the drive and approached the front door that my stomach began churning. I knew the goodbye was coming. One of the gardeners would be there to help unload the trunks from the car and carry them into the main marble floored hall.

On returning to school for each term, along with the large trunk for our clothes we had a smaller one which was filled with our sweets. We would form a queue after lunch outside the bathroom and, under the watchful eye of the weird and fierce matron, we would be allowed to choose three sweets. We would take as long as we possibly could choosing them . It was one of the few highlights. I would pacify myself dreaming of the following day when it would be 'sweets time' again.

Going down to the sweet shop at the end of the holidays was the best bit. I dreaded going back to school but the sweet shop trip made it bearable. The shop had every item of confectionery imaginable. The jars were all pretty, all colours, all shapes and sizes, row upon row of them neatly lined up on the high shelves. Miss Hill, who ran the shop, had a little ladder that she used to climb up, teetering on the top rung so as to be able to reach the jars on the very top shelf. It seemed I always wanted the ones on the very top. I would always say sorry as she scrambled up to get the jars down.

Painstakingly, she would weigh them out, usually a quarter of a pound; or sometimes she would kindly mix two sorts together so I could have just a few of each. They would be popped into a white paper bag. Golden-and-black striped humbugs, Fox's Glacier Mints, Everton mints, aniseed balls, Edinburgh rock (the delicious original which just kind of frothed and then slowly melted on your tongue). If she had it in stock, I would be allowed a box of Callard and Bowser's nougat. Oh, yum! Each little slab was individually wrapped in rice paper, which you didn't have to remove, it just melted as you ate it. It had nuts and cherries in it. The outer wrapping was beautiful, embossed silver paper which I used to smooth out and keep as treasure.

My mother would talk to the matron who greeted us back to school and told us which dormitory we would be sleeping in. The rooms each had the name of a flower: Daffodil, Sunflower, Forget-Me-Not, Poppy. I did not like being in Forget-Me-Not, which was a smaller, four-bedded dormitory; although I knew it was not so, I thought I might have been forgotten about. Sunflower was a bigger dormitory at the top of the stairs, which led on to the headmistress's room. We would find our room, safely tuck our treasures from home into the bedside cabinet and then go back down for the final farewell.

I hated having to wave goodbye to my parents as they disappeared off down the driveway and on to the main road, but it had to be done... and I had to get on with the term ahead as best I could. To start with I was at school with Anabel, and when she moved on to our next school Antonia joined me at Hethersett; so I was always fortunate to have a sister there with me at the same time.

Our whispered conversations in bed at night were usually all about our holidays, our family, our animals and our daily adventures. A girl who was in my dormitory one term lived in India. Her parents had sent her back over to England for a traditional education. Another was from Belgium, one from Switzerland. These girls' parents were not in the country, let alone the county. Gina had gone to a different boarding school as a weekly boarder. I always wished she had been there with me.

My sisters and I were the envy of some of the girls, as our parents used to come for an afternoon visit once a term. They would bring a picnic and take us out somewhere, often bringing the tame jackdaw with them as he needed to be fed on a regular basis and did not like being left alone! A little reprieve, a moment of escape. And yet, the fact that they visited didn't seem to make me feel any happier. I would look forward to their visit, but then we had to say goodbye all over again. I would long to go back home with them to the High Barn, to my own little bed, in my own little room, and be among all that I knew and loved.

We talked about the pets, how they all were, the menagerie, the garden, what was happening in the village, what vegetables were in season, and how they were off to Paris next week for a holiday. How I wished I could go with them. They said they would send us a postcard. I usually had to fight back the tears when they left.

Sundays were always the ritualistic letter-writing day. I remember that once, following the Christmas holiday, my letter read 'Dear Mummy and Daddy, I hope you are both well, I am. [All the letters started this way.] I love my new blue dressing gown. It keeps me very warm. Thank you very much for it. Love from Tookie.'

The matron would stand over you and read what you had written; she might suggest you said something else, like what a lovely time you were having. More often than not she would pass a very derogatory comment about your poor, untidy handwriting, correct your spelling and suggest that your parents would not think you were working very hard if you sent such a brief letter to them.

Tookie was my nickname. I think it originated from the incident when I was reading to my little sister in my made-up language. Or even perhaps when I was younger and I had difficulty saying 'book'. I used to say 'took' instead.

Sunday was the one day I enjoyed. We would walk in a crocodile along the pavement a mile to the church. I always loved singing the hymns and once sang a solo at a church concert, this beautiful hymn by Charles Wesley. I think my father must have been very proud.

May the grace of Christ our Saviour,
And the Father's boundless love,
With the Holy Spirit's favour
Rest upon us from above.

I kept it a secret that I liked singing hymns. I thought I would be teased and called a goody-goody, so I thought it safer to keep it to myself.

All through the term I dreamt about the holidays, being back at home. I was still trying to work out why I had been what felt like 'sent away'. I wanted to tell my mummy and daddy that I didn't like being at school. Years later I did attempt a conversation with my mother about our schooling, but it felt like a bit of a delicate subject. I knew they were doing the very best for us.

Sending one's children to boarding school was the norm among those families with whom they socialised. Compared with my mother's experience of being educated in semi-isolation with her various governesses, I am sure it was also intended as a means for us girls to engage in a healthy way with others. Perhaps it was also seen partially as a place of safety, but in all truth I never really knew. I have spoken to other people who asked me why I had not talked to my parents about what I felt, but looking back it was not something I ever considered. I was only young and, in those days, I just accepted this as normal.

The classrooms were cold, a single radiator which we would fight over to sit close to. The one I liked the best was the old, converted railway carriage in which we had our nature lessons. It was filled with everything that I found most interesting, including dead birds which we would learn to dissect and examine, and birds' eggs, in the days when it was not illegal to collect them. It was the 'hands-on' classroom. I never felt under stress when I was in there, which I did, almost without exception, with all the other lessons.

We would have a break mid-morning when we had to drink a quarter of a pint of cold milk with a straw. I could not swallow milk. It made me sick. So, I would wait until the teacher was not looking in my direction and pass my bottle to the girl behind who loved it – so, lucky for her! She would pass me her empty bottle under the desk. I was caught once doing this and made to stand outside the classroom in the cold with my face to the wall and miss the class altogether. The worst thing about that was if the headmistress came by and saw you. You would then have to go to her room and explain yourself. There was little leeway with respect to punishments it seemed to me, even if swallowing milk made you sick.

Endless research has been done, personal stories told, and educational theories expounded regarding boarding schools. Films made too, books written. One in particular, *The Making of Them* by Nick Duffell, which I have read, was received with critical acclaim. Another of his I have yet to read is called *Trauma, Abandonment and Privilege*. The titles alone sum it all up, speak volumes. Yet, difficult as I found it, the experience probably toughened me up, and I believe it's possible to turn adversity to advantage. It is a choice one can make.

During the summer holidays, we enjoyed the gathering-in of the harvest. When the corn had been cut with the huge, bright red Massey Ferguson combine harvester the stubble would be burnt. Before the burning of the stubble operation Dad would often go out and see if he could shoot a rabbit or a hare, which might have been hunkering down in the warm straw. If he was successful, he would take the rabbits back to the house and hang them in one of the sheds.

I used to love their little white fluffy tails and I would cut them off and keep them in a tin which I had painted pink. I took the tin to Hethersett with me and kept it in the bedside cabinet. I used to stroke my cheeks with the fluffy tails at night time to try to get myself to sleep. They were my comforters.

I also took a little carved wooden hippopotamus with me, which an aunt had given me. She lived in Kenya and had given us girls all sorts of carved animals over the years. I used to self-harm, bash my hands and wrists with the hippopotamus until I was bruised, then would run to the matron having made up some story about how I had tripped over. I learnt to tell good lies. I used to cut myself to draw blood and smear it on my clothes drawing attention to myself, and all in the hope I suppose of getting some sympathy.

You might be teased by other girls for being a cry-baby, or punished by the matron for keeping the other girls in the dormitory awake. The quick-witted ones, if they were caught talking, usually came up with a convincing excuse, and it was usually the goody-goodies who got into trouble.

Once when I was quite ill with mumps I had to be in the isolated sick bay for several weeks. When I was a bit better, I was allowed out for some air and was told to make sure I was back at a certain time. The matron had lent me her watch, but I could not tell the time and dared not tell her so. I was so petrified of getting into trouble and ashamed that I could not tell the time, I pretended I had lost the watch and that was the reason why I was late back. I had in fact hidden it in an old tree stump. The matron was furious, and I was told to go out again the next day and find it, which of course I did.

As well as self-harming, having said my prayers I cried myself to sleep under my bedclothes most nights. This was my favourite prayer. I learnt these first two verses by heart.

Matthew, Mark, Luke and John,
Bless the bed that I lay on,
Before I lay me down to sleep,
I give my soul to Christ to keep.

Four corners to my bed,
Four angels there aspread,
Two to foot and two to head
And four to carry me when I'm dead.

If I was caught making any noise in bed, I might get dealt a rather more curious punishment.

Chapter 5

Psalm 23

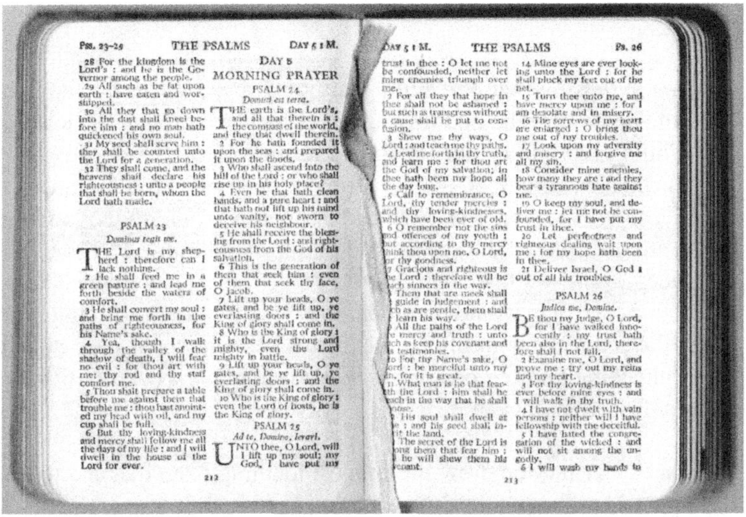

My prayer book given to me by my father on my Confirmation Day, 7th March 1959

A *shoe in the door* was the initial warning if there was a peep coming from the bedroom. The matron must have had her ear well to the door. She would grab one of our shoes and use it to prop the door open. I expect she then continued to eavesdrop in the hope of catching us at it again, which of course she often did. Next it was out on the landing. We would be ordered out of bed and told to stand in the corridor with our faces to the wall. If there were two or three of us (which there usually were), we would then be strategically placed at intervals along the corridor about fifteen feet apart. Matron would pace up and down checking that our posture was to her liking: upright, motionless statues, frozen in obeyance.

One particular matron drew the deepest loathing from me, and to this day when I conjure up a picture of her it sends a cold shiver down my spine. It seemed inconceivable that she could be a matron. I wondered if there was such a thing as job description in those days. How would the advertisement have been worded? Perhaps something like: 'Girls' boarding school requires a kindly woman to act as matron. Please apply to the headmistress.' Or perhaps it ran more like this: 'Girls' boarding school requires sadist to act as matron. Practical duties include administering medicines and providing very strict discipline of children at all times. A tendency towards cruelty and a punitive attitude would be considered an advantageous quality, together with an overall distaste for young children. Would suit spinster, witch or woman with a fierce approach and no kindly traits. Only tall dark, preferably frightening ladies with no redeeming features need apply'.

Whichever, the applicant had been this matron, who would stomp past as you were standing face to the wall. The headmistress might appear, just to check out what was going on upstairs that night. If you survived the first half-hour out on the landing, it was back to bed.

If, however, you twitched, itched, scratched, let alone sniggered, giggled or uttered a word – or were trying to hide the fact that you were blubbing – there was more to come. One of the worst positions to be ordered to stand was right at the end of the corridor, where the elegant, wide staircase met the landing. This was very close to the headmistress's bedroom. If she passed, she never spoke, just made a mental note that you were there, scowled disapprovingly, and made a strange face exposing her unfortunate teeth.

So worse was to come if either she or the matron decided that you needed to learn a harder lesson. The matron would lead you down the staff staircase to the main hall. The door was opened into an inner room, a dark place with no windows, which in turn led through to the dining room and kitchens. This was known as the 'Black Hole'. This eerie place was a kind of no man's land. No windows: therefore, even in daytime, no light. There were rows of lockers for our shoes, and some low benches on which we would sit when donning our gym or sports gear. It was an airless place, dusty and smelling of sweat, dirty socks and shoe polish. It was not difficult to understand why it was called the 'Black Hole; it was such a perfect description.

On one side of this area was a large wooden table which was used for shoe polishing. The headmistress's shoes, brogues and others, were neatly lined up in their pairs, in rows, along with the shoe-polishing kit which was crammed into a small, lidless wooden box. The matron didn't speak. You knew exactly what you had to do. One exposed light bulb hung over the polishing table, and the dim light enabled you, just, to see what you were doing. You could hear a pin drop, save for the regularity of the feverish brushing sounds as you polished away. Once your efforts were inspected and approved you would be led back up to bed, this time up the winding back staircase.

I have no idea exactly what crime I can have committed on the particular Saturday night in January when, following the shoe-polishing punishment, I was in for another surprise. Again I was led down the narrow back staircase by the poor, toothy headmistress through the Black Hole into the study where the 'Sunday letters home' were written. We then passed through the gym hall, which smelled of chalk and cheese – and smelly feet where we also used to do morning remedials if we had 'flat feet', which apparently I did have.

I was led along a corridor and into a classroom. Not my usual one. The light was turned on. The heating was off. During the daytime in class the antiquated heating system at best merely took the freeze factor out of the air and meant that the drip on the end of your nose did not materialise into an icicle. I was wearing my pale turquoise, cosy woolly dressing gown, a recent Christmas present, along with my grey-and-blue tartan felt slippers adorned with a bright little bobble. The classroom was a large one, normally used for examinations. It overlooked the garden but by now, half past nine, of course it was pitch dark outside, and all I could see was my reflection in the window.

The windows were those ones with stark metal frames – the only kind available after the war. I remember we had the same ones in the downstairs lavatory back home at High Barn. There were five rows of desks and chairs, five to each row. I was shown to the desk in the very centre of the room – third row back from the front, and middle desk in the row. I presume this position had been carefully calculated (well, maybe not, but it felt so at the time). It seemed to maximise my sense of total humiliation, isolation in the middle of a sea of desks, a sense of bewilderment as to what was happening and fear as to what might be about to happen next. After all, I was possibly only eight or nine, I think. Perhaps it might have been a little less humiliating had I been seated at the edge of the classroom. I could have hugged the wall for a bit of comfort perhaps.

Anyway, there I was waiting, wondering if I was just going to be told to sit there in the cold till midnight. I honestly didn't know. Then, out of the pocket of her grey-green tweedy coat, the headmistress drew a small book and slapped it down on the desk in front of me. The embossed gold crucifix shone out against the dull black leather cover of the prayerbook, and I remember thinking, 'I love gold.' I must have been fighting back the tears. I don't remember. The headmistress opened the book, turned the pages to Psalm 23 and said, 'Learn that. I will be back in an hour.'

'The Lord is my shepherd, I shall not want…'

I don't know what the time was by then, except that it was late and, anyway, I could not tell the time so that just added to my humiliation. There appeared to be no clock in the classroom. Like the colours in a spinning top that merge into one, losing all definition, so the numbers on a clock or on the face of a watch always seemed to me to be just a jumble of black and white marks.

I don't remember much after that. But eventually I was led back through the dreaded letter-writing room thinking that on the Sunday I would have to write again.

Dear Mummy and Daddy, I hope you are well, I am.
I love my new dressing gown, it keeps me very warm.
Thank you very much.
Love from Tookie.

Little did they know about the twenty-third Psalm episode. I never talked to them about punishments.

Recently I found the Holy Bible given to me by my Aunt Biddy, my father's elder sister, to mark the year of my birth in 1946. I treasure the Book of Common Prayer given to me by my father on my confirmation day, 7 March 1959. I was thirteen at the time, and by that time had moved to my next boarding school. A white cover this time, with an embossed silver cross. In the front of it I had written, 'Thou, Lord, are worthy of better worship than I can ever offer thee. Purify my heart, open my lips and stir my will so that what I give to thee may be the best that I can offer.'

And here I am. Determined to do the very best that I can. Somehow I have always managed to keep the faith.

Clearly, much of Charlotte Mason's philosophy was based on the Christian tradition. I am grateful for that, but less appreciative of the strange methods by which they chose to instil some of the Bible teachings. In the long run it has actually done me no harm. Or so I tell myself.

We did have some fun too in the bedroom, on the one night at the end of the summer term when we were allowed to have a midnight feast. We stayed awake and guzzled on all kinds of food that we had hoarded, and we shared a chocolate biscuit layer cake that my mother had made especially. So boarding school was not all bad.

There were other things I enjoyed as well as midnight feasts. I was pleased when Antonia came to Hethersett, because I had missed her. I looked out for her and used to go and meet her at break time and see if she was OK. I loved the singing of hymns. I loved taking off our boring grey school uniform after the school day was finished and changing into mufti, our own clothes – I felt comforted. And it brought the sense of home a little closer again. I enjoyed our gardens. We had little individual beds which we would tend, plant, weed and harvest. We collected seeds and recorded it all in our nature notebooks.

Very occasionally we might get invited in to sit with the headmistress and have a chat. Perhaps it was following a punishment session, her way of making amends. I have no idea, but at least I felt I was getting some individual attention and was not just an insignificant blur amid a whole sea of other girls. I liked it when I found I was to sleep in Daffodil.

Some girls weathered it well. I found it peculiar, primarily since the emotional wellbeing of the children seemed to have got lost somewhere along the way. There was little or no opportunity or indeed encouragement to voice what one was feeling. Being away from the familiarity of home and my parents I found hard. But it seemed a bit like the subject of money. In those days one never spoke about such things.

Having written about these early school days has inevitably made me think about the different learning styles:

If you tell me, I will forget.
If you show me, I may remember
If you involve me, I will understand.

The first issue for me when at this school was that I was obviously homesick. It did not appear that anybody understood this, or how it was affecting me and my ability to learn. On top of that I did not feel engaged with any of the teachers. I was fearing failure most of the time, and unable to study with any genuine enthusiasm or desire. I never really understood anything that I was supposed to be learning about. I was not able to take things in or gain any sense of achievement.

Education, what a vast subject. When I left Hethersett I knew I would be moving to a bigger school, another boarding school, but I hoped it might be a bit different. I was older by then – and, anyway, a long, hot summer holiday lay ahead.

Chapter 6

1953 and beyond

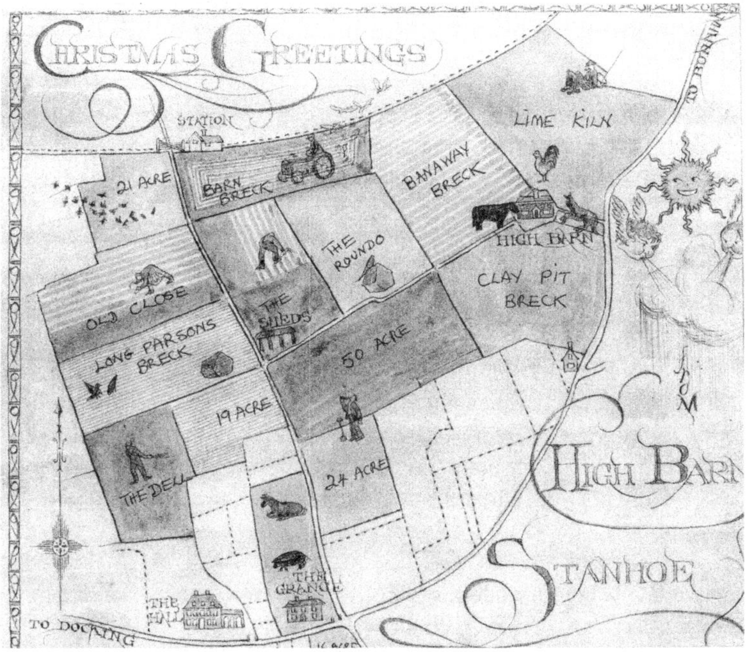

A Christmas card of the High Barn Farm map drawn by my mother

That year, 1953, was indeed a long, hot summer. It was unusual in that it was a prolonged late-season summer with temperatures breaking all records. More than twenty highs in the 80s and 90s Fahrenheit were recorded, by far the most of any year in those times.

Earlier in the year, on the fateful night of 31 January, the unpredicted storm conditions resulted in one of the worst flood disasters in history. The north Norfolk coast was ravaged by exceptional high tides, which broke through the sea defences. This was caused by a combination of North Sea high tides, atmospheric pressure, and ferocious hurricane-force winds: the perfect, imperfect storm. One hundred people died, and homes were swept away overnight. The sea literally raged inland, the storm-whipped waters surging relentlessly, creating devastation from King's Lynn eastward all around the coast to Yarmouth and beyond.

Nowadays a colour-coded weather warning would be issued from the Met Office from yellow, then amber to red, at which stage all families would be advised to evacuate and seek safety at inland locations. Seventy years ago, there was no such early warning system, and the people of Norfolk were literally in the dark since the defences were breached under the cover of the night.

It was not exactly what one might call a sightseeing jolly, to go and witness the aftermath of such a tragedy, but we did. We drove along to Wells-next-the-Sea and, as we passed Holkham, I remember shouting out and then crying when I suddenly saw that there were lots of dead sheep caught up high, hanging there bedraggled in the trees. It was impossible to believe that the sea had wreaked such havoc.

On the harbourside at Wells, a large fishing vessel had been torn from its mooring, and amid other piles of debris and smashed-up boats it lay forlorn on its side. Crowds of people were standing silently. After wandering for a while and taking in the scene we sat on the harbour wall eating fish and chips which we had bought from Mr French's famous quayside shop. On the return journey I remember hiding my face as we passed the dead sheep in the trees. I didn't want to see them again. I felt frightened.

A happier memory of 1953 was that of the Queen's coronation, Queen Elizabeth II. She was twenty-seven years old, having suddenly been thrust into the limelight the previous year when her father, George VI, had died suddenly. She had married Philip Mountbatten in 1947 at the age of twenty-one and unexpectedly five years later became Queen on 6 February. A period of nearly sixteen months passed between the death of her father and the time she was crowned on 2 June 1953.

Every city, town and village in the country celebrated all day, and danced the night away. The country was on hold. Street parties were held in every corner of Britain and the hardship of rationing was apparently banished for the day.

I was fascinated to hear from an elderly lady about some of the more specific aspects of how people managed during those years of rationing. A cake would have been a luxury – well, one of any reasonable size. So in towns and villages a street might club together and offer up whatever ingredients they had: sugar, flour, butter, currents, cherries, nuts, enough to make a fair-sized cake which they would then share out. On other occasions, when not enough ingredients were available, a little cake would be baked, whatever size it turned out to be. They would then make a large cardboard cut-out cover to place over the cake. What a wonderfully creative idea! Community was so strong, and was the key to survival and to keeping one's spirits up during those difficult times.

So I imagine there must have been a great sense of camaraderie as everyone prepared for the coronation festivities. It was particularly exciting since it was announced that it would be televised. Few people had a television, but those who did opened their homes for others to come along to view the spectacle. Some folk went out and bought one especially so they could watch it. Separate colour filming took place for showing in cinemas, but colour TV broadcasting did not begin in the UK until 1967.

Our little village of Stanhoe was no exception in its huge efforts to celebrate the day in style. The usual weather in June would have been mild and sunny, but strangely on 2nd June there was a near gale-force wind blowing into the village straight from the North Sea, bringing with it cold temperatures and deluging rain. The fancy-dress parade was practically a wipe-out, as people's costumes, often made from crêpe paper, disintegrated about them in the rain. Scantily dressed elves and fairies and numerous nursery-rhyme characters carried on enjoying themselves regardless. The competition was held in front of the Grange barns, which were all part of our farm buildings in the village. The celebrations carried on in the teeth of the wind and every child was presented with a coronation mug

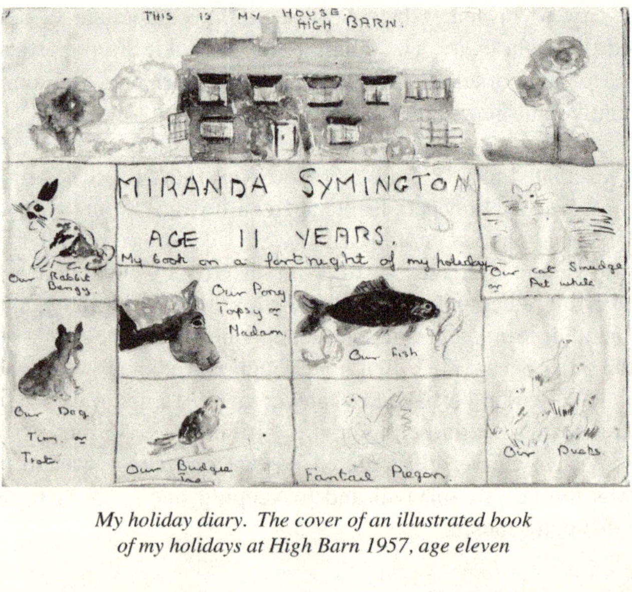

My holiday diary. The cover of an illustrated book of my holidays at High Barn 1957, age eleven

The banquet which was to feed well over 100 people was laid out inside the barns. Long trestle tables were decorated with red, white and blue tablecloths; the barns were festooned with bunting and the tables laden with food of all sorts. The main meal was cold meats, salad and hundreds of those unforgettably delicious tiny pickled onions. My father always loved a pickled onion. I wonder who on earth peeled so many. I have always found it impossible to peel a pickled onion.

The sports event had to be postponed until the following Saturday, as the field in which it was to be held had turned into a bit of a quagmire. I remember that so well. Mrs Footer, wife of one of our tractor drivers, was running so fast, determined to win the ladies' running race, that her big, baggy bloomers fell down. Rather rudely we all laughed, but she didn't seem to be upset!

Our dear Queen has passed away now. Her faith maintained her throughout her long and momentous reign. She was our sovereign for seventy years and 214 days, and is the longest-reigning British monarch and longest verified reigning female monarch in history. She bore, with such good grace, so many horrendous experiences during her lifetime. The trials she endured included the murder of Lord Louis Mountbatten (her distant cousin and uncle of her husband), the divorce of three of her four children, the death of her daughter-in-law, Princess Diana, and the terrible fire at Windsor Castle in which the Crimson Drawing Room was gutted and the private chapel badly damaged. All had been set alight by a lamp igniting a curtain. I know about fire. It's terrifying when not intended and out of control. The poor Queen had to face all these very personal dramas in her life while the world looked on.

We are now having to get used to saying 'our king', instead of 'our queen'. It feels strange. Charles will obviously have a bit of a hard act to follow and, since he is now over seventy, will have fewer years in the driving seat. The next era is going to be interesting, particularly with regards to the future of the monarchy. I wonder what will happen. Hopefully no more tragedy.

So, back to 1953. I remember on 29th May my mother being intrigued and wildly excited when the news broke that the thirty-four-year-old

New Zealander mountaineer Edmund Hillary and his Nepalese Sherpa guide, Tenzing Norgay, had accomplished their mission to conquer Mount Everest. We all sat round and listened on the radio. They were the first to achieve this, and many climbers had been lost in previous attempts. It took them a total of sixteen days to traverse the south-eastern ridge and reach the summit at 29,035 feet. The Sherpa people can acclimatise to the thinner air more quickly than other climbers, since they have adapted to living in the high altitudes.

I recently went to a talk by the charismatic Sir Ranulph Fiennes, who is to date the oldest British person alive to have climbed Everest, and who has crossed both polar ice caps. It was fascinating to hear him say how inspired he was by Sir Edmund Hillary. He said he was at a young, impressionable age when he heard about Hillary, who 'got right inside my brain and started scratching away and didn't let go'. Fiennes travelled to New Zealand to celebrate the life of this great man. What a lovely thing to have done. He said Hillary was one of three people who influenced and affected his whole life, along with Robert Falcon Scott and his own father.

My parents always seemed fascinated with the great explorers, those from times gone by and ones who were achieving amazing feats in their lifetime as well. Perhaps it's because such people served as role models, examples of what one can accomplish when one puts one's mind to an ideal and commits. In my father's case this was certainly true of his efforts to overcome adversity.

During the holidays we tried to help mother with her 'to do' list. There were always hundreds of things needing attention. I have adopted the same system. I love it and get great pleasure from ticking things off – and if I have completed a job that was not on the list in the first place (because I had forgotten to write it down) then I write it down just so I can tick it off. Well, that's just one silly way of giving oneself a positive mark when they are in short supply.

One of my young techy friends seems to think it's a crazy thing, having a 'to do' list, but I like to think that all the young living in the fast lane, as they seem to, have their lists secretly tucked away somewhere on their mobiles and they are constantly checking them to see what they must remember to do, or re-do, or not do, or undo or have forgotten to do.

My mother's handwritten list pinned up on her desk in the late 1940s might have read something like this:

TO DO
Pick fruit
Bottle plums
Mend curtains
Get butter
Make chicken stock
Check mole hills
Mend broken leg on chair
Sew up pillowcase
Make meringues
Bottle pears
Sweep
Find where chicken is laying, could be under hedge
Gather sticks
Go ragworting in the meadow
Glue the broken swan which Jackie has broken
Find out where I can get Muscovy ducks
Get weed from village pond
Polish table in sitting room
Take Topsy to Algie's for new shoes
Plant more daffs down drive
Make felt skirts for Xmas
Get a new dog bowl
Paint back door
Mix mud for nesting swallows
Empty old trough and refresh water
Check on tadpoles' development
Post letter and get more butter
Sort woodshed
Do church flowers
Darn socks

Meanwhile my father would be instructing us in the fine art of trimming the edges of the grass along the garden path at the side of the house. We were to use a Wilkinson Sword-edge razor blade! Yes, true. He was very particular about some things, so we always tried to make a good job of it. I always liked to try to help. I had fallen into that role of 'dear good little helpful girl'.

I would do anything to keep the peace too, keep things sweet, not rock the boat, be compliant. That seemed the best way, and it had unwittingly become my modus operandi and one of my coping strategies. I hated it when there were any arguments, or if I sensed an atmosphere of disquiet and feared there was some sort of a row about to erupt. I never liked conflict, who does? But as a child I didn't understand what had caused it, and didn't know how to resolve it, so my way of dealing with it was to do my best to avoid it. I sometimes used to run off and hide behind the barns and wait until I thought the storm had blown over before going back to the house.

In truth, surely we all like to look good. So, as the classic people-pleaser, I would always help my mother when it was her turn to do the church flowers. I was expected to by now. Years later when I protested and said I did not want to go and help her she was very upset.

Sometimes I would help bring in the wood for the winter fires. The woodshed was a small structure, attached to the larger shed but a little way off from the house behind the garage and tucked round the corner. It had a large, heavy, black wooden door and was kept shut by means of a huge iron latch that hooked over a bolt. Dad was always furious if we left the door open, as he liked the wood to remain as dry as possible. He didn't want the door to blow open and let all the rain in. So, it was on one of those 'bringing in the wood' days that I trotted off to help. We would load the barrow and ferry it back over to the house and stack it in another shed near the back door. The gardener-cum-handyman helper was good with an axe and sawed and chopped away splitting the logs into convenient-sized pieces. We trundled many loads on this particular day. 'Next load coming up,' and off I would rush pushing the heavy barrow.

After there had been a lot of chopping it was suggested I take a smaller load, not so heavy, as it was obvious that I was getting a bit tired. So that was kind, I thought, and off I went. When I returned with the empty barrow the door of the shed was shut. I opened the door to put the barrow safely back inside where it was always kept, and there the handyman stood. I think I had caught him out in a compromising situation. Oh! I didn't really understand. He looked askance and sorted himself out. We carried on, ferrying another barrowload to the house. Mother rushed out, so pleased that the winter wood store was getting replenished.

Some weeks later it was 'bringing in the wood' day again. So rather nervously off I dutifully went. I dared not say that I did not want to help.

I remember hiding my head under my pillow one night when I heard my parents talking about the Suez Crisis. I heard them mention the word 'war'. I had no idea what this might imply, but I knew I felt frightened. I was also worried, wondering if I dare tell my mother and father that I did not want to go back to school.

But in 1958, when I was twelve, I moved on from Hethersett to my next boarding school.

Chapter 7

Clifftop school

A moody teenager age fifteen. I cropped my hair. It seems rather short and brutal

My second boarding school, Runton Hill, was perched on the clifftop at West Runton, a little village further along the coast from Burnham Market towards Cromer. The bracing winds whistled, and fresh air blew straight into the small music rooms where we practised our piano; the glass doors rattled and we'd no choice but to shiver our way through our half-hour practice times, which were usually after tea.

The headmistress was an interesting woman. She had been a Wren (Women's Royal Naval Service) and she would often give us talks about her work and travels. She would usually start them, in the same way which amused us: 'When I was in the Sudan . . .' and off she would ramble. She seemed to take a bit of a shine to my mother, I think because she empathised with her spirit, sensing that my mother, too, was a woman out of her own time. Having retired as headmistress in 1972 she came up with the unusual idea of converting a fire engine which she then drove around the world. Pretty plucky in those days for a middle-aged spinster to travel alone, let alone in an old fire engine. Her book *Around the World in a Green Goddess* is fascinating. Her uncle, the Reverend Francis Kilvert known for his diaries written in the 1800s, no doubt was an inspiration to her. She followed in his footsteps and certainly was a character, although way back then she was of course just my headmistress. I have to say I have had to work hard on trying to forgive her. She did not always choose her words that carefully.

It was more of the same for me at this school. I found most lessons difficult. There was a terrible system called 'narration'. From the red book *Citizenship*, we had to read aloud a page or more, and then one girl was chosen to narrate what had been read. I used to dread being called upon. Owing to my fear of being chosen I had been unable to concentrate or remember a thing, and was then reprimanded for not listening.

I had several attempts at the English exam and failed. The maths teacher despaired of me and told me not to go to her class any more as she couldn't bear trying to drum figures into my head for another single day. She told me not to tell anyone that she had requested this, and told me that instead of going to her lessons I should 'hide' in the music rooms and practise my piano. The writing was on the wall. I was not an academic and was never likely to become one.

I loved art, nature and music. My father gave me a guitar for my thirteenth birthday. He hoped I would study hard and be able to play like Julian Bream and Segovia. I did get up on the stage once in Stanhoe village at some summer country bop for the youth club, and I strummed a few chords. I still strum a few chords but I have not devoted enough time to serious practice. Perhaps I will one day soon. It's never too late .

Domestic science was fun, although learning how to cook soused herring and make pink blancmange was a bit of an odd choice, I think. Games I enjoyed, but really only because we were out in the lovely fresh air. Light relief with an all-night hula hoop marathon at the end of term was fun, and with holidays looming and knowing there would be a break from the cold classrooms which smelt of chalk, I remember feeling excited.

The highlights were on Saturdays. In the morning we had 'eggy bread' for breakfast instead of porridge, which I hated. We were allowed to go to Cromer or Sheringham to the shops, let out for the day. On Sundays we had church and after that we might disappear through the village into the woods and hope to meet some boys from the Gresham's private school, which was a few miles away. We would sometimes go to concerts there, and I remember falling madly in love with one of the choirboys, 100 per cent convinced of course that he was staring at me all the way through the concert. Completely infatuated. Funny how easily one can delude oneself at that age, or at any age in fact.

I always loved receiving a letter from my father in his beautiful handwriting. At the top of the letter, he would always write:

Miranda
London. Paris. New York.

I think I always felt I would be a disappointment to him but I tried not to let it bother me.

Mother's letters were often about their holiday in France, what delicious things they were eating, Lobster Thermidor, Sole Veronique and Coquilles Saint Jacques being some of my mother's favourites. She would say that they'd see us soon. She always signed her letters 'ever-loving Mum.' I always sign off this way too when I write or message my children.

There was the usual rather odd collection of teachers. The poor science teacher was a character with a very strange voice. While doing an experiment in the lab she had spilled iodine over the only photograph she had of her fiancé, who had been killed during the war. She showed it to us. All you could see were his feet – the rest was just a brown splodge.

Except for one, the teachers were all spinsters. What an odd life it must have been for them too. I had no idea where their homes were or if they even had one. Presumably in the holiday time they returned to somewhere. The geography teacher was another very strange lady. Her bosom seemed to start from just under her chin and end at her waist. It was a massive kind of protruding platform on which she used to rest her book if reading, and balance her cup of tea. A bit risky, but I remember her doing that. We had a terribly unkind nickname for her which I cannot repeat. It was too cruel.

I had a couple of friends at Runton, but I wished that Gina had come to this school. She had gone as a weekly boarder to a different school along the coast in Cromer; so I always looked forward to seeing her during the holidays.

When back from school and at High Barn I always felt we were living in a kind of isolated, utopian bubble, protected from all the goings-on out there in the world. But occasionally we did hear about them. In 1960 (I was now fourteen), there was news of the earthquake in the Moroccan city of Agadir in which a local Norfolk businessman had been one of the casualties. Mercifully he arrived home safely. This terrible news seemed to bring the world out there a bit closer, particularly since we knew of somebody who had been caught in the disaster. Over 12,000 people were killed, a third of the city's population, and 35,000 people were left homeless. It was the deadliest earthquake in Moroccan history.

Once, when I came home from Runton for the holidays, I realised the beautiful white fantail pigeons were no longer flying around. I couldn't understand it. I think there were well over a hundred of them. The odd-job man had been ordered to shoot them all, as my father said that they made too much of a mess roosting in the various garages and outhouses.

There were two different houses at school, North and South. Eventually, when I was in the sixth form, I ended up being made head of North house. I presume it must have been recognised that I did possess some leadership qualities; but apart from the privilege of having one's own bedroom it was not an envied position. The other monitors teased me. It was thought, I suppose, that one must be favoured above others so there was a certain amount of peer jealousy. All that good-old boarding-school nonsense.

Occasionally some rather odd things used to happen at this school too. Whether I really was not much liked, being head of North House, or whether it was intended merely as a light-hearted bit of fun, a joke, I will never know. But sometimes at bedtime, as if aiming to imitate the solidarity, imposing strength and dependability of the Grenadier Guards, the monitors and sixth-form girls in my house formed two lines in the hallway out of which a staircase led to the bedrooms. They raised their arms, as if they were swords, linked hands forming a military-stye arch through which I was then invited to walk while they chanted, 'We hate Miranda, we hate Miranda, we hate Miranda.' Nowadays I guess it would be called bullying. These were supposed to be my friends. Once through the arch I fled up the stairs and hid in my very small bedroom, where more often than not I indulged in mild self-harming. I cut away at my hair with a razor blade, bashed my wrists with that same wooden hippopotamus or on the chest of drawers, bit my finger nails. Sometimes I might pacify myself a little by swooning over my pin-up, the film star Tony Curtis. I thought he was so smooth.

Even though I was older now I would often go to sleep crying, with my head under the pillow.

Boarding schools are bizarre places. But I can't possibly paint the full picture, because really it was all about the emotional disturbance that I was experiencing, and that's a bit tricky to fully explain even to this day. I think maybe you get the gist, though, that I was not boarding-school material. I have heard that some people fare well in that environment; but for whatever reason, and I think there are numerous ones, I didn't. I apportion no blame. I have thought about those early years over and over and have tried my best to come up with a balanced understanding of why I was not happy.

I tried to make the best of it, I suppose, and as head of North House, having a little authority, I and the head girl took the initiative when April Fool's Day came around. What an opportunity to do something a little more fun, creative and interesting and less disgusting than the usual boring prank of smearing the lavatory seats with marmite and marmalade.

We and the other monitors in North and South Houses decided to evacuate the school of all pupils. It was nothing less than a well-planned military operation. We engineered a secret meeting (we thought possibly some members of staff had got wind of our plan but never mind). We informed all the girls that they would be woken at

5 am, and were to creep out of their bedrooms without so much of a whimper or whisper and congregate out on the playing field where they would be given a marmalade sandwich and an apple. We would then advance to the Scout hut, which was outside the perimeter of the school grounds about half a mile away. We had discussed our intended operation with the Scoutmaster, and he thought it an ingenious plan, backed us all the way and agreed to meet us there at 5.30 with a key to let us in.

Perhaps he had tipped off the headmistress as to what we were up to but we successfully accomplished the mission, and by lunchtime we were all feeling a little weary and rather hungry. No one had come to find us. So, with our tails somewhat between our legs, we thought it best to go back and get some lunch. We marched back up the drive, humming the tune of 'Colonel Bogey'. We hit the headlines in the local newspaper, *The Eastern Daily Press*. My name was mentioned. A little fame at last.

Our parents used to visit, just for a day, once a term. They would bring a picnic. In summer it consisted of all the fruits from the garden and other treats – and most importantly they would never forget to bring Jackie along. He still needed to be fed, apparently at regular intervals. There he was, squawking away in his cage. The cage, which seemed to take up all the room in the boot of the car, was perhaps something that my father had made especially for him. I remember telling my mother how I hated the fact that we had to eat the porridge every morning, except of course on Saturday when we had that yummy eggy bread for breakfast.

The porridge was not nice, and I have never been able to eat it since. There was a huge aluminium pot, and a ladle was placed beside it ready for the serving. A thick glutinous film covered the full cauldron of now-cold porridge. The film had to be broken when the porridge was served by the ruddy-faced kitchen maid, who I noticed had bitten fingernails (just like mine). But a healthy serving of it each day would keep the dreaded lurgies at bay,we were told. A bowl of hearty oats every morning is what a growing girl needs.

In 1958, the year that I started school at Runton Hill, there was great excitement because it was when the first-ever crossing of the English Channel was made by the hovercraft. The craft was researched and finally built by Saunders-Roe on the Isle of Wight, and the daughter of Sir Christopher Cockerell, its inventor, was at our school. It took two hours to make the crossing from Calais to Dover. Revolutionary in its design at the time, it gave us a sense of fun that we felt part of such an important event in nautical history.

This was also the heyday of the infamous Barbie doll, and Hamleys sold out overnight at Christmas. I was content to rely on my rabbits' tails for comfort. The first picture of the earth from outer space was taken by Explorer 6 – I remember that. That year we went to see the film *Ben Hur* in the holidays. But then back to school for the finale: the drawing to a close of my school days, when I was seventeen.

It was surprising that in my last term at Runton I was allowed to attend Norwich Art School for one day a week to study dress design. I can only assume that somebody, perhaps our art teacher Cavendish Morton realised that this could be an avenue through which my creative talent might come to light. Or maybe my mother had discussed the possibility with the headmistress. I'm not sure. But it was a good feeling at last that somebody, besides myself, recognised that the arts was where my true passion lay. So off I went – and I loved it. It felt exciting, and I knew I was in the right place.

The only reason I was sad to leave school was that I would no longer have the Sunday experience of swooning over the choirboy at Gresham School with whom I had fallen head over heels in love.

Years earlier I had failed the Eleven Plus examination. At Runton Hill I'd passed five O-levels and two A-levels. Back in those days it was unusual for many pupils to carry on and to get into university.

I had imagined that leaving school was meant to be all about giving you a great send-off, perhaps with an accolade or award for something special you had achieved. It seemed to me it was an opportunity to create for each pupil a special memory that she could hold in her heart, hopefully hold dear for ever – a positive message to send her on her way out into the big, wide world. So, I was about to leave Runton Hill and the stage was set. All parents and the final term students had taken their seats in the main hall. Each pupil was invited up onto the platform, which you mounted via a small set of rather rickety wooden steps.

It was finally my turn to go up and accept whatever I was about to receive. The headmistress, taking my hand looked at me. 'Well, Miranda, we have never had a girl like you in the school before, and I doubt very much that we will ever have one again who has taken the English Language exam so many times and still has not passed it.'

With that, she handed me a book on wildflowers.

How strange that Miss Kilvert decided to make a negative comment about my failure rather than a positive one about my beautiful nature notebook.

Chapter 8

Nature notebook

Blackberrries. A painted illustration from my nature notebook when at Hethersett School aged eleven

During the holidays we would always go on our walks with my mother along the farm road and then strike off across the fields down to the old railway line. In the early days I can remember seeing the little train coming chuff-chuff-chuffing along, white smoke belching out of its funnel. You could catch a train at Wells-next-the-Sea, a few miles along the coast to the east, and travelling an eighteen-and-a-half mile single track you would eventually arrive at King's Lynn.

The track meandered its way through the small villages of Holkham, Burnham Market, Stanhoe, Heacham and Hunstanton. From King's Lynn you could then catch a train to London, which is what we did when we went on our Christmas trips. Sometimes the red carpet might be laid out along the otherwise rather grim, grey platform in readiness for the Queen's arrival, if she had been staying at Sandringham and was heading back by train to her palace in London.

In 1953, the year of the disastrous North Sea flood, the line between Wells and Holkham was severely damaged. Not considered worth repairing, the line was closed. Eventually the track was removed, the strip of land on which it had run incorporated into the adjoining fields.

It was during those in-between years when the line was no longer in use that we spent so many happy days wandering along the old track gathering wildflowers. My mother taught us the names of them all, and recently my sister set us a fun family quiz. She posted, on her very modern phone, a picture of a bunch of wildflowers and we had to identify each variety. You are not considered to be up to much in our family if you can't identify wildflowers! But the real test is being able to identify them by the leaf alone.

Down on the old railway line all these wildflowers grew in abundance: scabious, self-heal, speedwell and salad burnet, buttercup, birdsfoot trefoil, eggs and bacon, yellow archangel, ragwort, herb robert, yarrow, lucerne, loosestrife, toadflax, campion, willowherb, fumitory, cranesbill, plantain, teasel, agrimony, shepherd's purse, scarlet pimpernel, stitchwort, ox-eye daisy and mignonette. Then there was vetch, whose beautiful springy tendrils clung to the bushes. Knapweed, a useful treatment for bruises and wounds. Viper's bugloss, apparently very effective if you boil up the seeds – it can help the flow of a mother's breast milk. And legend has it that Mary gave birth to Jesus on a bed made from the flowers of lady's bedstraw. All such fabulous names. We knew all these and still do, just about. I can smell them all too, particularly the lady's bedstraw, a very sweet smell. Ragwort is poisonous to cattle and horses, and my mother, over the years, painstakingly pulled up every plant by hand and managed to rid the meadow of this deadly plant. 'The meadow' was the field in front of High Barn where our ponies and horses used to graze. She would go out every evening 'ragworting'. It was one of her tasks.

I am not very knowledgeable about herbalism myself, but the many people who are will know all the ways in which these plants can be used medicinally. In those olden days before farmers were using horrible, deadly pesticides, these flowers were living in their own little heaven down on the railway line. It was one of our heavens too.

We gathered large bunches and brought them home. We drew them. At school I always looked for the wildflowers too, on the playing fields, or by the roadside when walking to church or in the woods when we went to meet the boys on Sundays. I enjoyed trying to identify the flowers, then would press them and draw them in my nature notebook. I found my even earlier nature notebook in the loft the other day among school reports, letters and photographs. As I look at the drawings I can remember sitting there engrossed as if it were yesterday. I am so glad I didn't get rid of it in one of my impulsive clutter-clearing moments.

Chapter 9

Whatever next

London girl. Me in Portobello Road, London, buying fruit and vegetables, aged nineteen

My school days were now history, although of course not the impact of them. I had gained a smattering of knowledge about all sorts of things I suppose, but clearly I was never going to become a highly achieving academic, definitely not a bright high-flier, not university material ... So what would become of me?

I felt a bit of a dunce. I felt that anything arty was considered what one did if one couldn't do anything else. And, actually, I know that is how it is still viewed among some ill-informed folk. It's taken me all these years to get over this ridiculous idea. It's true that during my school days I always felt I was at the bottom of the pile, just a bit of a joke type of a person. But I did leave school feeling secretly very proud of my nature notebook.

I learnt some important things. I learnt about what worked for me, what I loved. I discovered that I cherished fresh air, nature, music, colour, design and making things. It didn't really matter what I made, as long as I was using my hands and creating something. I liked cooking, poetry, being in churches, singing hymns and the feeling of being in love – because there had been that choirboy, remember?

It was also useful to have learnt that there were things that I did not enjoy and was not good at. I found reading difficult and was hopeless at maths, geometry and algebra, and anything scientific or technical that required logic, calculations and collating. None of it made any sense to me at all.

I learnt all about resourcefulness, stamina, determination, along with ridicule, humiliation and failure. I learnt the difference between wants and needs. Although I was not getting what I wanted, at that young age I had not the courage to ask for what I actually needed. So, I learnt that it is useful to know what you don't want and like, even when you don't know what you do want or how to achieve it. Knowledge of that is at least a starting point.

But what was to become of me? It was not uncommon, in that era, that a supposedly well-educated girl would sit around looking as beautiful as they possibly could in the hope that some eligible young man might appear and ask her father for his daughter's hand in marriage – thus, conveniently taking her off her father's hands. Love didn't really come into it. It seemed that to get your daughter palmed off on somebody, somewhere was the priority, whether he was suitable or not. Provided he was not a rogue, anybody might do.

Well, it was not like that at all in our family, of course, but I feel we were on the fringe of that kind of thinking. We were not in that realm of social standing (or whatever you want to call it) so what I have described was not about to happen to me … although I did have a dalliance with a viscount whom I met at a dance. I rather regret giving him one of the charms from my bracelet, the gold heart. Just think; if I had played my cards right I could have been a viscountess by now, and all the family could be coming to visit me for tea at my stately home in Norfolk.

I have an inkling that perhaps my father had wished for a gallant suitor to appear out of thin air from somewhere and whisk me off my feet. He might have liked to see me rocketed to fame, supported by a wealthy husband who would finance my design business. And he would finally see my name emblazoned somewhere, everywhere, around the world. 'Miranda, London, Paris, New York.' His fantasy? His dream? That I shall never know.

I don't really know what he was thinking at this juncture. Was I simply going to be a disappointment to him? Was I just going to carry on drawing flowers, and with a light dusting of curiosity might I eventually channel my energies into something that might make me some kind of a living? Did he now have three daughters to support, and what was the financial future for us all? I imagine it might have concerned him. Did he ever wonder if all that money spent on a private education was worth it? I think it was my mother's money which had financed our schooling, but nevertheless he knew how hard it was to make money. I imagine he must have wondered, as he did about most things.

So what next? As a young child, as well as loving flowers I spent quite a lot of time parading about feeling important dressed in my Red Cross nurse's uniform, which I had been given for my seventh birthday. Sporting the bold red cross on the bib, I would trail my stethoscope behind me, eager to check out everyone's heartbeat, including the cat's. I thought I could cure anything in site; and if friends or family didn't have any ailments that needed curing, I would quickly invent some and imagine they were at death's door. I would assure them that I could make them better. I used to practise applying bandages by wrapping strips round the odd chair leg. So, the possibility that I might pursue a career in nursing had been vaguely lurking in the background ever since those early days.

Having left school, with the question mark still hanging over me, I would have to come clean with my father. I remember it clearly. I braced myself, went into his office and told him that I did not want to be a nurse but that I liked ballet. He carried on filling in his calculations in the Friday wages book.

When I was tiny, I had been to ballet classes, and at the age of six I was awarded my first certificate. A Primary Pass. But I had not continued in any serious way, and I had shown no particular talent in that direction. So it was just a bit of a fantasy of mine that one day I would fly across the stage at Covent Garden just as I had seen Margot Fonteyn doing that Christmas. This fantasy had always been a little secret that I kept. I had been spellbound, and knew by the age of twelve that I would never be a nurse but believed perhaps I might be a prima ballerina! I guess every other little girl has this fantasy. But the little secret which I kept seemed to hurt. I knew I had no talent; how would I ever be spotted, particularly since I was no longer even having ballet lessons?

I still love to dance, not that I do much ballroom, or anything serious like that (although I still might one day). But at the age of seventy-seven I have been going to Lindy Hop classes, which are a real laugh. You can't not smile when you are dancing – that's what I like about it. You go home feeling alive, all singing, all dancing, and ten years younger.

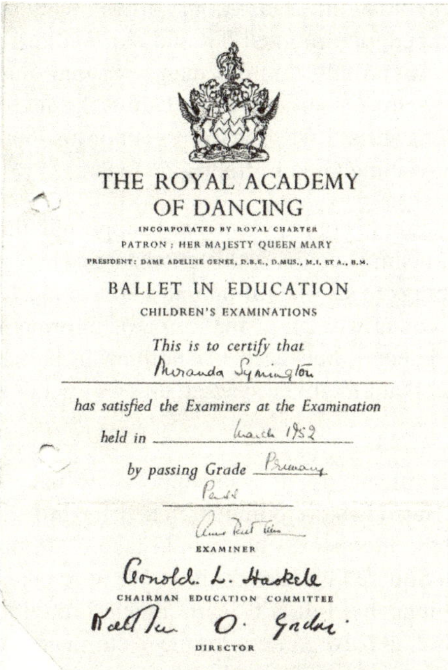

THE ROYAL ACADEMY
OF DANCING

INCORPORATED BY ROYAL CHARTER

PATRON : HER MAJESTY QUEEN MARY

PRESIDENT: DAME ADELINE GENEE, D.B.E., D.MUS., M.I., ET A., B.M.

BALLET IN EDUCATION

CHILDREN'S EXAMINATIONS

This is to certify that

Miranda Symington

has satisfied the Examiners at the Examination

held in March 1952

by passing Grade Primary

Pass

EXAMINER

CHAIRMAN EDUCATION COMMITTEE

DIRECTOR

My ballet exam. Primary Pass, aged six

So back to whatever next! Not a nurse, not a prima ballerina. A dressmaker perhaps ? The summer was spent pondering, I guess. I had various little odd jobs to earn some money. I used to bicycle about five miles down the farm road and across two very bumpy tracks to the main coast road where there was a well-known pub called the Jolly Sailors in Brancaster. I used to waitress there at lunchtime, earning about £3. The best thing was that, when I had finished my shift, I was allowed an ice-cream with the most delicious chocolate sauce. I used to greedily smother the ice-cream in it.

Eventually, it was announced that I'd best go off to London, and I was signed up for a rather strange course called 'Look and Learn'. But I suddenly felt a bit more grown up at the prospect of going to live in London. Having been all these years at boarding school and then living in semi-isolation at High Barn, here I was at last stepping out into the big, wide world on my own. Gina and I shared a bedsit in the small, terraced cottage in Chelsea, just off the King's Road. It was a pretty but cramped, one-roomed flat and our landlord rather gave me the creeps. He was a tall, thin old man with long fingers, grey hair, and he had a weird lecherous voice. I think he had a penchant for glamorous young girls. I was far from glamorous, but Gina certainly was with her ravishing Gina Lollobrigida looks.

The 'Look and Learn' course was what I suppose in those days would be called a 'finishing course', designed to teach one a few useful rudimentary things to set one off on one's course in life. The intention was to give a young woman a smattering of information, expand her knowledge in general, but teach her nothing in particular. The hope was, I presume, that I might be sparked up by something and find some direction.

Quite what significant use it was supposed to have been for us to discover that Harrods storerooms stretched for miles underneath the park and that the number 14 bus would take us from Putney all the way to Russell Square I will never know. We were taken to 'look' at all sorts of odd things, but I didn't 'learn' much. I did find the trips to St Paul's Cathedral, to Kew gardens, to the Victoria and Albert Museum, to the Royal Mint and to various theatres fun and interesting. Mostly I just liked wandering about in London discovering that I felt quite safe in the big city. There was a lot of exploring to do.

Gina had a boyfriend, and so did her friend, Sally, and they used to sit in the afternoons in our flat painting their toenails in readiness for their dates in the evening. I didn't mind not having a boyfriend. I felt free. I had been a little sad when Jimmy, my first-ever sort of boyfriend from Norfolk whom I met at a dance in the school holidays, had disappeared off to Canada. He wasn't my type. But I hadn't a clue what was my type. Somebody artistic perhaps? An adventurer? Unconventional? Non-conformist? A bit out of the box?

Once the three-month course was completed, of course the same question reared its ugly head yet again. What next? My parents were still hooked on the idea of me pursuing a nursing career of sorts, so they came up with the idea that I might like to train as a 'nanny'. Hmm! I was not at all sure about that. A Norland Nanny training was the one that to this day offers the world-renowned best training possible. That is if one wishes to be employed by the great and the good, the upper crust or royalty. A Norland Nanny must always be dressed impeccably, formally, neatly, boringly, and must adhere politely with the notion that pampering the little darlings who have been entrusted to her care is of prime importance.

In days gone by the babies would be pushed out for sedate walks in the park in their regal, well-cushioned Tansad prams while their parents sipped tea at the Savoy. The nannies would then administer tea to the children in their nurseries and, as they grew up, would instil into them the old-school values that 'children should be seen and not heard', and should 'never speak unless spoken to'. 'Big boys don't cry.' 'When at table you never leave until you have finished every mouthful and have asked if you may get down.' Table manners were of the utmost importance. You would be taught that, having eaten sufficiently, you were not to say you were 'stuffed' or 'full' but would politely state that you were 'replete, thank you'. Rigorous bedtimes would be kept.

Once trained, a Norland Nanny would reap the reward of a good wage. As I understand it, nothing much has changed today with the strict Norland philosophy still in place. But perhaps that's not a bad thing, since manners these days seem to have virtually gone out of the window, and some poor parents seem to be run ragged by their children's unruly behaviour – they could well do with a dose of good old Norland Nanny discipline.

So the idea of me becoming that Norland Nanny had to be given a whirl. Off I went with my mother to London and then on another train to Chislehurst, which is where the training took place in those days. I knew full well when we were on the train this was definitely not my vision for the future but went along with it as best I could. Needless to say, my lack of enthusiasm during the long interview did not impress.

On the way home I owned up and told my mother it was not the career for me. She tried to persuade me that it would be a good way to earn a living, that my father would be pleased, and that if I was offered a place I ought to accept it. I might end up travelling to some interesting countries and perhaps even working in a royal household. I put my foot firmly down. I feared that on my returning home Dad might be cross at my decision and go into one of his downhearted moods.

I was worried, as he used to behave strangely sometimes. I think it must have been because he was feeling depressed and pressurised or disappointed when in his eyes we appeared to be ungrateful or unappreciative. It usually happened at mealtimes. He would suddenly put his leg up on the dining room table and thrash it about and shout.

I did feel this curious kind of pressure as to what would happen to me in life. It seemed that being brainy was the only way of guaranteeing that a hopeful path might lie ahead. The only other path of course was to be saved by the sudden entrance of that knight in shining armour.

But as is often the case, the creative gene shone through. I calmy announced one day that I was going to study dress design, and that I wanted to return to London. I am sure my father wondered how financially secure this career would be, but perhaps he was pleased and knew in his heart that I was following my dream, doing something with my hands, being creative, using my imagination. And perhaps he too might have his dream fulfilled after all and see my design label up there one day alongside other famous names.

The Katinka School of Dress Designing was in the Cromwell Road, West London. It was a small, independent school, with only about twenty students. I would be awarded a diploma if I stuck out the one-year course. I had not plumped for the more well-known and established London School of Fashion, although I did attend there for a short period having completed my year at Katinka's. We were set assignments, were taught pattern making, cutting, tailoring, fine hand sewing of rolled silk hems, and hand buttonholing. All the usual dressmaking techniques were covered: stitching, costing and marketing.

With each assignment there was usually a tight brief which I often found difficult to stick to, always wanting to go off doing my own thing. We would design, pattern-cut and make the various garments. I remember making a very formal, grey, pure wool suit. Not my style at all, and whenever I wore it I felt a bit odd. It was a 'Little Miss Neat' outfit. Another was a striking calf-length linen dress, half white, half black, with a squirly squiggle down the front. Very challenging to make and very original, I thought at the time. One of the tutors, a rather austere Italian lady, told me it was far too way-out. It was deemed to be an eye-catching design, but one which would be too costly to make, was not elegant, and would have limited appeal.

Some years later I found in a fashion magazine a photograph of exactly this dress, designed by Ungaro, a French dress designer who founded his fashion house in 1965. I always wondered, not meaning to blow my own trumpet, whether he had ever seen my design. Or had I on some subliminal level seen his somewhere along the line? Or was it just a case of great minds thinking alike! I liked that dress anyway and wore it a lot.

During my dress design period I was no longer sharing a flat with Gina but had moved into a bedsit off Gloucester Road, just round the corner from the school. It was rather grim, a basement, with a window with a grille over it, down which people used to peer from above into my little cavern below street level. I put money into a slot meter to run the gas, cooked on a green enamel stove, and had a one-bar electric heater. The bathroom was upstairs, and I had to walk through a spacious hallway and up a rather grand staircase to the loo and bathroom. An odd collection of people lived there whom I might just pass on the stairs, but never spoke a word to. I occasionally had a friend for supper. I used to open a tin of spinach and we'd have tinned orange segments or tinned pineapple for pudding. I didn't do much cooking.

I went to a concert at the Albert Hall, and met an Italian called Angelo while queuing for a ticket. He asked me to go and have a meal at his place in Bayswater Road. While we were in an Italian shop buying spaghetti (because he wanted to show me the right and proper way to cook Italian spaghetti *al dente*), the news came over the radio that President Kennedy had been shot: 22 November 1963. One of those moments I will never forget. What a charismatic couple he and Jacqueline were.

I made a few garments for friends and put notices in the local shop window in South Kensington. I used to go to my bank in Sloane Square and cash £5. Of that, £3 was for my rent. I lived on the other £2. I must have eked it out somehow, together with top-up money which I earned from various waitressing jobs. I also worked for a Japanese businessman, two days a week. He didn't seem to have a clue how to do anything. His wife was away somewhere and she instructed me to leave him meals in the fridge, iron his shirts and tidy his apartment, and generally make sure he stayed alive.

I went to Pitman's college thinking that learning to be a shorthand typist might be another useful string to add to my bow. I got a cleaning job with some weird man who requested clean sheets on his bed every day – I did any odd job to make ends meet.

My father was at the time giving me a small allowance, most of which I tried to save. It was customary in those days, I think. Your parents helped you out if they could. My father used to come up to London to go to Sotheby's. He liked to go to the auctions and would sometimes put in a bid for a seascape that took his fancy. He bought two lovely paintings by the Dutch painter Willem van de Velde, one of which I had for many years until I fell on hard times and sold it. He would take me out to lunch to some very smart West End restaurants: Wheeler's, Scott's, Pruniers, Quaglino's (the well-known Italian restaurant in St James), and Veeraswamy in Regent Street. I don't remember him ever coming to see where I was living.

By 1964 I was still feeling that I was in limbo. I'd made few friends, but I was not aware that I was lonely. Antonia was still at Runton Hill school, and I only saw her on one of her half-term breaks, or if I went back home to Norfolk for a weekend. I always wondered how she was doing as, rather like me, I don't think she fared very well at our boarding school.

Anabel was studying at the Byam Shaw Art School and lived just offNotting Hill in West London. She was a real live beatnik, beautiful, slim, with typically huge made-up black eyes, dressing mostly in black, and always with her black winklepicker shoes. She seemed to me to be leading an interesting, arty life. In comparison I seemed to be leading a boring, somewhat sheltered one in my grim bedsit in Gloucester Road, doing odd jobs, not doing anything specific, just bumbling along. But I did have one old school friend who invited me to visit her in Cambridge. She, Lizzy, was a high-flier, unlike me. She had got into university, which was quite unusual for pupils from Runton Hill boarding school.

So it was a big excitement when I went to meet her and spend a weekend in Cambridge. Wonderful. A mini escape from London, and what might happen? She introduced me to some of her friends. It all seemed fun, a welcome change from my rather isolated life in London. We went to the Fitzwilliam Museum, to various debates held in basements, went to a folk club, walked along the Backs, the river, went punting, swam in the river Cam, ate at the cheapest little Stockpot café. I went to King's College to attend evensong. Lizzy seemed to think that I was being all a bit '*holier than thou*'. I defended myself. We had a kind of row, and I went off on my own in the end, to hear the 'angels' voices'. I love them.

I listen every Christmas to Carols from King's. I never feel it's Christmas until I have heard that wonderful service. I feel I am being transported to a very special place, a place where I like to be.

Lizzy and I made up after the King's College row and she invited me again. Having caught the train back to London to continue with my week's work, I sped back to Cambridge in eager anticipation a few weeks later. There was some 'special party' we could go to – she had a plan. There were some guys whom she wanted to meet and she wanted me to go with her.

I don't recall where any of us met, where we went or what we did, except that I had immediately fallen for one of the guys, called Jeremy. But there was a problem. Jeremy was in love with Lizzy, unbeknown apparently to Lizzy! She had not even noticed him. I had not logged any of the other chaps who were there on that evening, either, because now I only had eyes for Jeremy. But one of the others, Kendall, had apparently logged me, and seemed to be making a beeline for me. I had not been instantaneously captivated by him. Ah, well. It all felt so complicated. Eventually Lizzy disappeared off with Jeremy, abandoning me, and I was left trying my best to make polite conversation with Kendall. As the evening wore on I slightly warmed to this bright, good looking intellectual undergraduate, a rugby enthusiast who played for Saracens, of Scottish origin, studying economics. I was feeling rather out of my depth though, and was wondering, what next? We met again some weeks later.

We 'ding-donged' about for a while. Kendall would visit me in London, and I would train it to Cambridge and stay over for the odd weekend. He took great pride in his dark-blue MGB sports car, which he had bought from a local Cambridgeshire classic car enthusiast. We would go for drives out into the countryside and stop for a romantic tea somewhere by the river. We drove up to Norfolk for a weekend and surprised my mother and father. Kendall was so proud of his car, and had spent hours one afternoon washing and polishing it. My father in his usual way, fond of playing practical jokes, then spent hours that evening, unbeknown to Kendall, sticking shiny cellophane filaments onto the car door to simulate scratches. The alarm was raised! Kendall went into meltdown only to realise, after a while, that it was all a trick. After that, my father and Kendall bonded, so all was well.

I was by now enjoying London a bit more, perhaps because Kendall was in the background. I created a kind of weekend routine. On Saturday mornings I would often go to Portobello Road antique market and scour the stalls looking for cheap treasures. I would always come home with some little gem that I had managed to bargain for. It might be a pewter candle-holder, a brass bracelet, an odd earring, a book, a rustic Portuguese plate, a sweet teacup with no saucer, an old piece of lace, or a carved picture frame which needed a picture to fill it. All these unexpected little finds accumulated in my flat in Gloucester Road. And although it was far from a real home, like my true and real High Barn home, it gradually began to feel a little bit more lived in.

As well as the antique market of Portobello there was also the fruit and veg market. It was always fun on the way back home to see what exceptional bargains I could find. The stall holders, now at the end of the day, seemed eager to clear the decks and get rid of the tired-looking cabbages, bananas, lettuces and the odd orange or pineapple. So, I would often return home with enough fruit and veg to keep me going all week, usually having paid nothing. I had also been busy searching in the gutter for all the unblemished oranges and apples that had rolled away off the stalls during the course of the busy day. Wonderful. All these a welcome change from my usual tin of spinach.

On Sundays I often went to Speakers' Corner in Hyde Park and listened to the various orators getting up on their soap boxes and on their high horses about something or other. There were usually some heated discussions and a lot of heckling. Sometimes it became a little too heated for my liking.

There were quite a few nutters, too, who were simply enjoying the fact that they could draw an audience. They might be off their trolleys and talking gibberish, but it was always entertaining. The person I did love listening too was Lord Soper. A British Methodist minister, a socialist, a pacifist, he was for many years the mainstay of Speakers' Corner. Very controversial, very CND, very interesting, he was a clear-thinking, clear-speaking, influential, charismatic gentleman.

My weekend entertainment took me all over the place. I went to services in St Paul's Cathedral where I enjoyed once again singing hymns. On Sundays I often went to Kew Gardens to sit in the hothouses and draw the flowers. The Victoria and Albert Museum was another haunt, and I'd just wander about London enjoying finding my way around.

Days were often spent looking forward to my various evening classes. I didn't last long at Car Maintenance or First Steps in Accountancy. To this day I haven't a clue how my car works and although I persevered with the maths, I'm still not ace when it comes to balancing the books. I enjoyed the upholstery class and made a pair of heavy gold velvet curtains for my flat, and covered a rosewood Victorian chaise longue in a sumptuous floral fabric. My fave rave class was the Martha

Graham contemporary dance. I loved it, leaping about and flying around deluded, imagining I still might one day perform at Covent Garden I suppose.

I did seem to be always on my own, though. I didn't seem to have many friends or know quite how to make them. I think my parents were slightly worried, not that they ever actually said so or even asked how I was doing, but they could see that I was a bit of a loner. Perhaps in truth I was a little like both of them, rather solitary, self-contained, unsure of where or how or with what I truly fitted in.

I walked one day into the City, all along the Embankment, and ended up off Fleet Street. I wanted to find the plaque that had been placed at the supposed birthplace of Samuel Pepys. How times have changed, beyond all recognition. To think that Samuel Pepys had witnessed the Great Fire of London and written about seeing scorched pigeons falling from the skies. He had witnessed the Plague and recorded it all in his famous diaries. He wrote daily detailed accounts of what was happening, what he was experiencing.

Kendall and I had been on and off as it were; it didn't seem to be too serious a commitment. He was seeing another girl in Cambridge, anyway, so he told me, so I wondered. I didn't know how he really felt about me.

One of my mother's lifelong friends was a Swiss lady who lived in Norfolk. She had two daughters and a son. They were all high-flying academics, very brainy. Her son, Scott, was also at Cambridge, but I don't think his path had ever crossed with Kendall's. Scott was tall, dark, and not exactly handsome, but interesting looking and very intelligent.

His father had been a doctor and had committed suicide. Put a gun to his head. His mother, my mother's friend, was a Christian Scientist. They were an intriguing but clearly somewhat troubled family I always thought, living in a large, grand house outside Norwich. The garden had one of those ha-ha sunken walls, which always fascinated me. It gave the illusion of an unbroken slope down the garden to the meadow beyond, while at the same time cleverly restricting the sheep from entering the garden itself.

The Swiss lady had a maidservant from India whom she had taken under her wing and for whom she was providing a home. I was astonished whenever we went to tea there. The lady would ring a bell and the servant would come, be given her orders, dutifully disappear and return with another jug of hot water, more biscuits or whatever had been requested. It seemed my mother and the Swiss lady were good friends, although I am not sure of the origin of their friendship. I got the feeling that there was concern about the son, since he seemed to have no girlfriends and my mother was a little worried about me and my lack of any social life in London. So, whether the two mothers hatched a plan I am not sure.

But out of the blue one day I received an invitation to accompany Scott to the Oxford and Cambridge Boat Race Ball at the Dorchester Hotel, Park Lane. My heart leapt! Incurable romantic as I was (and still am), I wondered: was he going to propose to me on the dance floor of the Dorchester? What would I wear? Anyway, I accepted and said I'd love to go. I made a dress out of an old, white-lace tablecloth which I'd found in the airing cupboard up at High Barn. I lined it with aqua-blue taffeta, which made quite a nice kind of shivery, rustling noise as I walked. It was long, plain, simple, with a round neckline. You'd never see a dress like this anywhere else – not made out of an old tablecloth, anyway – especially at the Dorchester.

What about my hair? I'd never been one for doing anything much with my hair, let alone having any particular hairstyle. I've always just let it hang about however it wants to. At the time it was not very long, but I decided I had better go and get it tidied up perhaps, get along to the hairdresser and at least go through the motions of having made an effort for the ball.

So off I trotted to a salon off Gloucester Road early in the morning on the day of the ball. I sat for the longest three hours ever while the kind girl patiently washed my hair, conditioned it, discussed the trim, trimmed it, blow-dried it, fiddle-de-diddled about with it, engaged not very successfully in the endless hairdresser chit-chat, all in a vain attempt to make my hair look like something. I was going up the wall with all the fussing about – and by the time she had finished I couldn't really see any difference. I was desperate to get out of the place. I had agreed to meet Scott before the ball for a light lunch, and over polite but slightly strained conversation he said that he presumed I would be going to the hairdressers in the afternoon and he would come and pick me up from my flat, following my appointment, at around 6 pm.

I had just spent all my hard-earned waitress's wages at the hairdressers and I was mortified. I bit my lip and told Scott that, yes, my appointment at the hairdressers was at 3 pm, so if he were able to pick me up at 6 pm that would be perfect. I slinked back to my flat feeling more than a little despondent. I quickly cobbled together a blue bow made from the remnants of the taffeta lining of my dress and thought that would do. I'll stick that in my hair somewhere. To hell with what I look like, I've done my best, and I'm off to the Dorchester.

I remember nothing about the evening other than being pleased with my lace tablecloth dress and the emergency bow for my hair.

Some years later, Scott, like his father took his own life.

Chapter 10

Escaping London

My father on a Cross Channel Ferry holiday

I liked to escape London at the weekends as often as I could, so as well as my occasional trips to see Kendall in Cambridge, I would drive up to Norfolk. I pined for some fresh country air, particularly the Norfolk air, which is well known for being exceptionally invigorating, bracing, and refreshing.

The drive took about five hours, since in those days there were no speedy motorways. The final stretch was the winding route from the town of Swaffham, but it was not until I had passed the village pond in Stanhoe that I felt I had arrived. My parents were always pleased to see me.

My mother would usually have a delicious meal prepared. Perfect timing. Just as I tumbled in exhausted through the back door, the roast pheasant would magically appear from the Aga, along with all the trimmings, including the essential toasted breadcrumbs, a must with pheasant. Oh and delicious, home-made giblet-and-red-wine gravy just to top it all off.

My mother and I often walked out along the zigzagging marsh path at Burnham Overy. When you reach the beach after the half-hour-long walk, you are greeted by a vast expanse of gold, of sand, of blue, of sea, of sky. I always feel I have arrived in heaven on earth. It's a special, magical place. Another of my heavens.

We walked in the woods at Holkham. The pine woods themselves are fascinating. Their trunks and branches have grown every which way, twisting and turning, creating beautiful and extraordinary sculptural artworks which my mother loved to paint. One in particular is like an elegant candelabra, its branches reaching out and upwards. The wind whistled through the tall trees, and the trunks rubbed against each other making an eerie squeaking noise, or sometimes a strange groan like that of anguished lovers in a desperate embrace. We gathered fir cones for the winter fires and returned home for warm cups of tea and cake around the Aga.

I would gather a selection of delicious fresh veg, baskets full of whatever was in season: spinach, asparagus, potatoes, runner beans, lettuces – I know what a fresh vegetable is! Then in the summer came all the fruits, gooseberries, raspberries, strawberries, blackcurrants, apples, pears and damsons. And a big bunch of flowers too. I remember once filling up an old empty manure bag with earth for my London window box, in which I managed to successfully grow mint and chives.

I used to observe my father. He so often seemed to be labouring with one job or another either in his workshop which adjoined the old farm barns, or in one of the larger barns where farm machinery and tractors were kept. His workshop was filled with every tool imaginable, and there was almost always something that needed mending, adapting or completely refashioning. He was very ingenious in the way he applied his wartime attitude of 'make do and mend'. He would get so annoyed if one of the tractor drivers had not put a tool back in the place where it belonged, knowing that as a result of their laziness neither he nor anybody else would be able to readily lay their hands on it when it was next needed for a job. He had tried to overcome this problem by making a shelving unit out of rough wooden planks. It covered the entire end wall of one of the smaller barns, on which he had written in white chalk on one of the planks:

THERE IS A PLACE FOR EVERYTHING,
EVERYTHING IN ITS PLACE.

I am not sure that it did solve the problem, as few people were as meticulous as he was in maintaining a sense of order with all the numerous tools and bolts and bits and bobs. But he, the boss, the farmer, knew that anything and everything might one day come in useful and save him money; so everything was kept just in case.

He often seemed irritated even when trying to complete a small task, such as removing a seized-up rusty bolt or replacing a fuse in a plug. Most things seemed to be an effort. If he were not in his workshop tinkering away, he would be seated at his desk in his office, which was a small room off the passageway which led to the back door of the house. (My mother always used to say in winter when the wind was in the north: 'There is nothing between the back door and the North Pole.')

My father overseeing the operation of grading, weighing and bagging up the carrots grown on the farm, outside the barn at High Barn

One of my father's weekly tasks was to do the accounts, the farm books. They were all neatly written in his elegant handwriting. He calculated the wages for the farm workers, and their money would be popped into a little brown envelope which Reg, the foreman, collected on a Friday afternoon. The average wage for a week's work would be eight pounds and fifteen shillings. There would be discussions about the plan of action for the following week, but that would also depend on what the weather was up to.

The forecast was a continual worry, with the weather reports being less detailed than they are nowadays. It was a crucial factor that had to be considered almost hourly, especially in the summer. We would all sit round the table at lunchtime on tenterhooks, and would have to be silent while we listened to the midday forecast. If it was not favourable, my father might disappear back to his office in a glum mood. At that age, of course, I never really understood the amount of stress he must have been under. Nor did I know what his mood might be from one minute to the next. I felt worried by the unpredictability that was often in the air. His moods could be a bit like the weather. Changeable.

In addition to his own physical and emotional challenges I now think that he must have been wondering if his beautiful wife was truly happy; and to what extent did he feel her happiness to be his responsibility? It appeared that my mother did not take a great deal of interest in the day-to-day running of the farm. Well, a wife would not have been expected to in those days. People had their traditional roles and largely stuck to them. I remember my mother standing behind my father once as he was seated at his desk and saying: 'Do something.' Who knows quite what she was meaning, feeling or referring to, but presumably she had sunk into one of her dark moods and needed his reassurance that she would get through it. I recall hearing her words quite frequently too: 'This too will pass', and ' Worse things happen at sea', but never really having any understanding of the extent of the emotional aspect of her doubts, fears or worries.

My father's concern about how to support and console her must, I imagine, have added to his own constant worry about how to keep himself emotionally afloat. She, though, was obviously in the perfect environment in which to pursue her love of nature and the great outdoors. She took an interest in the history of the local area, and the people who had worked the land. She was fascinated by the remains of a Roman villa which had been unearthed on one of the fields on the farm.

They shared a love of history and the arts, of culture and literature, and of the natural world and its wildernesses too. Their regular trips to look at châteaux in France, or to tour the English cathedrals and castles, or to return to the wilds of Dartmoor where my mother grew up, were perhaps partially a way of keeping her stimulated and content. But I will never truly know.

But as far as I could see, my father's life had always been one of hardship, worry and toil, and was still a struggle in so many ways. My mother was doing her best to play the role of farmer's wife. She contributed to the local community and ran elementary first-aid classes for the Red Cross, for young girls in the village. She taught them the basics, how to fold a triangular bandage and make a sling for a broken arm, how to roll up bandages neatly and secure with a safety pin without pricking the invalid. She gave art classes at High Barn for ladies in the local community, and also taught in Norwich at a centre for disabled elderly folk. She was often busy preparing mounts for her students' pictures, or making a frame in which to put them.

I imagine she was happiest when she was just carrying on doing the things she was best at. She might be baking meringues, which she had got down to a fine art, the Aga being the perfect oven in which to bake them. Or she would be attending to a lame duck that had been injured when a dog had terrified it by chasing it through the farmyard. She might be gathering flints and lugging them home to paint, being fascinated by the patterns and colours of their cut surfaces. She might be painting a chest of drawers some obscure colour or rearranging the furniture, or taking a door off its hinges: she didn't like doors, despite the fact that they might have helped exclude the winter draughts. She would be writing a poem, or sitting painting the moon rising over the meadow, or of course arranging flowers.

She kept busy with all these activities, but all the while I think she was concerned about the more significant questions of life and death: what was the meaning of it all? Deep down she felt disquiet about the state of the world: was it progressing or not? As a young woman she had always contemplated everything, constantly wondering and often worrying. She gave me a copy of her favourite book, by Alan Watts, *The Wisdom of Insecurity*. I have two copies of it now, one of which funnily enough I keep in the lavatory.

One of these weekend visits home – I suspect for my birthday on the 29 April – I remember with crystal clarity. It was time to leave, hit the road back to London. I had spent a lovely few days and my mother had helped me pack up all the goodies, including a fruit cake she had made especially for me. My car, a white convertible Triumph Herald, was laden. Mother, as she usually did, had wandered off down to the bottom of the drive. She would always stand up on the bank on the right as I turned onto the main road and would wave wildly until I had disappeared out of site up the hill. Dad stayed up near the house at the top of the drive and was standing beside the little, ornate, wrought-iron gate which led into the kitchen garden. We had all said our farewells. I started the engine and was about to drive off, but seeing my father standing there alone I felt sad. I wondered what the forthcoming weeks and months would hold for him and my mother and their life together at High Barn.

Spontaneously I stopped the car, jumped out, ran round and gave my father another farewell hug. With a strained expression on his face he said words that summed it all up: 'I shall die in harness.'

I didn't say anything. I did not know what to say. I just kept looking at him. I wished I could have smiled.

But I jumped back into my car and, with his words ringing in my ears, I set off down the drive, off back to London.

Chapter 11

All change

A painting by my mother based on a churchyard scene

I stopped at the village pond in Stanhoe, fighting back the tears, my father's words still ringing in my ears. I wanted to go back to see Dad. I wish I had done so. But for some reason I didn't. Was it that I feared not knowing what to say to my poor father? I had never really talked to him much about anything. He was just Dad, he was always there with his one leg, just being Dad. What could I have said? How could I make things any better? What could I possibly do? What difference could I make to his life of toil? This dear man, my father who seemed trapped in his weary body, troubled in his mind, and whose spirit was far from broken but clearly struggling, I think.

All I could have said, perhaps, was that I loved him and admired him. But I didn't. I wish I had.

I thought of my mother too. I imagined it must have been a somewhat unsettling life now for them both, a difficult juncture, perhaps, with the family, all three girls, now growing up. All the childhood years will have flown by so quickly, so many months spent separated from them at boarding school. Although Antonia was still at Runton Hill school, Anabel and I now were now living in London. So, naturally and normally, but still perhaps traumatically, they were having to face up to the empty nest syndrome.

All these thoughts were tumbling round in my head, and I sat ruminating on it all and had a good old cry. Eventually I composed myself, but I was still worrying as I drove back to London, having decided that was for the best.

The long journey in reverse now seemed to take for ever. Swaffham, Newmarket… and eventually weaving back through north London to my flat in Gloucester Road, Kensington. I don't remember any such thing as a parking meter, I just found somewhere to park. There were very few restricted areas. In Mayfair the first meters were installed in 1958, and you could park at one for six old pence for one hour.

The High Barn memories and my concerns about my mother and father gradually faded as I became busily swept up in my Londonish life again. I had my various mundane weekly waitressing jobs, and I made the odd skirt or dress for whomever I could. I called home regularly.

One day I had decided I would attempt a new hair look. I stuck my head in the wash hand basin and lathered my head with a cheap, instant, black hair dye. Whoops. What a mistake. I looked in the mirror and seemed to now have a head of hair, deadlier-than-deadly-dead black – no glisten, no sheen. I called my mother in tears. Poor mother: initially I think she thought this was serious and that I was about to break the news that I had crashed the car or something even worse. On discovering that this was not the case, she couldn't think what all the fuss was about. She assured me that my deadly black hair would soon grow out, which of course it did.

My career path remained unclear – well, it was non-existent really. I dibbled and dabbled in this and that, but quite enjoyed the variety at the same time. I moved in to live with Anabel for a short while in her flat in Aubrey Walk, just off Notting Hill Gate.

Earlier in the year, in January, I had been to Westminster Hall to the lying in state of Winston Churchill. I am so glad I experienced this ceremony. I shall never forget it. Churchill had died aged ninety on 24 January 1965, and was lying in state from the 27th to the 30th. According to the records over 320,000 people passed by his coffin in those three days. Although I had no direct memories of the war as such, I knew this man had seen the country through the most terrible of times and I felt I wanted to pay my respects.

I queued all through the cold night, crossing over the Thames via Lambeth Bridge, and then shuffled my way with hundreds of others along Millbank and eventually entered the hall in the early hours of the morning. Four guards stood vigil at the corners of the coffin with their heads bowed. A reporter for the *Illustrated London News* described the procession as having 'the mesmeric effect of a river flowing past'. That is exactly as I remember it. There is a wonderful oil painting by Alfred Cooper of the occasion. The gentle, subdued sunlight is seen streaming in through the gothic windows. What a gift and talent to have managed to capture the mixed emotions that were being felt at that time.

Churchill had suffered a stroke in 1953, after which it had been feared that his death might occur at any moment. So 'Operation Hope Not', as it was called, had been in the planning for twelve years before his actual death. It was the first state funeral to be held in the United Kingdom for a non-royal since one in 1935 for the politician Lord Carson. So, it was a momentous occasion, in a way an act of mourning for the imperial past, and one which honoured Churchill's extraordinary leadership through the war years.

Kendall and I had been bumbling along, but we were often getting into huffs with one another, and not really having a lot of fun. At the age I was, nineteen, I did not have a sense that the relationship had much of a future. But seeing him and meeting up in Cambridge added interesting interludes to my week so I just stuck with it for a while.

In the spring of 1965, I went to Cambridge for a weekend, and he decided to drive me back to London in the famous blue MGB. That was one of the best things about him: I loved his car. I didn't like the fact that, while we were driving along, he announced that he would like to be king! I thought that was rather an odd thing to admit to. Or perhaps it was just the male equivalent (and no different from) every other little girl dreaming of wanting to be a princess or in my case dreaming of becoming a prima ballerina! But he was clever in a way that I am not: logical, clinical. We were different personalities altogether, and it concerned me.

On this particular return journey to London, we ended up having a ridiculous big row, one of those silly shouting matches: 'I'm right, you are wrong.' Stupid, naïve, a battle. We eventually calmed down and talked about just being friends. I couldn't at the time really see the point of this idea, but it seemed like it might be a stepping stone and a way round things for the moment.

We arrived back at the house at Aubrey Walk. In our final tentative conversation, before I got out of the lovely car, we agreed that our relationship was not really very satisfactory and it would be best to call it a day. I was sad, but also felt slight relief, as I had not enjoyed having these ridiculous rows.

Kendall was a gentleman and walked me to the door of the house. It was a slightly gloomy building, I always felt. Two storeys high, it had those bleak, wartime metal window frames and festoons of greenery tumbling round the slightly hidden doorway. Anabel was leaning out of one of the upstairs open windows as we walked along the street towards the front door. Perhaps she had heard the car coming, since MGBs do have a very recognisable engine purr. But maybe she had been looking out for me because, seeing me approach, she screamed out of the window: 'Dad's dead!'

Oh my God. I rushed up the stairs in hysterics.

No! No! No! But it was so. My father had died.

Chapter 12

A marriage of sorts

A photograph of me sitting beside a tombstone in Stanhoe village church shortly after my father's death in May 1965

It was inevitably a very strange period following my father's death. His death was so sudden, it came out of the blue. His poor heart must have been under great strain for so many years. And, in the end, he had suffered a major heart attack.

He and my mother had been married for just twenty-four years; he was sixty-one and she was only fifty-one. My mother lived on at High Barn for a further thirty-one years without him. It was obviously not what she had expected, to be bereaved so suddenly and relatively so young. Her touching words written eight years after his death express so perfectly how she felt about him .

'No one but you, You were the only one. No one but you'.

I was nineteen at the time of my father's death. What seems odd is that we never really talked about it. I never saw my mother cry. She never seemed to want to talk about it or how it was for her, even in later years. I imagine she was, like my father, just doing her best to put on a brave face. Death was not talked about in the way it is today. Like that of money, the topic was considered rude, and it seemed to me that it was regarded as intrusive to engage in any conversation on the subject other than to offer one's initial condolences.

I remember very little about the immediate weeks or months following my father's death. I have no recollection of the funeral. He is buried alongside his mother in the churchyard at Old Hunstanton, the church where we used to attend Sunday School. I like to visit his grave with flowers whenever I am in Norfolk.

Despite the steaming row we had just had, after I received the devastating news Kendall kindly offered to drive me up to Norfolk during the night. We stayed with my mother while all the arrangements for the funeral were made. What would happen next? My immediate response was to pack my bags, leave London and go and live in Norfolk with my mother.

Kendall had by now graduated from Cambridge and decided he would get a job near where I was now living – feeling somewhat sorry for me, I think. He managed to secure a position in King's Lynn, where he lived in a rather gloomy bedsit on a roundabout on the outskirts of the town. I remember the song *Mr Tambourine Man* was playing on the radio the night we loaded all of his stuff out of the car and into the dreary bedsit. Whenever I hear that song it has an instant impact. I am immediately transported right back there with him unloading the car into the dreary lodgings.

We had kind of ignored the fact that we'd agreed our relationship was going nowhere after the big argument on the day I'd heard of my father's death. Here Kendall was, back in my life again.

I set up my little dressmaking business at High Barn, in a small room which led off from the kitchen. When we were children, it had been our playroom. I put a notice in the local shop window in Burnham Market hoping that a few Norfolk society ladies might like the odd hem turned up or old dress transformed, adjusting the neckline for a little more of a décolleté look. One very grand lady wanted a black velvet dress made for a cocktail party. Velvet. Oh no. Such tricky material to work with because, when you iron it, it must be placed on a needle press so that the pile of the velvet does not get crushed down and marked. I found this difficult, but I said yes – and made a complete hash of it. When she came along for the second fitting the sleeves seemed to be very ill-fitting and looked all kind of wonky. I had sewn them in the wrong way round. Whoops. Never mind. I managed to refit them and I gave her all her money back (which was only £5 for the entire dress), so she forgave me, I think. But of course that little mistake did not exactly help me earn a reputation in the area as a brilliant seamstress.

I used to charge two guineas to make a skirt. (For all you young ones out there who remember nothing other than decimal currency, or don't even handle real money any more because now you just use your credit cards, a guinea was twenty-one shillings. In other words, just over one pound.) My heart was not really in the business, though, and my mother encouraged me to go back to London, which I did for a short while. But I didn't know quite what to do next. I was always feeling so sorry for my mother, now on her own.

Kendall was still playing for the Saracens rugby team, and I would don my wellies, prepared for a muddy pitch, and leap onto the Piccadilly line tube and leap off at the end of the line at Cockfosters. His name hit the headlines in the Daily Telegraph, which was exciting: 'New winger Carey helps Saracens to a sparkling win'. We all celebrated; we needed something to celebrate.

Suddenly, out of the hazy blue of grief, Kendall suggested we should get married. I was twenty. I don't remember any romantic proposal. Was this just a classic 'on the rebound' situation? A wedding would be a nice thing to do, something to plan for, something to look forward to, a way of cheering myself and my mother up. We announced our engagement in the Telegraph. This was one of the normal formalities and traditions in those days.

The wedding date was decided upon for the following year: September 1966. I remember we went off to the famous Hatton Garden in London, home of all the top jewellers, silversmiths and goldsmiths, to buy the wedding ring. For some reason we chose a platinum ring. I never really liked it. It seemed to have no life in it, it was grey and dull.

In the spring before the wedding my mother and I drove to the south of Spain in her white Triumph Vitesse convertible. She sat and painted on the quiet secluded beaches, as they were then, while I sunbathed on the rocks. We lived on seafood and tomato salads, soaked up the sun and tried to talk Spanish in the markets. I remember one night walking alone back to our beachside apartment in the little village of Jávea ('little village' as it was, then) having been for a lone ramble somewhere. A wild eyed Spaniard with gold teeth leapt off his rickety bicycle and pushed me off the road into the grass and beat me about a bit. It was terrifying. But I got home safely and didn't mention it to my mother.

Homeward bound, and it was time to make the wedding plans. First things first: the customary pep talk with the vicar. The dos and don'ts. So along we went to the vicarage in the nearby Norfolk village of Bircham. Unlike today, when 'pre-nuptial' precautionary agreements are apparently so often undertaken, it was hoped that a marriage would last, was founded on good and sound Christian principles. It was quite usual for the vicar who was to undertake the marriage ceremony to invite you to a series of meetings in which he would give advice, suggestions and have a general chat about marriage, love, loyalty, faithfulness, commitment, consideration and the importance of compromise. I remember it clearly. This was his take on things: guidance for a happy and long-lasting marriage. I liked it that one of the things he read to us was from Corinthians:

Love is patient and is kind; it is not jealous or conceited or proud; love is not ill mannered or selfish or irritable; love does not keep a record of wrongs; love is not happy with evil but is happy with the truth. Love never gives up; and its faith, hope and patience never fail.

I hoped all his sound advice would help.

The next most important thing was to arrange the customary wedding list. Such a good idea, so that invited guests did not risk duplicating things. One could avoid being in receipt of six irons, two ironing boards, four kettles and two dinner services. Also, one could make one's own choice. We chose Denby for our dinner service – a deep-blue, heavy pottery ware, classical 60s style.

We fancied a fondue set. That was on the list and I still have it to this day. Kendall's mother gave us the canteen of silver arranged in a beautiful teak box. She also gave me an incredibly heavy, old-fashioned hand wringer, one for wringing out the clothes having done all the washing. I was about to become a domestic goddess, I could see. Best be a good wife and keep on top of the daily chores.

Following the wedding list was the guests' list. Most of the guests were friends of my mother and one or two of Kendall's friends from Cambridge. Gina came, of course, but I can't think who else.

My mother bought a lovely lime-green suit from a smart shop in King's Lynn and I made my wedding dress. I went to Liberty's in Regent Street and, true to form, bought curtain material. It was a fine cotton lawn with see-through dots woven into it. I lined it with silk. The train, which was attached at the shoulders, had no lining, so my idea was that the light would shine through the diaphanous dots. It was kind of pretty, with a frill around the neck. I had a 24-inch waist at the time, so I looked pretty slim. The wedding photograph, to me, is one of innocence and naivety.

My mother's cousin gave me away. Mother and I had done the flowers for the wedding in the village church of Stanhoe. We arranged colourful little posies on the end of each pew and one wild arrangement near the pulpit, rather reminiscent of my mother's wedding bouquet. I never recall having a single thought about Dad. I don't remember feeling sad, wishing he were there, or having any reference made to him during the speeches. Kendall's young niece and nephew were bridesmaid and page. I had never met them before.

The reception was held at High Barn in a large marquee in the garden. I 'went away' in an orange suit which I had made. I was also wearing a black turban – was that a subconscious symbol of grief, I now wonder? I had decorated it with those delicate orange Chinese lantern flowers which had been growing in the garden. We drove off in the dark blue MGB with tin cans on a string rattling behind us all the way to Cambridge, where we stayed the night in the Royal Garden Hotel by the river.

The honeymoon was spent in the Dordogne. We had not booked

anywhere to stay, but we eventually found a bed for the night in a rustic wayside inn, and were shown to a very dusty room on the top floor. I don't think it had been used in fifty years. On that first night the whole woodwormy bed frame collapsed off its metal frame and we ended up spending half the night trying to put it back together. It was not much of a night of passion.

Wedding day. My marriage to Kendall at Stanhoe village church, in September 1966. I made my wedding dress out of cotton lawn curtain material. My mother, on the right, looking very slim and elegant in her lime green dress

We went adventuring. We came across an old cowshed in the middle of nowhere on which there was a notice: 'À Vendre.' Understanding it to be up for sale, we wondered about having a possible bolt hole in France. We eventually tracked down the farmer who owned it, and he appeared the following day at the cowshed with an enormous key in his hand. When I say enormous, I mean it was about ten inches long, heavy iron, ancient. He opened the weighty old door, and we peered inside. I thought I could live in there very comfortably; the good life, the simple life. The farmer said it was £50, but if we touched the key it was ours, and we would have to give him the money on the spot.

How silly we were to walk away from that one, but we did, and returned home a week later to our rather boring little house in Port Vale, Hertford. This house had cost £3,000. We had each put in £1,500 towards the purchase of it and once again I set up my dressmaking business in the small spare room upstairs. The usual notice went up in the window of the front room: 'Dressmaker. Please knock if you would like any alterations done, dresses or curtains made. Wedding dresses, skirts, shirts and waistcoats.'

The same year that I got married, Gina's mother died. She was the first person I remember being aware of who had passed away, apart from my father, of course. She died of cancer. At the time it was the dreaded 'Big C', that terrible disease which one never dared mention. It was as though a dust sheet had been laid over the whole sad family situation. Poor Gina. We never spoke about it at the time, but I was always wondering how on earth she was managing, having lost her mother at such a young age.

In October of that same year, 1966, we all listened to the horrific news of the Aberfan disaster in Wales. It was truly tragic. A colliery tip had collapsed and 116 children from the local school had lost their lives.

I didn't get much dressmaking business, so I took a job in the nearby town of Welwyn Garden City, where Kendall also had a job. I worked at the Cresta dress factory. I was on the line of the finishers. The clatter of machines all day was deafening, frightful. I hated it. My job was to sew on the hooks and eyes at the top of the zip, sew on the dress labels, do final hand stitching of hems and sew on buttons. It was piece work, you only got paid for what you did, so you had to work fast. The work was always inspected by 'the checker'; mine was often sent back to be redone. Same old story, never good enough. I didn't last long there.

I can't remember anything very romantic about our years together except cheering on the Saracens at Cockfosters. I used to spend many an hour standing in the cold, in the wet, in the driving rain watching these massive bulldozer guys pushing each other about in a mud bath. I did enjoy it, though, when the ball was passed out gracefully along the line. It was 'musical' to me when it all went according to plan, the ball was grounded over the opponents' goal-line and a try was scored.

I did attempt the odd dinner party. Having invited a doctor and his wife for dinner, I remember serving up tinned Campbell's mushroom soup, followed by tinned steak and kidney pie with peas, and very smart tinned pineapple for pudding.

The dining room smelt of fish and mud for a long time, not because I was always cooking fish or making mud pies but because the river flooded, completely covering the playing fields at the back of our house, flooding the garden and the two downstairs rooms. Kendall had called me one day and exclaimed that the dining room was 'full of fish', a slight exaggeration. But any flood leaves a terrible wreckage and smell. I thought the vicar of Docking who had given us the pep talk would have been proud of me, as there I was down on my knees scrubbing the floors and skirting boards, still with a smile on my face and able to get a meal on the table for my husband.

We muddled along together for three years. There was never any talk of wanting to have a family. It is impossible to say now how I was feeling, or what I was thinking. I wonder if I was simply just numb, dumbed right down after my father's death and with constant worry about my mother now living alone.

I think this was when my mother developed the idea of what she called 'friendly attacks'. She realised she could well have become somewhat of a recluse. To some extent she was perfectly happy with her solitary life, but she also had the wisdom to know this would not be a healthy and sensible way to continue, so she made a plan. She grasped the fact that she would have to make more of an effort, and about once a month she would rather impulsively invite someone for tea or visit somebody in the village. If I am truthful, I seem to recognise a similar trait in myself; I have recently had a major 'friendly attack' moment and invited all sorts of friends and strangers for a New Year's Day gathering!

The marriage-of-sorts was clearly on the decline. One day Kendall suggested that perhaps if I became a model, I would be more loveable. I wasn't clear exactly what he meant. Did he think an injection of something different might lift us out of the doldrums?

I signed up to a modelling agency in the West End, Bond Street, and came slinking back home with a collection of rather ridiculous fashion photos of myself. Once, following a photographic session in London, I was invited to a party and had way too much to drink (sangria, I think it was). I somehow made it to King's Cross station and caught the last train home to Hertford. I fell asleep, and on waking up at about four in the morning found myself slumped in the seat, stuck in the railway siding about half a mile down the track. I stumbled off the train, wandered back down the track in my glad rags and limped home. Kendall didn't seem at all bothered about where I had been or why I had not come home the previous night.

I continued my day trips to London but, as to be expected, after a few months, once the 'sticking-plaster effect' had worn off, we agreed to separate. We were amicably divorced. I found it shocking that the lawyer tried to encourage me to 'sting him' for a lot of money, but I stuck to my principles and stated clearly that all I wanted in the form of any settlement was my share of the money which I had invested in the house. In those days 'irretrievable breakdown' was not a valid reason for filing for a divorce.

I moved into a bedsit the size of a jam jar in Nevern Square, Earls Court, West London. It had once been a large, lofty house with many spacious rooms, each of which had been divided up into about three or four rooms, so the walls were paper thin. The truckle bed resembled the one I had slept in as a child at school. The one-bar electric fire didn't work. I cooked on a one-ring gas appliance which stood on the floor. The one window would not open because it had been nailed up. The loo and bathroom were located down a thin, narrow corridor. The cast iron bath was filthy and usually before bathing I would blitz the whole bathroom.

The lady who was living in the room next door used to incessantly tap on the wall at night and then on occasion would bang on my door. If I opened it she would appear dressed very provocatively in either her frilly pink baby doll pyjamas or her revolting pale-green lace negligee. She would shout horrible things at me when I told her I was not interested in joining her for a glass of wine.

There had been a murder in Nevern Square two weeks before I moved in to my bedsit.

So, there I was back in the big city wondering what life as a model in the sixties might be all about.

Chapter 13

Modelling days

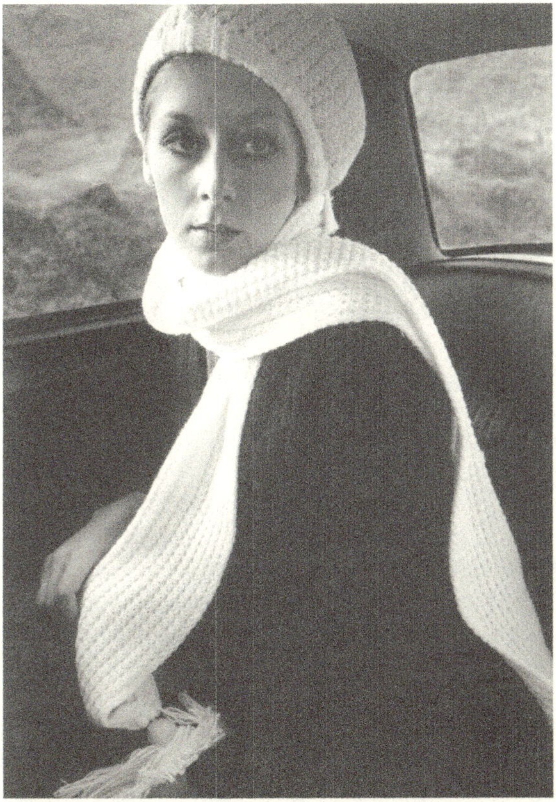

Looking a little sultry. A shot for my modelling portfolio taken in the back seat of a car. Photography by Brian Morris

I look back on it now with laughter, but at the time I didn't think it was at all funny. In fact I was mortified. It was during one of my very first encounters with a sleazy, stocky, greasy-haired, Greek photographer in his studio in Bond Street. He was taking shots of me for my modelling composite and suggested in no uncertain terms that I would be going nowhere fast in my modelling career unless I had plastic surgery on my legs. They were too fat, and there was an operation I could undergo which I should seriously consider. I had visions of a kind of ham slicer – of having my legs carefully pinned with spikes between a metal clamp, while fine slices of my flesh would be magically removed. And, hey presto – I would be on the front cover of *Vogue* the following week.

I didn't return to his studio for any further photo shoots and I did not take his advice. OK, I have never had the greatest legs, and now I am in cellulite country, but there's always been a limit in my mind as to what lengths I am prepared to go to fit a stereotype which is largely manipulated by whatever is the faddy fashion of the day.

In the late sixties, when I embarked upon this crazy quest to become a model, it was the Twiggy and Jean Shrimpton era. The ultra-thin, stick insect look, into which category I obviously did not fall. I could have starved myself, slimmed down a bit, I know that. But I thought I was a reasonable shape and size at the time, only ever eating steak and spinach.

I could of course have made it easier for myself and taken a different route. I could have indulged in more Portuguese custard tarts and croissants and gone for the outsize look, at which I understood one could make quite a reasonable living. Doing outsize catalogue work was especially lucrative. But I just carried on as I was. My modelling composite profile and statistics, very neatly printed out, read as follows:

……………….Miranda Carey…………………

Height 5' 8", bust 35", waist 24", hips 35"
Shoes 6, gloves 7
Hair fair, eyes blue

A fair-haired, blue-eyed country girl with a 24-inch waist.

I had joined an agency in Brompton Road called *Penny Personal Management*. Other well-known agencies at this time were *The Lucie Clayton School of Modelling* and *Top Models*. The system was: first get your composite printed, which consisted of a four-page brochure with a selection of photographs; wait for a phone call from your agent to go for an audition or attend a photo shoot; and hope for the best. The competition was fierce, particularly in the field of advertising.

A lot of walking around in the West End was required. I trudged with my huge black-leather bag visiting photographers' studios in the hope of getting selected for a job. Into the black bag I had stuffed a selection of wigs, Carmen heated rollers, special combs for back combing, shoes (always a dark pair and one light pair, just in case), jewellery, underwear, stockings and tights, and the massive bag of makeup, false eyelashes and blush sticks, powders and cheek-bone highlighters, lipsticks, etc. Once you were booked for a 'shoot' there was a lot of sitting around, waiting for hours titivating oneself rather obsessively in front of the mirror while the set was being arranged, clothes ironed, and lighting adjusted.

I think the ongoing back problems that I suffer with today are partially due to the fact that I hauled that heavy old bag miles and miles around the streets of London for three years or so.

Me with a 24"waist, backcombed hair and black leotard. Those were the days. Photography by Robert Dibué

I had some fun jobs. I remember lying on the bonnet of a pale-blue Jaguar car in Covent Garden doing the Schweppes ad: 'Shhhh, you know who'. I don't remember the name of the very suave, grey-haired gent who was the lead for that ad. But I do remember he was a dish.

I shopped at Barbara Hulanicki's Biba in Kensington High Street, and got close to doing some work for them, but I was pipped to the post by somebody with the perfect look that was needed. I was photographed for the front cover of a restaurant menu, lying amid a pile of discarded cardboard boxes in a Soho back street, looking rather sultry, wearing a white crochet dress. A very strange, unappetising choice for a restaurant, I thought.

Whoever came up with these crazy ideas? They are even more obscure these days, and it is often hard to work out what on earth is being advertised or quite what the subliminal messages are meant to be. I had the opportunity to wear some extraordinary garments. I was interested in the fashion aspect since, after all, I had studied dress design and had been making clothes for several years.

I remember being photographed with three other models outside the Royal Festival Hall. At low tide we had to stand on the muddy foreshore of Old Father Thames in very weird glittery catsuits, thigh-high boots and minks. We turned a few heads on that shoot.

Lying on the cardboard boxes in Soho. Photography by Robert Dibué

For the occasional weekend away I sometimes went to see Antonia, who was married with two sons and living in Norwich. Once I took myself off there on a day trip. It now seems a peculiar way to have spent a valuable Sunday off. But since I had apparently not had the time to get to the launderette round the corner from my grim bedsit, I took all my dirty washing with me and went to the launderette near her house.

With 1969 came the Apollo 11 space flight. Man had set foot on the moon. One of the highlights was sitting with my mother out in the yard at High Barn on 20 July and gazing up at the moon. With a small piece of white chalk, I scratched on the red brick farmyard wall 'MOON LANDING 1969', imagining Neil Armstrong taking that 'one small step' and also knowing what a 'giant leap' it was for mankind. To have landed successfully was a miracle. I wished I could do the same. I felt I wanted to come to land somewhere. But somewhere that felt safe, and maybe I could start living and having some fun again.

In 1970 the divorce decree absolute was granted. This was a turning point. There was a finality about that odd and brief period of my life, one in which I had not really been very happy.

My mother never asked where I was living. I imagine she was immersed in her own grief at the time and did not have the energy to be concerning herself with anything else. When I told her a little about my dreadful bedsit in Nevern Square, she suggested I find somewhere else to live.

On returning to London after a weekend in Norfolk I found that yet another seductive message written on a pretty postcard had been shoved under the door from the weird woman who was living in the room next door. I decided I must indeed move on and find some different accommodation. This rather depressing and seedy area of Earls Court did not quite fit with the supposedly glamorous world of modelling. And I did think I deserved somewhere a little more salubrious.

Scouring the Evening Standard newspaper was tedious, but I finally found a flat overlooking Battersea Park, on Prince of Wales Drive. It seemed a much more up-market address. The long, sweeping, grand drive of red-brick mansions built around the turn of the century flanked the park. I lived in Cyril Mansions, No 39. I made it home. Having painted the walls of the small kitchen bright orange and mauve, I filled my window box with red geraniums. I was determined that I would be turning a corner and that things would look up from now on.

I bought a bicycle and rode to Regent Street in Piccadilly where I was a model for Aquascutum, showing their latest season's collection of beautiful but very heavy coats. I twirled about on the catwalk showing off to the regular buyers and individual invited customers. I bought one of their camel coats, but felt the style was way too conversative, strait-laced and boring. At least it did keep me warm, and I think I felt quite smart.

Being a house model was the only reasonable way I could see of making any kind of a living at this game. I was always in hope of getting rebooked for the next season's show. I also worked for Cojana, another traditional, classy label, modelling elegant coats and suits. But again none of them were my style at all, more like the rather conventional Norman Hartnell, Hardy Amies look. But attempting to make a living was the objective, and so I stuck with it.

I then struck lucky and landed another rather fun job as a house model for Silhouette swimwear. The showrooms were located in Baker Street, so I would pedal up Park Lane, whiz around Marble Arch and then scoot off down Baker Street. Lots of sweet-smelling deodorant was needed after the rather sweaty bike ride to work.

This job, looking back on it, was another of those ridiculous ones. The bikinis might as well not have existed, scanty little triangles of fabric tied with a shoestring in a neat bow at the hips. But with my then-slim figure I guess perhaps I must have looked rather ravishing. This job took us, me and two other models, travelling up and down the country for the season's shows, to Manchester and Nottingham. We were taken out once, when we were up in Manchester, as a diversion, to a football match. Tottenham Hotspur vs Manchester United. Georgie Best and all that. Lots of cheering, and then back to our luxury hotel for dinner. I still only ever ate steak and spinach. No wonder I managed to stay so slim. I still have reasonable eyesight. The spinach must have helped. All that vitamin C.

Once, when I was mounting my bicycle leaving a photo shoot off Bond Street I was asked if I was the film star Catherine Deneuve. What a compliment. I think it was just the jaw line.

Fame came at last. I landed a job for Heineken.

The audition was most humiliating, with about 100 of us, all jostling for position. We had to strip down to bra and pants and stand behind a white screen, thus exposing to the critical eyes of the advertising team our torsos. Whereupon a tape was placed round our waist showing the exact measurements – 24" – and I got the job. I presume this was claiming to be some sort of a low calorie lager, hinting that as such, it would not be likely to damage your waistline.

So, there I was up there on the hoardings of Piccadilly Circus. No head, therefore no face, no proof that this was me, after all that … No obvious claim to fame. Ah well, never mind (I've got used to saying that). Just my torso and my 24-inch waist, but a little success at last. Yippee! Bicycling back to my flat in Cyril Mansions, after the booking had been made for a shoot for the following week, I was buzzing.

With a twirl and a swirl I continued giving the catwalk modelling jobs a whirl for several seasons. But I longed to be having a bit more fun, showing off some more way-out designs.

Is it coincidence, serendipity, random chance or what, I wonder, that the day I decided to start writing this chapter about my modelling days was the very day, 29 December 2022, on which my hero, Vivienne Westwood, passed away. She has always inspired me, not only because of the originality of her wild, out-of-the box designs, but also because of the delightful unpredictability of her approach to everything. Her very nature and confidence to push the boundaries in every way I find uplifting.

I once watched her being interviewed on TV, and it was of great consolation to me, because everything she said seemed to match exactly how I think. I had no difficulty in understanding every word she was saying – but the poor interviewer, with his staid style of questions and answers was completely at sea.

The show I'm talking about was a regular slot on a Sunday night, and Vivienne was the star guest. As to be expected she swept into the studio eliciting a 'wow' from the audience. Her wonderful red hair, piled high, looked a bit like an apricot meringue. She was wearing a rather stylish but shapeless shift dress, which was of course adorned with bows and bits and bobs, all colour and razzmatazz. The interviewer shuffled in his seat looking dull and drab in his dark suit compared to Vivienne. He seemed a little nervous, but asked her tentatively what to date had been the main inspiration for her way-out creations.

He was obviously expecting a simple, straightforward answer to his question. Vivienne paused for quite a while. It was clear that no instant flash-in-the-pan response was going to come the interviewer's way. She glanced upwards and to the right. This, apparently, is the stance one takes when deep in creative or contemplative thought. There was no eye contact. She remained gazing heavenward and then a waterfall of words began to flow from her. In writing I have taken the liberty of putting words into Vivienne's mouth, but having got the gist of her way of expressing herself I have had fun expanding on some of the images she described. 'I remember seeing these fluffy yellow baby ducklings swimming across the pond, and the ripples on the surface of the water as they swam and the snowdrops dancing like fairies around the cherry trees in the garden behind the pond. I think they actually were fairies, and anyway, even if they were not, anyone who does not believe in fairies goes down several notches in my estimation.

'And I can just remember the crisp sound as my feet crunched on the carpet of frosted oak leaves, having created a mystery scene of delicate lacework, nature's garden weaving its designs, and the unfurling pale green fronds of the woodland ferns. The lattice puff pie pastry crust too on top of the blackberry and apple pie which my grandmother always cooked on a Sunday, when blackberries were in season, which was usually late summer, and the apples in the orchard, a glory of colours, and then coming in for tea after picking baskets full for the pies, and seeing the dust that lay silent and thick like a sample of dress velvet on the sideboard in my grandmother's hall. I traced a pattern with my finger in the heavy dust and the sheen of the walnut veneer which I had exposed would shimmer with delight ... her clothes would be blacker than any soot black could be – she always wore black, nothing else.'

The agitated interviewer looked away and towards the audience, presumably in the hope of gaining some reassurance from them, and perhaps even gaining a glimmer of a clue as to what on earth she was talking about. Clearly, to him, it appeared that she had not heard nor understood his question.

He looked decidedly embarrassed and asked: 'Excuse me, can I ask you again, can you tell me…?' And as Vivienne turned her head and caught his eye she carried on with yet another delightful creative ramble. But alas it was in vain.

'Excuse me, Vivienne, can I bring you back to the question please. The question of your designs.' The poor interviewer was trembling, lost, exasperated. 'I am afraid I'm not able to follow you. I thought I asked a simple question?'

Yes, he had asked a simple question, but there was no simple answer. She could only answer it in her unique way, which she did to perfection. She went off on a tangent time and time again. Every single thing around her and every second's little tick-tock seemed to ignite her; she was constantly alight with an image which might eventually translate into an idea. She answered in pictures, in colour, in shape, in every possible creative way available to her. She fearlessly allowed herself to go freefalling, wildly uninhibited, with her imagination running riot, and this way her magical creations were born time and time again.

The interview came to an abrupt close with an apology from the interviewer: he had not found himself in this awkward position before.

I felt strangely comforted. I understood her, exactly. The images. Her thoughts, turning into ideas, seemed to be running on one from the next, effortlessly. I felt that there was some hope that somebody might understand me one day.

Rather as I sensed she did, I think, in pictures, I tend to see words in colours; they form themselves into shapes as I write and speak.

Sometimes I find it difficult to express myself coherently. I can't seem to think quickly enough, because I am enveloped in the image I am seeing. I find I am unable to find the right words in the moment, and if I am 'hurried up' my thoughts then get jumbled up. As I become frustrated, and embarrassed at my inability, my emotions can then get in the way and I can also then end up feeling humiliated. Not understood. I then find myself on a downward slope. Any confidence is instantly eroded and clear thinking goes out of the window. People do become impatient with me.

I am not suggesting for a moment that Vivienne had the same problems that I sometimes have when attempting to communicate but I observed that it appeared the interviewer could not follow her train of thought and I found this fascinating.

How I would love to have met her, perhaps worked with her and had the chance to show off some of her wonderful creations.

So … I was still in search of something a little more exciting in the fashion field, an opportunity that I might hold as one of my memories of a lifetime. It might be a trip somewhere enjoyable, a commercial, a front cover … and then suddenly there I was!

I got a double-page spread in the Evening Standard. It was during my period as a house model for Cojana. To my surprise I was selected for a photo shoot to launch the new season's collection. I was driven to Ascot in a plush limo with the photographer, a dresser, stylist, makeup artist, hairdresser, chef and all the photographic paraphernalia. I had to stand in the middle of the racetrack, motionless, wearing a rather boring beige woollen suit, while two mounted jockeys on beautiful white steeds, with thundering hooves, advanced from behind and at great speed skimmed past me on either side. Why did I not get paid danger money, I wonder? I can't remember what the fee was, but definitely not enough to break any bank, that was for sure. The caption in bold capitals across the top of the page read:

COJANA. EVERYONE A WINNER.

A week later I was booked to teeter on the parapet of a building overlooking Piccadilly Circus wearing a bright green full-length dress, draped in a white feather boa, hair flowing. 'Rather Raquel Welch,' I remember the photographer saying, as he encouraged me to inch my way to the very edge of this treacherous location. I'm not sure quite why it had been chosen, and again no danger money was ever mentioned.

The following week I was sprawled over the bonnet of a white Aston Martin at the Earl's Court Motor Show and had to serve champagne and canapés to likely purchasers, having my photograph taken alongside

Teetering on a Piccadilly Circus parapet

them as they fantasised, sitting in the driver's seat behind the wheel. I did get asked out to dinner by a smarmy American but declined, and slinked off back home on the Tube.

You might be wondering if one had to 'sleep one's way' to get anywhere in this game. Well, it was not the route I ever wished or chose to take, although I believe some girls did. It was hard to make a living, unless by some miracle one had been spotted.

I supplemented my income by waitressing in the evenings at various restaurants. One was in Dover Street … oh, what was the name of it? My brain cells must be fading … And there was another in Victoria. I do remember the name of that one. It was the called The Avocado. There often seemed to be a drama going on with the chef at The Avocado, either because the steaks were overdone, or the vegetables were not al dente, or the sauce was too salty. There was a lot of hurling of knives in the dungeons of the kitchens, screaming and shouting, and staff marching out and refusing to ever come back and even forgo their wages. But we served delicious food there. I remember pushing the sweet trolley around. I got it stuck once between two tables, and all the cheeses and tiramisu crashed to the floor. Oh dear! But I didn't get the sack.

While working in the restaurant in Dover Street I met Julia. She had moved from Hartley Wintney in Hampshire, where her mother lived, and had come to the big city in search of fortune. Restaurants were not as numerous as they are today. Fine dining had not been invented. Vegetarians were considered hippy weirdos. Foodies had not arrived on the planet and the planet itself was not under the threat of extinction. The coffee artist baristas were yet to emerge from Italy and the café culture was yet to hit London. It was unusual to find a pavement café, so there was a real buzz in the air of how we might reinvent ourselves, follow in the footsteps of Europe, become more cosmopolitan. The British climate, of course, had a lot to do with the reduced potential for al fresco dining. But the occasional café sported its bright umbrellas, and people even dared sit out under them in the rain enjoying a glass of something sparkling and pink in the summer months.

Julia had work to do. She transformed the restaurant in Dover Street, soon became the manager, and came to live with me in Cyril Mansions. We would often work together in the evenings, share out the tips and travel back to Battersea at dead of night on the bus. We became such good friends, and spent our weekends drifting about London together, sampling other cafés, visiting galleries, gardens, shopping in the King's Road. We were doing what young girls did in London at that age, just drifting about. I think now it's called 'down time' or 'decompressing' after the busy week.

I still felt I was limping along as a model, not really enjoying the scene as much as I had hoped. I spent the occasional evening in various photographer's studios lounging on sofas being semi-chatted up, listening to the Beatles' *Sgt. Pepper*.

I sometimes wondered what my father would have thought of me now, living this life in London, hoping no doubt that I might have a lucky break, make it big-time perhaps. I often used to think of him when having a photo shoot. The photographer more often than not would say, 'Face to camera square on, please' ,which I thought I already was. It was my crooked nose which had thrown things out. When I was born, apparently my nose was sort of squashed to one side, and my father told me how he used to stroke it while I was lying in my pram as a baby, trying to straighten it out. No wonder the photographer had a problem. Now I understood.

On and off I had quite a lot of work. It dribbled in slowly. But I experienced a strange dichotomy between this life and the lack of any expression of my more authentic self: the person who thrived on country air, and who loved being out in nature. I satisfied that need as often as I could by kicking off my shoes, dumping my heavy bag and going to see mother in Norfolk. In London, too, I walked by the river and paid regular visits to Kew Gardens and to the parks.

I spent quite a lot of time sitting in churches, listening to organ recitals and singing hymns. I used to go to the Mormon Church in Exhibition Road. It seemed a friendly place, quiet and peaceful. At one point – it must have been a moment of desperation – I decided to go to Earl's Court to experience the laying on of hands by Billy Graham, the evangelical crusader. He asked Jesus to save me. Would it make any difference? Would I see the light? Make a triumphant discovery? Have that long-awaited eureka moment?

I did not like it that, around this time, my family adopted the idea that I should be called Mandy. To be precise, it was 'Mandy Rice Pudding' they used to call me. The government was still trying to recover its reputation, thoroughly upstanding and respectable, but this was proving difficult following the very long-winded Profumo affair back in 1963. John Profumo, the Secretary of State for War, had been involved in an affair with a young model, one of whose friends was also drawn into the whole outrageous and scandalous drama. Her name was Mandy Rice-Davies. Thanks to endlessly repetitive news coverage, when all the dirty washing of the affair was paraded for some years, for some ridiculous reason I was given this infamous nickname. I was a little puddingish, to be fair, compared with the real Mandy. But to this day if I am ever called Mandy I wince, and always correct people. Likewise, if I am called Matilda, which for some inexplicable reason a dear male friend seems hell-bent on calling me, I politely have to remind him that in fact my name is Miranda.

I was so pleased and excited for Julia when she told me she was in love. She had fallen for a guy who had chatted her up in the restaurant. I was not so pleased when she told me they were planning to go to South Africa the following month. But off she went; they disappeared together into the blue yonder, travelling on a ship, and arrived in Cape Town a few weeks later. Sadly, the rose-tinted spectacles had fallen off before the couple made their landfall, but she quickly recovered herself and moved into a flat there with a Canadian called Norman and his South African friend called John. John, or Skeets, as was his odd nickname, had shacked up with his girlfriend, called Hazel. For about a year I would receive regular letters from Julia describing the minutiae of the daily lives of this jolly little foursome.

Meanwhile, I drifted into doing more work in photographic studios as an assistant set designer, and arranging props for shoots, which I really enjoyed. Having been briefed as to what was needed, I would go off to Bermans & Nathans, the famous costumiers in St Martin's Lane, and rummage around among fabulous vintage numbers and also racks of smelly old Afghan coats and piles of tie-dye garments, hunting out whichever costumes and items were needed for the job.

Once I remember the task was to cover all the old furniture in Fablon, the self-adhesive plastic sheets that were all the rage. You could transform your furniture overnight – instant, op-artish, stick-on designs were busy and colourful. I had to find all sorts of old furniture which we could cover with this horrible sticky stuff, so I raided all the skips in Soho and hauled them back to the studio in Floral Street.

Floral Street, such a pretty name, is a narrow road leading straight into Covent Garden, which in those days was still the fruit and vegetable market. The massive delivery lorries would rumble their way right into central London and somehow skilfully manoeuvre through the narrow streets and offload their produce. There was a wholesale warehouse above the studio where I worked in Floral Street, and the lorry would stop outside, blocking the street for hours while being divested of hundreds of crates of oranges. They would be loaded onto a wooden platform which had been lowered down from an overhead gantry, then hoisted up and reloaded onto a sack truck and taken through to a storeroom behind our studio. The flirtatious, kind 'fruit man' used to hide a box of oranges for me behind the door and blow me a kiss as he left. I was so happy with a free box of oranges and a flying kiss.

During this period of working in advertising I hung around with a photographer on and off. He had a proper girlfriend hidden away somewhere, I think. I never quite knew, since he would never come clean. But being somewhat infatuated with him I would accept any invitation from him that came my way. He knew all sorts of people in the interior design business, and through one of them he ended up living in a beautiful little garden studio apartment in Kensington behind this lady's house. She in turn seemed very well connected; one of her friends, apparently, was Princess Margaret.

So, when I was invited to a cocktail party by this photographer friend and was told Princess Margaret might be there, I thought, oh what fun, and said of course: 'Yes, I'd love to go!' We were briefed at some considerable length about royal protocol, etiquette and all that stuff. I found it all very amusing and a little ridiculous. We were told to be there an hour before her possible arrival time; not to stare at her when she entered; not to speak to her unless she opened a conversation with us; not to move towards her. If she did appear to be advancing in our direction, we were to open up a pathway so that she could move wherever she wished.

Well, eventually she did arrive. She was wearing a weird, slushy pink (probably officially called 'crushed raspberry'), flouncy long dress with a white stole draped over her slightly plumpish pale shoulders. A stole was one of her trademarks.

Yes, she wandered in, it all seemed very informal, and I could not think what all the fuss was about. But all the briefing had left me feeling like a nervous automaton. I felt I was bound to put my foot in it. I kind of just stood there hugging the wall, doing my best to behave. She milled about for a bit among the twenty-or-so guests, all of whom I presumed she probably knew. Then she seemed to be moving in my direction.

Initially, I felt a bit like a frightened rabbit, frozen in the glare of the headlights, but I quickly moved aside as I had been directed to do so that she could pass by with graceful ease: a good little girl doing as she had been told. But she then stopped, and we were pretty well face to face. I wondered if she was thinking 'Ah, here's a new face, I'll go and have a chat with her.' Well, she smiled, I smiled, I did a sort of bob, bow or something, and then the words popped out of my mouth as they so often seem to with me, not engaging my brain. And without any concern for adhering to the royal rules, in a very polite little voice and with an even more syrupy little smile, I said, 'I do hope you have had an enjoyable day.'

I had not expected her reply to be so interesting. 'Well,' she said, 'it's not been a very good one. I am tired. I had to go to some awful place in the south of London and open this hall. The trouble is, my sister has always had all the power and so she gets all the top jobs and I get the boring ones.' I smiled politely and didn't quite know what to say. There was no answer to that one.

I would have loved to have had a normal conversation with her about how she had obviously always struggled in her role as a royal; she was the one who broke all the rules, found it difficult to toe the royal line, conform, while her sister, the poor Queen, dutifully carried on, top jobs and all. I felt sure dear Princess Margaret just wanted to go home to her comfy bed. She drifted off and mingled with the other guests making formal conversation, and I was left feeling a little sorry for her and so grateful I had not been born a princess.

Through this photographer friend I worked on a book called *The Art Director's Index to Photographers*. It was his baby. It was an interesting project which involved gathering all the required information, profiles, personal statements, sample photographs, and details of about fifty photographers from England and Europe. Some texts had to be translated. Part of the job was liaising with many different people in different areas of publishing and pacifying the odd stroppy photographer when he was not happy with the proofs. This was yet another challenge for me, since collating information was not my forte. But I managed it, and I was beginning to get over myself, get a handle on things and allow myself to believe I had the capability to head up a proper project.

I discovered too that I was a reasonably good 'people person', able to be diplomatic and polite even when the going was getting a bit tough. The job involved a lot of hiking around London, walking miles to and from studios, leaping on and off buses, seeking out studios hidden away in delightful little mews. It was yet another way of discovering some hidden gems in the heart of London and meeting interesting people.

Then out of nowhere I got a phone call from Julia. She was back in England with her husband, Norman. They had got married in South Africa. It was Norman's birthday and she suggested we should meet for a drink. I was so excited. We met in a pub off Gloucester Road, and Julia was all things bright and beautiful. It was so wonderful to have her back in England again. And who should be there with them but Norman's friend, the famous John, the South African, otherwise known as Skeets. John whom I had heard all about in Julia's letters to me.

A fair-haired, bearded figure, settled himself comfortably in a chair in the corner of the smoky pub. I don't remember him talking much at all on that evening. Was he shy? Where was Hazel? I gleaned that he had split with her and that he and Norman, having become somewhat disillusioned with the unpredictable political situation in South Africa, were fancying a change of scene. Would the grass be greener in London?

On parting that night, Julia and I agreed we would be picking up where we had left off and would be seeing a lot more of each other.

The following morning I received a phone call from John asking if I would like to go for a walk in Richmond Park. I was surprised, since I didn't think he had really logged me; but I was curious and agreed to go along.

Chapter 14

Surprise surprise

The Swinging Sixties. A modelling agency shot. Crochet and crazy op art.
Photography by Ivor Ashmore

After Julia had vanished off to South Africa, I had been unable to find another suitable flatmate. So I had left my place in Prince of Wales Drive and located somewhere cheaper to live. It was another rather grim bedsit off the Gloucester Road in South Kensington. I found another job, in the Bistro Elegant on the corner of Brompton Road. I was supposed to be working there in the evening of the next day after that first meeting with John, but now that he had suggested we meet and go for a walk I was in a bit of a quandary. I decided that I would leave the afternoon and evening free. I didn't want to feel the pressure of getting all ruffled and having to dash back to work. So, I cancelled my shift. They were none too pleased, but I am afraid I thought, oh well, what the hell.

With heart slightly racing on this autumnal day in October 1973 I busily prettied myself up and set off to meet John as agreed outside South Kensington Tube station. Ten stops to Richmond – or perhaps I could take the lead and suggest we alight at Kew, one stop before Richmond, and I could take him to some of my favourite haunts in the gardens there. I could show him the giant water lilies which I was so intrigued by. Like huge, resting pizza pans, they are utterly extraordinary.

I felt slightly uncertain about meeting him, since I knew a little about his personal life: Julia had shared much with me in her missives from Cape Town. I had heard all about their time together there, so I felt almost as though I had been living alongside them all for a while. But I had to erase any thoughts I had about his past and just enjoy what was to be now, live in the present and meet him for real. I wondered what he was going to be like in actuality.

We jumped onto the first Tube that came along. I was pleased that he seemed a lot more sparky than he had the night before. He said he liked my name. It was a strong name, and pretty too. His surname of Shuttleworth I thought was interesting. I wondered if his family had any connection with the Shuttleworth Aeronautical Collection which I'd heard of, but later learned this was not so.

John appeared to be a gentleman too, I could tell. He held the door open for me when we stopped for a coffee. Nowadays, some poor women consider it sexist if you like a door being held open for you by a man. I think they probably have some emotional baggage they could well do with offloading. I think it is plain and simple polite behaviour to hold a door open for anybody, male or female, young or old.

Anyway, John was scoring quite a few Brownie points by now. I had been rather dreading that I might feel disappointed. I felt slightly dubious since he had not made much of an impression on me the night before in the pub. But now that we had time and were able to sit quietly and chat on our own, rather than straining to hear each other in the noisy and smoky pub, I realised he was clearly a bit of a character and a man I would like to get to know.

I can see us now, sitting on the bench in Richmond park. That beautiful late autumn light, the sun setting behind the trees silhouetting the savannah-like grasses in the foreground. Geese were calling hauntingly from across the lake, competing with the imaginary sweet strains of violin strings, which were by now playing between us. John put his arm on my shoulder, then an arm around me, and we kissed. Was this to be the beginning of something very special?

As we snuggled on the bench together, I began to tell John a bit about my life. There had recently been a lot of toing and froing to Oxford where my sister Anabel was living. We had a brief attempt at doing bed and breakfast, which amused us. It was near-nigh impossible in her house to find a matching teacup and saucer, let alone one that was not chipped. We both had uncontrollable giggles when I served breakfast in bed to some strange man who had booked in for several nights. Having asked him how he liked his eggs cooked, we then could not find an egg cup in which to serve them. Wearing a white frilly apron (I was hoping to pass as the housemaid, I suppose), I teetered up the stairs and served his eggs in an egg box with toast on the side.

Anabel and I had recently been off on a brief holiday to Crete. We slept on the beach at Loutro after walking down the Samaria Gorge with all our belongings stuffed into wheelie bags. Having packed ready to leave from Oxford, we realised that we could hardly lift our very heavy rucksacks. We were worried about our poor backs. So we had dashed off to the market and bought these brightly coloured little shopping trolleys on wheels. We thought they would be more convenient. Stumbling over all the rocks and boulders of the Samaria Gorge, one of the longest and most challenging hikes in Europe was treacherous, far from easy, especially with our 'shopping trolleys'. It was a ridiculous disaster.

I had ditched my trolley and gone to Athens and bought an antique rucksack in the flea market, having met Antonio, who was a wild-eyed, devastatingly good-looking Spaniard. He joined us on our travels for a while. Turned out he was mad. He was running away from some drama back home, although we never discovered quite what it was. A child had tragically died somehow, we had thought, and I had a hunch that he was wanted by the police. Sleeping on the beach one night he asked me if I thought I needed protection, and with that he drew a large knife from his bag and hurled it over my head. It landed in the sand two inches from my right ear. He turned up in Oxford some months later and stole all the lodger's rent money which Anabel had hidden in a cornflake packet in the kitchen cupboard. He faked a burglary by leaving the kitchen window ajar, disappeared, and we never saw him again.

I told John I had written a lot of poetry but kept it under lock and key. I liked dressmaking and would be capable of making him a bespoke shirt with hand-stitched buttonholes. I explained how my father had died very suddenly, and that I was worried about my mother living alone. Since going to boarding school at the age of seven, I told him, I had fought off the sense of being a failure almost on a daily basis. Deep down I was shy, not confident. I was so thrilled that Julia had returned to England. Essentially, I supposed I was an artist, but had difficulty with the label.

I told him all about my more current life in advertising, and that I was still dabbling with a bit of modelling, still a busy working woman and still deliberating as to whether I should go and train as an occupational therapist. It might be an avenue for getting into more meaningful work. I would like to be working in the caring professions. Some called it doing the 'worthy work'.

The training would involve an interesting combination of physiotherapy and art therapy, craft and counselling. A certain amount of medical expertise was required too. If I decided to go this route I would have to go to Derby, live in student accommodation, wear a grim uniform which resembled a J-cloth (but it was brown-and-white check, not blue-and-white). It might also mean that, having completed the training, I would be able to command a reasonable salary. That would be a significant point in its favour.

As we talked I realised that I was trying to convince myself that this idea was a good one, while knowing at the same time it was definitely not for me. If I qualified as an OT, I would be destined to wear a uniform for the rest of my working life and have to tie my hair back very neatly. That mere fact was enough to tell me that I didn't quite fit this bill. And I very much doubted that I was clever enough anyway to be able to get my head around all the medical stuff. What would be the point of reinforcing my sense of failure?

Yes, that job might provide a stable income … but as we wandered back through the park, hand in hand, we spontaneously burst into song: *'I don't care too much for money, money can't buy me love!'*

Strange the random collection of things I chose to tell John on this first date, I think it was a case of slight nerves and verbal diarrhoea. Surely it was all enough to make him wonder if I was slightly off my trolley.

But he seemed to be attentive, all ears, listening. I did of course ask him a few questions, but he seemed a little reluctant to share much other than the fact that he was feeling a little displaced having decided to leave South Africa.

John needed to find employment, and after going for numerous interviews he did in the end get offered a well-paid job, having graduated as an electrical engineer. I never quite understood exactly what that meant, although he tried to explain it to me on numerous occasions. He seemed to spend hours gazing at complicated electrical circuits, designing them or refiguring them somehow, in order to make them work more efficiently, I guess. I used to drive him out along the Great West Road beyond Chiswick to his place of work.

John had moved into my bedsit, which was far from a romantic little pad, so we searched yet again for something a little more cosy and found a flat off the Bayswater Road. We spent that Christmas in Norfolk with my mother. Julia and Norman came along too. We piled into a hire car and loaded it with goodies for Christmas. My mother seemed a little in awe of these two bright young men, but so long as I was happy, which I seemed to be, she was not worried.

I had committed myself to waitressing work at the Elegant Bistro on New Year's Eve, desperate to save some pennies, so we dutifully returned to London after the short Christmas break. On the way back in the car Julia and Norman dropped their next bombshell. They had decided to go to Toronto. Canada was Norman's homeland and Julia, as ever, was up for her next travelling adventure. They were going to book their tickets within the week and depart. I was so sad. Would I ever share the fun again? We always had such good times. We were going to wave them off at the airport but, in the end, I decided I couldn't face yet another goodbye, so we had a little farewell supper party together in our flat.

New Year's Eve, and I was working at the bistro. John decided he might as well go to the party he had been invited to, so we agreed to meet on the doorstep of a friend's house, which was just round the corner from the restaurant. The friend was away, so the house would be a handy place to spend the night, a sensible arrangement. I would not have to waste all my wages on a taxi back to Bayswater or risk walking back home having to avoid the New Year's Eve drunken revellers.

We kissed goodbye and John disappeared down the flight of stairs leading to the Tube station at South Kensington. 'See you after your work,' he called back. 'I'll just stay a short while – I won't be late, promise.'

His words filled me with excitement. The harsh reality of all the hours and years of rather weary waitressing work seemed to have been transformed in an instant. The tired, aching feet and the lonely bus ride home to an empty bed… all thoughts of this past life fled away as I skipped across the road, dodging the traffic.

As I entered the Bistro, I felt I was stepping over the threshold into a new world. The black apron was tied neatly but loosely around my hips. I worked with fresh enthusiasm knowing that, having served up a few fillet steaks and some steak tartares, I would soon be off to meet my love.

I didn't like having to make steak tartare at the Bistro. The thought of the combination of raw beef and raw eggs, parsley with a little seasoning of Lea & Perrins, turns my stomach over. It did then and it still does. But there were lots of orders for that dish on this particular New Year's Eve for some reason and I found that, when I left the restaurant, I was not in a particularly good frame of mind. But I thought, oh well, I could blame my bad mood on the steak tartares.

Not having had much of a fun evening, with everyone off to their jolly parties, I felt a bit of a clot having volunteered to work that night, particularly since I had just met this interesting man. But the night was young. We would soon be together.

Just after midnight I rushed back to the rather grand, freshly painted white house with its imposing portico, smartly painted wrought iron railings and wide steps leading up to the front door. What an impressive place to spend the night, I was thinking. But no lights were on. No sign of life. John had sworn he would be back shortly after midnight since the party was not far away. He had a key, and I just had to ring the bell, he would let me in and we would celebrate together. I reasoned that he must be busy putting the champagne on ice and arranging the ambient lighting, setting the stage for our romantic evening.

Having rung the doorbell twice, I thought I had better bang on the door. I rang the bell again, banged on the door again. Oh well, he's not back yet. Never mind, he's bound to be here soon.

Rain. Ah! No umbrella. I hate umbrellas. There are not many things I hate but one of them is umbrellas. But now I was getting wet, and I had waited nearly an hour. It was 1am, 1.30am, 2am. The odd taxi passed. Was John going to leap out? No, none of them stopped outside the house. By now I was pretty well soaked. Well, it's decision time. Do I spend all that hard-earned money on a taxi home? Then I wondered, but is John OK? Or has something terrible happened to him? The other option was I could start walking home. It was by then 2.30. I stood and waited. Then 3am. I stood and waited; 4am. I stood and waited; 5am. Am I a complete, half-witted idiot?

I asked myself: Why am I not walking away from this ridiculous situation? Where is the stupid man? He is in serious danger of losing all his well-earned Brownie points now. Well, he has already lost half of them, that's for sure. How was I ever going to recover from this, how could I possibly forgive him? At this stage in our embryonic relationship, surely if I mean anything to him, he would not be treating me like this. I was fuming and by now completely drenched. Even if I'd had the good sense to use an umbrella I don't think it would have held off the driving rain on that stormy night.

Dawn was by now breaking. The first sweet bird calls cheered me up, and for some reason I suddenly saw the funny side of things. I realised I could turn this ridiculous situation on its head, if I chose to. All the crazy things one does and puts up with when smitten and deluded in the first throes of love! The infatuation, the obsession, the blinkers and the rose-tinted spectacles are all designed to obscure any rationale.

All sensible decision-making goes out of the window. Any reasonable course of action seems dull and boring. All rude, dishonest or vulgar behaviour is ignored, or instantly forgiven, and time itself becomes distorted. I imagine I might have stood on that doorstep for another forty-eight hours and lost track of reality altogether.

A figure appeared at the end of the street. Flamboyantly, romantically (of course) there was John, singing his heart out, twirling his umbrella, dancing obliviously down the street, with a broad grin on his face. 'I'm singing in the rain...'

All was forgiven, and despite my sopping wet hair we drew the curtains and tumbled into bed.

On waking at midday, I wondered: had I walked away, what a different story might have unfolded over time. I reflected on those hours waiting on this unfamiliar doorstep. Everything else was unfamiliar, too. I was in love. That was not something I'd been expecting, either.

When a loved one dies, time seems to stand still. The world around one ceases to exist, because one is consumed with the momentousness of what has happened. Life has been snatched away. Grief to me is love with nowhere to go.

Being in love is grief in reverse. That love is itching to just let itself be, it has everywhere to go, it wants to give everything, take everything, share everything, be everything. It is everything. It lights you up, it shines through you. It shows you who you should truly be. It's not anything you can control. So that's why I just kept standing there. Standing in the love.

I had feared that my head would allow my stupid, proud little ego to get in the way. I had felt disappointed and angry. But I didn't let it get the better of me. I also realised that the waiting had presented such a joyful opportunity. I remember having all kinds of random thoughts as I stood there on the doorstep, ones that perhaps under normal circumstances might have just slipped by unnoticed. I loved the dawn, just as I did the dusk. Dusk is that beautiful time of day when the world falls still. In towns and villages the people scurry home after a busy day to meet with their families, prepare meals, gathering together the threads of the day and sharing in cosy conversation. At dawn the world has yet to stir itself, and it's when I feel God's presence. It's intangible. It's a new day that has never lived itself before.

I had taken in every simple detail of the street, listened, heard every sound. Wondered about every waking soul, those who were being born, those who were dying. Thought of all those whom I loved, those whom I should have forgiven but had not, wondered how they were. Thought about those I didn't know, those whom I might meet. Wondered about the crossing of paths, the ships in the night. Was John going to be one of those ships in the night after all? I had thought about some of the moments when I wished I had said something to somebody but had held back. I thought of course about my father. I knew that I was lucky. I seemed to know that waiting there, in the greater scheme of things, was precisely where I was meant to be.

It wasn't long before John became disillusioned with his mundane job out along the Great West Road. And in all honesty, I had become more than a little disenchanted with driving him to and fro from work. He seemed to be losing his sparkle, which worried me, so I asked him one day what he would really like his future to look like. What kind of job did he fancy? What did he want to do with his life? He didn't answer for a long time, hesitating, but eventually told me that what he really wanted to do was to build his own boat.

I thought that sounded interesting. My reply – 'Well, why don't we?' – surprised John a little I think, but we said no more about it. Perhaps it was just one of his crazy dreams.

We were happy. He could look for a more rewarding job all in good time. We were meeting new friends, enjoying going to the alternative theatres and folk clubs, and spending weekends away.

In June we decided that a wedding might be a good idea.

I had secretly been searching for a more interesting wedding ring than the previous platinum one. We went along to the Burlington Arcade in

Picadilly and bought a beautiful little gold band, inset with three of my favourite opal gemstones.

John and me on our wedding day leaving Paddington Registry Office in June 1974. We were both wearing brown shirts. I made my skirt and John wore his trendy white bellbottoms

We rang my mother and told her we had just got married at Paddington Register Office. On hearing this news her words 'Oh, that's lovely darling' amused me. We had rushed off on the spur of the moment. The registrar officiating was a charmingly smiley lady who said she had tried her best to make it a lovely joyous occasion for us both, but it was difficult sometimes, especially when she had to fit in six or eight other marriages on a busy day. I think she felt a little sorry for us as we only had one friend of John's as witness, no other guests.

Her kind words seemed to ignite John's imagination. As he spontaneously grabbed me around the waist we flew off down the steps, laughing. He was wearing white bell bottoms and a brown crimplene shirt. I had made my skirt, different colours in diagonal panels. I was wearing a brown shirt too. We invited one or two people round for a meal afterwards and I cooked a huge leg of lamb. We bought loads of fresh strawberries from the Portobello Road for pudding.

The following morning after our wedding I made a little boat out of a walnut shell, a matchstick for the mast and paper for the sails. I floated it in John's teacup and took it to him as he was sitting up in bed. I scrambled in beside him and asked: 'Well, when are we going to start building this boat then?'

Chapter 15

Blood, sweat and tears

I embroidered this Painted Lady butterfly on the front of my iconic red cotton drill Fisherman's smock

I had not fulfilled my dream of becoming a prima ballerina, but I did have another dream. A simple one really. I had always dreamt of being in love with an interesting man and of going off on some kind of adventure together.

John had nurtured his own dream from an early age. He wanted to cruise around the world – go off in his home-built boat on an adventure on the high seas. So here we were, in love.

I think that John, having met me, was a little surprised that 'this woman' was apparently saying she'd love to help him fulfil his dream. And although I was not sure about the high seas, I thought I might be within reach of fulfilling at least part of my dream too.

So, time now for a reality check. Between us we had savings of approximately £4,000. If we were seriously intending to build a boat, obviously some money would be essential to get the project off the ground. But more significantly, I thought, it would require copious amounts of energy, enthusiasm, stamina and commitment. I wondered if we had all the necessary ingredients. I did think we would make a good team. But would it be fun, or would it just be a relentless and miserable slog? Deep down, however, I never remember having a single negative thought about the idea. I just kept repeating the question: 'So when are we going to build this boat then? Why don't we?'

John had learnt to sail with his father. They'd built a small dinghy together when he was seven. Then later John had sailed with an Australian friend (also called John) from Cape Town to Recife in Brazil in the friend's home-built multihull. He told me that this was the kind of boat he had dreams of building.

A trimaran has three hulls, unlike a catamaran which has two hulls, or a monohull which has only one. Knowing very little about boats myself at this juncture I was a bit confused. I was wondering if we were in fact talking about building three boats. It seemed to be getting a little more complicated. But John patiently explained the difference and his reason for preferring a trimaran.

Our conversations as we were sitting up in bed drinking our early morning tea were getting more serious. Was this just that crazy idea, a dream, or was it really achievable?

I dared to suggest that, once one has a goal, one has to make a plan, otherwise it is just a wish. So, was it really his goal in life to build a boat and go adventuring? If so, I was willing to put my savings towards it, and I would help him make a plan – and why on earth were we wasting any time?

But where could we possibly build it? High Barn perhaps?

So, full of enthusiasm I made yet another surprise phone call to my mother, asking if we could live with her as we had decided we wanted to build a boat. She didn't seem at all fazed or surprised, and after only a slight pause her words heralded the next chapter of John's and my life together. 'Build a boat, how exciting, oh yes, well do come, darling.' We packed up our flat and within a week were heading for Norfolk like two excited children. We were off on a mission.

John had been doing his homework and fancied the idea of building a Derek Kelsall design. Kelsall was a well-established, revered boat designer who specialised in multihulls. With my limited knowledge I had not understood that an ocean-going vessel, particularly one in which we could live in reasonable comfort, would need to be a fair size. So, after a lot of deliberation we decided on a 40ft-long design.

The specification for the trimaran:

Length overall: 40 ft
Beam: 22 ft
Draft: 2 ft
Sloop-rigged 40-ft mast
Engine: 10 hp Yanmar diesel, housed under cockpit sole
Full standing headroom in saloon
Outriggers for storage only

It would be almost as wide as it was long, so there were all kinds of considerations before we could possibly begin building. We sent off for the plans and waited eagerly for the first drawings to arrive. High Barn was eight miles from the sea, so how on earth were we going to get a completed boat to the coast?

First things first. We contacted the police to find out what the maximum wide load restrictions were, since it would not be much use spending years building a boat and then finding we not able to transport it to the sea. We felt reassured when we were told we would be given a wide-load police escort when the time came for the launch. This whole idea was very rapidly becoming a reality.

Next on the list was firming up where exactly to build the boat. There were various large barns at High Barn, but these were still in use for storage of machinery. There was a lean-to barn adjoining the larger one and we asked the owners if we could use it. They agreed. It would be large enough to build the two outriggers there, but not the main hull.

So, this was where the work had to begin. We needed to build a shelter adjoining the lean-to, of sufficient size to house the main hull. I was beginning to wonder how much fun this was going to be. I was finding the planning stage so frustrating. Endless days were spent on discussion, deliberation and measuring, and all the essential financial calculating.

It was an exciting day when the postman finally delivered a large packet with the first line drawings. We had a celebratory dinner, and my dear mother, while exuding enthusiasm, kept asking John how on earth he knew how to build a boat. Fi-Fi, the treasured and handsome long-haired black-and-white family cat, seemed to be tuning in as well, and joined us at the table as we cracked open another bottle of wine. Having a propensity for tears I cried and couldn't quite believe what we were about to undertake.

We set up a design office in the loft above one of the garages. John used to spend every evening poring over the design and planning what was necessary for the next stage of the building. The loft was also a useful little bolt hole when we needed some time and space to ourselves.

My mother was very long suffering and never ever complained about having had her home and life somewhat disrupted since our arrival. But she did drive John nuts when, every time he walked past her through the kitchen, she would ask, 'Where are you going? What are you doing?' His reply was usually, 'I am going to the lavatory.' She was not used to having people around her all the time, after living on her own, and always wanted to know exactly what we were up to and where we were going.

We found a very well-stocked demolition yard nearby and bought all the heavy 2" x 4" posts and ceiling rafters with which to build the fifty-foot-long shelter. We dug massive holes and cemented the posts into the ground. Having erected the strong and stable shelter I raided the barns and fields, gathering together all the empty plastic manure bags and sewing them together to form the cover to go over it. I used my faithful old Singer sewing machine, which was still going strong after all those years of dressmaking. We did also buy a few rolls of very expensive heavy plastic for repairs, but our boat was going to have to be built on a shoestring so we had to be ingenious and save every penny wherever we possibly could.

We had estimated that it might take us about a year to complete. By the late summer of 1974, with the shelter finally completed, it was full steam ahead. With John at the helm, we started on the build itself.

The foam-sandwich method of construction was interesting and unusual. At the time the most popular method for producing boats was to build in glass fibre, or more traditionally of course wood, steel or concrete. I could never get my head around the idea of a concrete boat. But the critical factor when building a multihull is the weight. It needs to be kept to a minimum and therefore the half-inch-thick Airex foam method, with outer and inner layers of glass fibre, provided a lightweight and strong hull.

All the materials required had to be calculated and ordered from manufacturers up and down the country. Massive pantechnicons were beginning to arrive every week delivering huge barrels of resin, heavy rolls of glass fibre, and large sheets of the Airex foam. I set up a work-station area in the smaller lean-to, taking a page out of my father's book. 'There is a place for everything, everything in its place.' I enjoyed getting everything organised before we actually began. Buckets galore, catalyst for the resin, paint brushes, rollers, thinners, hammers, nails, screws and screwdrivers, bolts, pen and pencils, saws, Stanley knives, spirit levels, masks, and the essential emergency first-aid kit – along with all the electrical tools, a full-scale workshop was soon up and running.

We started work in the late summer, the weather still being reasonable. The grand plan was that, if it became impossible to work in the shelter in the colder winter months, we could carry on in the lean-to working on the smaller outriggers, the rudder, windvane, and the dinghy which we also planned to build. We must have been mad. Can't think why we did not just buy a dinghy. Money, I suppose. John also built a beautiful, working, scale model of the boat so that he could tank test it. I deeply regret that years later I allowed it to get damp and fall into disrepair in our leaking garage and finally waved goodbye to the remains of it in a ceremonial bonfire.

So, next it was off to the demolition yard again in search of suitable planks with which to build the 'strong back'. I always liked that term. It was necessary to build a heavy base which would support the boat itself. Very hefty planks, 8" x 2", were joined together forming a sturdy framework. This was all set up on the ground and all had to be dead level. John was a perfectionist and he paid particular attention to the measurements, wanting them to be absolutely spot on. Onto the strong back we then attached the frames of the main hull of the boat. These frames would be discarded later. These were made out of wood, cut into shape by a hand-held jigsaw. I very nearly chopped my little finger off one day when I struck a nail in the wood and the saw jumped sideways. Lots of blood on that day. We got through copious jigsaw blades too.

Off to the scrap yard again to source thinner wood for the stringers. We managed to find some old floorboards from a hotel which had recently been demolished, but they were covered in black pitch and had to be sanded smooth before we could use them.

Tea break. A shot of John and me taken through the wooden framework of the main hull of the boat with an outrigger behind

I got the shakes having spent hours using an orbital sander in an attempt to get rid of all the tar. The boards then had to be carefully cut into one-inch strips and laid onto the frames, bent gently round, gradually taking up the shape of the hull. Each stringer was screwed onto the frame, the screw holes all having to be countersunk first. When completed the wooden mould resembled a huge resting whale, which the chickens fancied roosting underneath at night. They made a lot of mess.

Next the fun bit. The large sheets of Airex foam had to be laid over the stringers of the wooden mould and screwed into place from the inside. We took turns with this job, sitting inside the cage of the mould. We calculated one day we had used more than 5,000 screws. There were a few blisters too after that job. The foam had to be cut and shaped so as to fit round the concave and convex curves, and various shapes had to be cut to fit into odd corners. It was reminiscent of making a dressmaker's pattern. I enjoyed that job. Progress always seemed so slow, with every stage taking twice as long as we had planned. We rarely reached our daily target.

My mother was always so supportive and encouraging and used to bring us cups of tea and cake to cheer us along. Gina arrived one day, just to check on progress. She had turned up in her white, open-top Mercedes, looking so glamorous wearing her grandmother's old fur coat. I was permanently covered in dust and had worn nothing but a boiler suit for months.

We lived with the smell of resin, ghastly itching from glass fibre fragments, and almost continually had to wear masks to avoid lung damage from the dust and toxic fumes. We worried about the finances of the project and we'd feel daunted and uncertain and wonder if we would run out of steam and money. There was more than the occasional drop of blood, a lot of sweat and the odd tear.

But we kept going. We had not really discussed where we were intending to sail; the adventure for now was focused on building a boat.

At first I had no idea how the glass fibre aspect was meant to work, but I quickly learnt on the hoof. The unidirectional cloth that we used was very difficult to cut. Loads of scissors ended up blunt in the bin. Two layers of glass fibre were placed diagonally across the foam, then painted and rolled with resin. The catalyst enabled the resin to harden within a certain time, so one had to work fast before that happened. The temperature affected the working time available, so if it was hot and sunny we had to get our skates on. If it was cold and chilly, we worried that the resin might not harden sufficiently.

We had only one disaster in that respect, when we were both so tired that we had forgotten to add the catalyst to the resin. The following morning, as we were all set to carry on with the next layer of glass fibre, we realised the previous one had not set. What a calamity. But we managed to recover the situation.

The next stage was to apply a fine microballoons filler over the glass fibre. This then had to be sanded with an orbital or belt sander until it was very smooth and ready for the paint job. Three layers of hard-wearing marine paint were applied, and antifouling paint below the waterline.

Then the rather tricky, nerve-wracking process. Having hired a crane we lifted the hull and turned it over with the frame still intact. This way it would safely retain its shape while being turned over. We next had to remove all those 5,000 screws. The crane hoisted out the wooden frame. We then repeated the same processes we had used on the exterior, this time glassing the inside of the hull.

Hard at it. John and me in 1975 building our boat at my mother's High Barn home. The hull taking shape

We now had something that was beginning to resemble … well, not a boat, but a vessel of some description. It's exhausting for me even to be thinking about the work it took, but I am a lot older now.

Winter was on the way, and Norfolk winters can be bitter. It became obvious that we could no longer work outside in the shelter on the main hull. So just before Christmas we covered the boat up in layers of newspaper and wrapped it in sheets, blankets and anything we could lay our hands on. My mother gave us some of her old sheets from the airing cupboard – that self-same airing cupboard in which I had found

The crane lifting and turning the main hull. A hairy operation

the lace tablecloth that I'd made into my dress for the Boat Race Ball at the Dorchester. Finally, we wrapped the hull in plastic, tied it all down with ropes and put it to bed.

We continued work during the colder months in the lean-to, making the two outriggers. In comparison to the size of the main hull these were small fry, but still a lot of work. They would be used mainly for the storage of sails, anchors, fenders, jerry cans etc, so once the hulls were completed there were lots of more detailed jobs. These included fitting watertight hatches onto their decks and making solid, glass-fibre pads for attachment of the stanchions. All this we managed to achieve through that first miserable winter.

When Mr Ayres, the coalman from the village, came with his delivery one day, he was intrigued to know what was going on in the yard. We proudly gave him a conducted tour and he promised to take the boat to the coast on his low loader when the boat was finished. We couldn't quite believe at this stage that it would ever be completed.

It had been such a tough winter. We had a strict routine. Up at 7am. Start work in the yard by 8am. Stop for lunch at 1pm. Work on till 6pm. I might slink off at 5.30 to start making some sort of a meal, but we knew and agreed that the only way this was ever going to reach completion, just like any other big project, was as a result of total dedication and commitment.

Snuggling down in bed together after these long, physically testing days was tough, especially when we had been working with the glass fibre. We had to lie several feet apart, while reflecting on the day's progress. The tiny fibrous filaments caused terrible irritation to the skin, and the constant itching and desperate desire to scratch was horrible. Even touching would set off the itches, so on many a night we would just have to grin and bear it and calmly say to each other: 'Don't touch.'

By the spring of the following year, we took a rain check on progress, finances and logistics. We drew up a schedule and did our very best to stick to it, but it seemed we were always running to catch up. Sometimes progress was held up because the next batch of materials had not been delivered on time. It was so frustrating. We realised this boat was not going to be completed within a year, nor did we have enough money to complete it.

I decided I would run a cake stall at the weekly market at Wells-next-the-Sea. Crazy. Can't think how I ever thought this was going to help the financial situation.

We needed to get a little more serious and I applied for a job at a holiday home for disabled children in the nearby seaside town of Hunstanton. I was offered the role of assistant activities organiser and occasional kitchen hand, and worked part time which brought in a little bit of money. We both went to work on another man's boat in Wroxham, on the Broads. This poor man had embarked upon a huge project, solo, desperately hoping to fulfil his dream, but he had run out of steam. He needed any help he could get, and anything to boost his morale. We rented a bedroom in a pub in the nearby village and spent a few months working for him. For days and days we undertook the tedious task of sanding the hull. But we managed to save a little, so it was worth it. Every penny counted.

Having spent hours enveloped in clouds of choking dust we rewarded ourselves most evenings with supper of fish and chips from the family-run business around the corner. A regular-sized piece of cod cost 10p and a portion of chips was 5p, all neatly wrapped in the local newspaper which we then enjoyed reading when we had finished our gourmet dinner. Sometimes we splashed out and bought a pint of lager for 25p. I smoked the occasional cigarette: a pack of Player's No. 6 cost 21p.

We returned to High Barn eager to crack on with our own boat.

I remember one night going into meltdown. I sobbed and sobbed and had a rather unladylike screaming and shouting fit. I seemed to have lost all energy and enthusiasm for everything. John and I had noticed we had become pretty short-tempered with each other, a bit twitchy and tetchy. We were worn out, not having had a single day off from the project in over a year.

We were contributing towards the household electricity bills at High Barn, of course, while knowing that we were so lucky to have this perfect location in which to be building, all for free. But living with my mother was not always easy. She was still driving John potty, always asking him where he was going and what he was doing. We took stock and decided it would be in everybody's best interest if we took a break.

A friend had mentioned that he knew of an idyllic cottage in Wales, called 'Acorns', and that we might be able to rent it for a week or so. We eventually tracked down the owner, who told us that the cottage was unique, in a beautiful location, fairly isolated; it might be a little difficult to find, and not in particularly good shape, but it was very cosy. There was no need for a key. We were not sure if it sounded like the perfect retreat. But we set off regardless, feeling ever so slightly curious but also excited, trusting that a change of scene and a refreshing romantic little interlude would rejuvenate us, with no dust, no itching, no questions from Mother.

Driving into the depths of the Welsh wilderness seemed to go on for ever. In those days, with no satnav, we realised as it was getting dark that finding the cottage was going to be impossible. Having driven round in circles down narrow, twisting lanes for two hours we finally gave up and slept in the back of the car. Next morning, we were hoping that daylight might be useful in helping us locate the cottage. Well, it did help a bit. We had been told the name of the hamlet, and it had been suggested we leave our car in the layby which was close to the sign with an arrow for 'Acorns'.

We had not been told that to get to the cottage we would first have to hike across three fields (two of which were full of sheep), negotiate two heavy farm gates which had been intricately laced with barbed wire, stumble through a forgotten wood, cross a stream, hike across yet two more very muddy fields, scramble through several overgrown hedges and eventually, there in the distance, nestling in a little dell, we would see the cottage. Well, just getting there and finding the cottage was an adventure in itself, and I had wanted an adventure after all.

Having finally arrived at the cottage – which one might more accurately describe as an abandoned ruin – I thought it worth reminding myself that one can always choose to learn something when faced with unexpected situations. This was completely unexpected. It's also worth trying to remain delighted by the unexpected, if that's remotely possible. At this point we were not sure.

Having lugged our gear and provisions all the way from the car we thought, let's put the kettle on, have a cup of tea and celebrate.

That turned out to be a bit of a fantasy. There was no kitchen to speak of. We fought our way through the brambles into a little back parlour where there was a three-legged broken table propped up on an old orange box with evidence of mice having taken up residence. We investigated the potential of the workings of the delightful old cast-iron kitchen range. Having found a saucepan we filled it from the water butt that was around the back of the cottage. We smashed up the orange box and lit a fire in the range and in no time had the saucepan bubbling and made a cuppa, knowing we had to look upon this little escapade as a welcome break from boatbuilding. In terms of its safety the staircase was questionable, but it was a relief to find there was at least a mattress on the floor upstairs.

The room was strewn with dirty old clothes, bags of rubbish and not a lot else. We imagined it had been a squat for some poor homeless family or a down-and-out's secret hideaway. We took turns in sitting in the one comfy armchair. We sat out under the stars beside the ancient old oak tree and agreed we would have no discussions about the boat building. We needed to forget it for a while and just be. We 'fairytaled' the place by lighting a few nightlights and settled down to our first night of romance at Acorns.

Surprisingly, we slept well on that first night and rustled together some breakfast, after which I decided I would like to have a wash. I stood outside in an old, galvanised-tin tub which we had unearthed from a pile of rubble from behind the cottage and I happily lathered myself, covered in sweet-smelling, foaming soap suds, using the water drawn from the butt in which we later found a dead rat.

A swarthy, broad-shouldered man walked past and, having said good morning, asked me who I was and what I was doing there. I said my name was Miranda and I was on my holiday and was having a strip wash. I asked him why he was walking with a sheep on a lead, and he told me he had just managed to disentangle it from a broken barbed-wire fence further up the hill and was taking it home. He and his lady wife would be eating it for Sunday lunch in a few weeks' time. With that he said, 'Well, enjoy your holiday,' and wandered off.

We had noticed on our first journey across the fields that there was a standpipe close by, so there were endless trips to gather water in any receptacle we could lay our hands on. I remember rushing back one day, shouting to John: 'Quick, quick, there's a hole in my bucket, my bucket, my bucket, there's a hole in my bucket, oh deary me!'

We had no alternative to seeing the funny side of things. We had also not realised we'd be so far from any shop with which to replenish our meagre stores. When we finally ended up in ration mode after a few days we decided it was time to pack it in and head back home. I had half hoped John might suggest we stop at a comfortable bed and breakfast for the night on the way back to Norfolk, but he didn't. Knowing how tight things were in the finance department I didn't sulk. We had enjoyed the peace and quiet and needed to get back with renewed enthusiasm to the job in hand.

A luxury holiday. Having a strip wash in Wales during the boatbuilding days

My mother was surprised but delighted to see us back home so soon. Amid plenty of merry laughter we regaled her with tales of our Welsh holiday. It had not been the holiday of a lifetime, one of lying on a beach sipping cocktails, watching the sunset. But perhaps that was all to come.

No time was lost, and the next morning it was on with that elegant boiler suit again. A bit like unwrapping a birthday or Christmas present we excitedly unwrapped the boat and picked up where we had left off.

The glassing of the inside of the hull was the first job, then installing the crossbeams. These were made of six-inch-diameter aluminium tubes and had to be glassed into the main hull very accurately and strongly with hundreds of small pieces of chopped-strand matt glass fibre. This material was more flexible than the unidirectional type and could more easily take up the acute angles around which it had to be folded. Having secured the beams in place we then inserted the four bulkheads, which basically divided the boat up into five different compartments and provided strength and stability throughout the hull.

The layout of the boat was excellent. As with any small vessel it was necessary to make use of every square inch available. From bow to stern there was the forward anchor locker, which was accessible only from the deck; then the forepeak, in which there would be two berths; the main cabin with a pull-out double bunk, galley and chart table; the cockpit; and in the stern an aft cabin with a toilet.

We fitted out much of the interior with all that was needed: cupboards, chart table, bunks, windows, steering gear and seacocks. We built in a forty-gallon water tank underneath the cabin sole, before finally fitting the deck, which was supported by iroko beams.

Iroko is a very dense and durable medium-hard wood suitable for taking the enormous load of the 40ft-tall mast. Grown on the coast of West Africa, it is said to be rot proof, so we thought that sounded a good idea. It is also a very pretty, warm-honey-coloured wood. John painstakingly, with great skill, trimmed all the bulkheads with iroko. When we had finished the interior, along with all the patchwork cushion covers which I had made, it felt to me more like a sweet little old-fashioned cottage.

It was a thrilling day when we fitted the gas bottle into the compartment in the cockpit, then installed the two-burner cooker. It all worked perfectly, and we invited my mother to come and have a cup of tea on board. She had made one of her delicious fruit cakes and, as she scrambled up the ladder to join us down below, I called out: 'Don't rock the boat, Mother!' We could see the light at the end of the tunnel. Although we were still a long way from completion, we knew we had turned a corner.

One day the postman delivered a package addressed to us; we wondered what could it be. John's Australian friend, the other John with whom he had sailed the Atlantic, had sent us something rather special. Having opened up this very carefully wrapped parcel, we found inside a five-cent piece, a coin from Rarotonga, one of the Cook Islands in Polynesia, where John was now living on board his trimaran. This was not any old coin. It featured Tangaroa, the Polynesian god of the sea, god of all creation, the god of fertility. We learnt that this present was all to do with an ancient practice which is said to have originated in Rome: in order to bless the ship and have good fortune one must place a coin under the mast step. This serves as a symbol of one's faith that all will be well as one voyages across the oceans. What a truly thoughtful gift.

The Māori believe that water is energy, with many, many moods – as no doubt we would be finding out before too long. It can be calm and life-giving, or dangerous, treacherous and destructive. This energy they call Tangaroa. In their mythology, Rangi is the Sky Father and Papa is the Earth Mother. They sprang from a gap in the emptiness of all darkness, and they had seventy male children who became their gods. One of them, Tangaroa, is God of the Sea.

When the time came to fit the mast, Tangaroa in all his glory was placed safely in position on the mast step, fixed in place with resin. I believed he would keep us safe on our travels.

The cockpit under construction

Were we, actually, going to set off sailing on the high seas, voyaging across oceans? It had not really dawned on me until now. I knew absolutely nothing about how to sail a boat, but John assured me it was easy, and I'd soon learn.

Having painted the deck with non-slip paint, I made netting out of thick rope by tying thousands of tight knots using a bobbin. These nets were attached with hundreds of little lugs to the main hull and then stretched across and attached to the outriggers. A nice little lounging area, or kind of trampoline of sorts. That was a tough job, hard on the hands. We put in a last push to get the outriggers and dinghy finished; John made a self-steering windvane. We made a storm jib. My trusty old Singer was still going strong and we had only just enough money to place an order with a Suffolk sailmaker for the mainsail, jib and spinnaker.

We took a day off. I wore a dress for the first time in a year, and felt slightly feminine again after the endless days of wearing my dusty, smelly old boat-building garments. We went off to a marine auction in Hull, hoping to pick up some bargains. We were now getting to the stage of finalising details of all the hardware that was needed: the winches, winch handles, anchors, chain, fenders, rope, stanchions, pulpit, steering gear, life jackets, wet-weather gear, oars, boat hooks, compass… the list was endless.

I love auctions. I have fond memories of the days when I used to meet my father in London and go with him to the auctions at Christie's in Bond Street and watch him bidding for a seascape. When John and I went to boat auctions I had to try to restrain myself, but I often got carried away and once ended up with three pairs of oars. I had been waving to John across the room and the auctioneer had misinterpreted my gesture and thought I was putting in a bid. The three pairs of oars came in useful though. One can never have too many pairs of oars on a boat.

It was about time to call Mr Ayres and ask him if he was serious about taking our boat to the coast. We needed to call the police too, and arrange the police escort which they had promised. A date for the transportation to the coast was confirmed, and we rushed about like crazy making all the final arrangements and tidying up the yard.

The interior of the main hull was now finished, and the plan was that we could comfortably live aboard on the quayside at Wells-next-the-Sea while we fitted the outriggers onto the crossbeams. John had been so clever in working out exactly how all this would be achieved.

A massive crane rumbled its way up the drive at High Barn. It was all too unbelievable for words, and I of course was crying and laughing as the crane lifted the hull onto the coalman's low loader.

I think this was honestly the very first time that I registered that what we now needed was some water in order to bring our beautiful boat alive. Making her grand exit down the drive was not possible since the load was too wide, so Mr Ayres bravely struck off across the ploughed field with his heavy vehicle chucking up clouds of dust as he went. He made it onto the main road through a convenient gap in the hedge, and with two police cars, one in front and one bringing up the rear, we were escorted on our eight-mile journey to the coast. John and I and my mother followed behind in our red Citroën 2CV. Our kind, friendly coalman then did a second journey and delivered the outriggers down to the quay.

I took a tape player with us and, en route to the sea, I put on one of our favourite Elton John albums, *Goodbye Yellow Brick Road*. We had up to this point not come up with a name for the boat, but when we heard the song *Sweet Painted Lady* we suddenly realised this was who she was about to become. Although still on dry land, that first night sleeping on the boat we christened our bunk bed and the boat. She would be christened the *Sweet Painted Lady*.

When we got up the following morning we seemed to be surrounded by a large crowd of curious onlookers. The council had granted us the rights to use a small piece of foreshore for two months in order that we could finish the boat on site. It had been a redundant car park, but was about to be reinstated as a public garden for the use of holiday makers and the locals. Unbeknown to us there had been a bit of a fracas within the council as to whether our sojourn should be allowed. It seems there had been some disagreement, but it was finally given the green light. The thinking was that our project might attract visitors to the area and bring some money into the small tourist town. It seemed to be working already.

It was lovely to find that there were so many enthusiastic folk genuinely interested in our project, but the downside was they came all day, every day, even at night in the dark. They would peer through the portholes. They wanted to talk endlessly, whereas of course we had work to get on with, The clock was ticking. They wanted an answer to their every question.

They wanted to know how long it had taken us to build. Why had we wanted to do it in the first place? What inspired us? Did we know how to sail? How old were we? Where were we going? When were we going? Why were we going? Did we have a life raft? What did our parents think? Did we have parents? Why did we paint the boat red? Why did we choose a multihull? What would we eat onboard? Did we like fishing? Were we vegetarians? What would we cook on? How would we manage without a fridge? Did we have a TV? Were we going to have children? What would happen if we fell overboard?

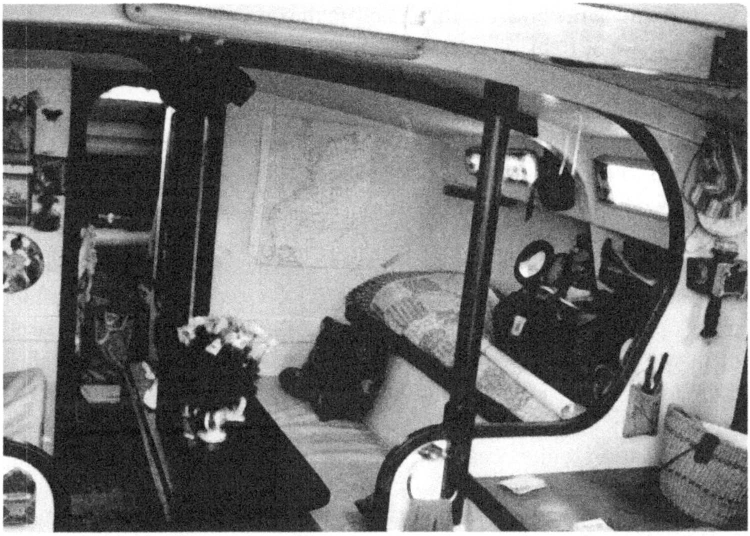

The interior of our floating country cottage, Sweet Painted Lady

Were we afraid of storms? Had we ever been in one? Were we going to the Pacific? Were we going to sail across the Atlantic? Where would we stop at night? Were we going to sail to the Mediterranean? How were we going to make money? Where had we got the money from? What were we dreading most? Where were we going when we left Wells-next-the-Sea? Could they please have a look inside? When was the launch day?

Their curiosity was endless. On and on it went, until one day, in exasperation I felt like being rather rude, under my breath asking one lady who was her auntie, and where did her auntie live?

Most of these questions I myself could not even give an answer to. So, having been as polite as we possibly could for the first few weeks, we finally agreed that, enthusiastic as the public were, it seemed to be a case of feast or famine. We would just have to shut them up. Tell them they were very welcome to watch but that we had to crack on, suggesting in the nicest possible way that they might like to look out for our articles in the local rag. With that we'd wish them a happy day and hope we could get on with our work.

We were up at the crack of dawn before the crowds arrived. Sometimes we went for a treat of a 'full English' at the quayside greasy-spoon café. We busied ourselves madly, joining the outriggers to the beams. There were a few complaints from locals. They were not happy that we were stinking the place out with the horrible smell of resin, and objected to the relentless sound of our whirring orbital sander. These things we just had to ignore. Not much we could do about it.

We applied the final coat of antifouling to the main hull. Antifouling paint is designed to reduce the growth of weed on the hull, which grows particularly when a boat is on a mooring or static in a marina or in warmer waters. Our paint had a toxic copper content; nowadays there are much stricter regulations as to what paints one can use. Only environmentally friendly products are sold, in the hope of reducing contamination to the oceans .

My mother used to come along in the evening, often bringing meals on wheels, and we'd sit in the cockpit dining out under the stars with a bottle of wine. It must have been strange for her knowing that in a few weeks we would be disappearing off on the high seas and she would be back at High Barn living on her own again.

It was truly an exciting time as launch day was fast approaching. We had absolutely no money left at this stage, and my mother very generously offered to pay for the mainsail, and kindly helped us provision the boat for our first voyage. We filled the lockers under the seats in the saloon with all kinds of goodies, a lot of tins and dried pulses, coffee, teas and some exciting treats. Lychees and pineapple were our favourites.

A wee suggestion if you are ever considering building a boat. It's wise, having done your calculations about the length of time it might take, and your costs, to multiply your estimated figures by two. We had imagined the boat would cost us approximately £4,000. In fact, it cost us £8,000. We were unrealistic at the outset, and overconfident, and had imagined we could build it in one year. It took us two years. I have this information backed up by a young gentleman who is in the business of yacht design; he agrees with me, and wisely says that whenever he is quoting for a job he wildly overestimates. So you have been warned. We were very fortunate that we had no time restriction when we started out on the build.

The final big expense was to hire the crane for the launch. When I was working at the holiday home I had secretly saved part of my wages in an envelope and marked it 'launch party', and so I was able to produce my little surprise nest egg, pay the crane driver and buy a few bottles of Prosecco. We had invited lots of friends, and of course family too. They were all assembled on the quayside. With all the local interest as well, a huge crowd of people had gathered.

Almost two years to the day, finally in the late summer of 1976, the huge slings were placed around the hull, and as the good ship *Sweet Painted Lady* was hoisted up and swung out over the water, guess what? I was in tears. The boat was lowered down – and then, panic stations! A bell seemed to be ringing on the crane, presumably alerting the operator, giving a warning that the maximum weight lift limit had been reached.

Launch day. We were holding our breath as Sweet Painted Lady was lifted by a crane and lowered into the water

But mercifully there was no drama and just before the boat kissed the water, I jumped on board clutching a bottle of champagne. *Sweet Painted Lady* was afloat. She had finally been born.

Eastern Daily Press, Saturday, August 14, 1976 15

Mr. and Mrs. John Shuttleworth seen on board their trimaran on Wells quayside . . . a craft they have built themselves and which will soon be launched.

Preparing for world travels

BOATS of all types are part and parcel of the everyday scene at Wells, but one has been attracting particular attention from local people and holidaymakers.

A 40-foot ocean-going trimaran, now in its final stages of construction, is on the section of quay at the bottom of Standard Road.

The trimaran is being built by South African-born John Shuttleworth and his wife Miranda. They started building it at the Stanhoe farm where Mrs. Shuttleworth's mother lives, and transferred the hulls by lorry to Wells for the final building stages.

The trimaran, a Derek Kelsall designed K39, should be launched in the next three or four weeks by crane. Then, after the Shuttleworths have sailed it locally, they will head south, and will probably go to the Mediterranean next year. They intend to sail around the world.

Mr. Shuttleworth has had experience of sailing a trimaran across the South Atlantic to South America, and in the West Indies.

The red-hulled trimaran on Wells Quay is 40 ft. overall, has a 22 ft. beam, draws just over 2 ft. of water, will be sloop-rigged with self-steering gear, and has a 10 h.p. engine. Its 40 ft. mast has been delivered and is ready for stepping. The interior has been fitted out, and the main living quarters in the centre hull are tall enough to stand up in comfortably.

Chapter 16

Southward bound

Sweet Painted Lady tied up alongside in Ramsgate harbour, heading south in the autumn of 1976

I shall never forget that first euphoric moment when she floated. She was bobbing about. She was moving. She had come alive. She was dancing her dance on the water, no longer static, stuck, imprisoned in a makeshift, dusty farmyard boatyard. Where, I wondered, did she want to take us? What might her dream be?

It may well have been a bit laborious, reading about the building of the boat with all the specific details, but I hope perhaps it has given you a feeling of what was required. While it was of course exciting seeing the boat take shape the work was relentless and we just had to keep at it day after day after day, for two years.

I hoped we were now able to enjoy the fruits of our labours. A whole new life about which I had no knowledge was about to be revealed. Building our beautiful boat was one thing, but living on board and sailing was another voyage into the unknown.

I learnt on that very first night on board that not a lot ever goes according to the plan with 'boat life'. There's often a drama of one sort or another.

We had picked up a mooring buoy in the small, tidal harbour of Wells-next-the-Sea. A local fisherman had showed it to us at low tide. It consisted of an old car tyre filled with concrete. But John was not confident that it was adequately secure. As the tide came in we were swinging on the mooring all over the place, with the risk of crashing into other fishing boats which were anchored out in the narrow channel. Boat life had begun.

The wind seemed to be increasing a little, and John decided it would be wiser to tie up alongside the harbour wall for the night. So now, in the dark, at the top of the tide, we started the engine. At least it started up straightaway. I grabbed the fenders out of the anchor locker and tied them to the stanchions to avoid any damage to the top sides. Here I was, having my very first experience of throwing a line ashore to a stranger who luckily happened to be up on the quayside at the exact moment. In the dark, nervous, with the wind increasing, my cheery mood was rapidly changing to one of despondency.

I remember for a flash of a second questioning why on earth I had been so stupid as to spend the last two years of my life in that hell-hole, building this boat, and deluding myself that sailing was going to be enjoyable. The truth was, of course, that I was genuinely terrified and was completely out of my depth. I could only trust that John knew what he was doing and that everything would come right in the end. There was no sleep that night. We bumped about, crashed up and down. We had to constantly adjust the mooring lines as the tide was now dropping, and all I wanted to do was escape, abandon the whole idea, leave John to it. I was not happy.

John managed to keep his cool but, all in all, for both of us, after the exhilarating launch day, this was more than a bit of an anti-climax. It was a very testing night that I found completely nerve-wracking. I was a little sad, as well, that we had not been able to calmly and joyfully celebrate together on that first night afloat. I prayed that the wind would abate during the night. My prayers were answered, and the following morning all was calm.

We had yet to christen the dinghy, so at low tide we both piled into the boat, armed with a picnic, and took it for its maiden voyage around the little creeks. The wind was a little fluky, and with water overlapping the gunnels the picnic turned into a soggy mess. It seemed to me to be a very tippy little boat, but who was I to judge? I clung on, doing my best to look as though I was having the time of my life, all the while wondering after that first traumatic night aboard how this sailing adventure was going to turn out.

We stocked up with fresh fruit and veg. After a few days we finally waved goodbye to my mother, and sailed off down the estuary of Wells, heading out into the Wash. I went up onto the foredeck, and with the shackle attached the jib to the forestay in preparation for the first hoisting of a sail. With a gentle force 4 forecast, we slipped along at four knots to the strains of Gordon Lightfoot's *Minstrel of the Dawn* playing on our little tape player. This is one of my happiest memories – my first romantic moment aboard. I rushed back to the cockpit and gave John a huge hug.

The Wash is notorious for its constantly shifting sandbanks and shallows, so with our charts at the ready we carefully picked our way through the narrowly marked channels. I had recovered quickly from that first initial night of horror and I thought that, after all, this was going to be a doddle. It seemed to me to be more like driving along a winding road. For quite some miles we were able to identify all the port and starboard buoys, and we just followed along having them as our guide. It was not until we were some miles out at sea that we needed to plot our course towards Lowestoft where we stopped for the night. The next day we enjoyed a slight detour and plied our way up the River Stour, spending a night at Mistley for a well-earned rest.

We had made no definite plans for our next port of call but we had mentioned to Derek, the designer of the boat, that we might be calling in at Brightlingsea, so we thought we'd stick with that idea. While we were checking in at the harbour master's office, by chance I happened to notice an envelope propped up on the shelf in the office. It was marked 'TRIMARAN SWEET PAINTED LADY'. How fortuitous that I spotted it. Derek had sent us a brief message suggesting we call in at his office in Sandwich to show him the boat.

We headed off, rounding the North Foreland of Kent, stopped overnight in Ramsgate and finally plied our way up the narrow river to Sandwich. Derek had not realised we were on our way. When he spotted us the following morning he rushed out along the riverbank and gave us a warm welcome.

He was very complimentary about the finish of the boat and loved the red paint job. There was one thing I had yet to do and that was to paint the Painted Lady butterfly on the transom. So, while John went into the office to chat with Derek, I got to work with my paintbrushes.

John returned after a couple of hours with a very large grin on his face. Derek had clearly been very impressed and had offered John a job in his design office. We were down to our last £100. The winter was fast approaching and, although we had hoped to get further south and find work in a boatyard, suddenly out of the blue we had been presented with this amazing opportunity. Of course, John did not hesitate.

We took a day or two to settle in and John started work while I trucked off to the Job Centre in Ramsgate and got a job working for Social Services as a care assistant.

The winter took hold, and in the worst of the icy conditions we had to hammer open the hatch which had completely frozen up. We rigged up an electric cable ashore and ran a tiny fan heater in an attempt to keep warm and dry, but this caused terrible condensation and every morning the cabin walls would be dripping with water. We struggled into our miserably damp clothes. Never mind, I felt sure all this hardship would toughen us up. We would enjoy the heat all the more when we could eventually head south to warmer climes.

We felt a little frustrated after not sailing for more than a month. So, on Christmas Day, just for fun, in a wild snowstorm, we invited our new friends Julian and Sheenagh, who were living on their boat up the river, to come out for a sail. I think they thought we were a little crazy. The visibility was appalling, not helped by the snow of course, but they were up for it and it turned out to be an unforgettable and unique experience. Sailing in a snowstorm transports you deep into yet another weird, wonderful and mystical world of white.

By March of the following year we had saved just enough money to contemplate moving on. Heading to the Mediterranean was going to be our first real adventure.

The ideal time to cross the Bay of Biscay is around June; this is in order to avoid the first of the winter storms which usually hit around September. While in eager anticipation of what the next leg of the voyage would bring, we were also sad to be waving farewell to our newfound friends. Was this going to be the shape of things to come? A taste of the cruising life already? No sooner had we made friends with new and interesting people than we were having to bid them farewell.

We had ordered more charts and had made arrangements to pick them up from a friend in the Isle of Wight. Fair weather took us south on a gentle sail and we moored up in the island's beautiful Wootton Creek. We had by now done some two-night sails. We each did four-hour watches, while the other attempted to get some sleep. Each day we were gaining confidence, getting familiar with the system of making sail changes, even in the dark if necessary. We were very pleased that the boat sailed well to windward. We both enjoyed helming and we each seemed to be falling quite naturally into our various roles, developing routines when handling the sails and anchoring. John always took charge of the navigation, while my mind was on what I might produce from the galley for the next meal.

By now in early May 1977 we were keen to get on our way further down the coast and so, with a force 4 forecast, we left the island in very high spirits. Sailing off down the Solent, we passed the spectacular landmark of the Needles and then headed on out into the English Channel.

Our Wootton Creek friends, Edward and Faye, had given us a lovely bunch of flowers from their garden which I threw into the sea. This ancient custom apparently ensures one's safe return to familiar shores. I hoped that would be the case.

I had started work on my therapeutic project, a multi-coloured rainbow-striped jumper. I was sitting happily in the cockpit knitting and keeping a watchful eye on a vegetable stew which was simmering on the stove down in the galley. Our friends had given us a delicious-looking home grown cabbage, and I thought it best to eat it that night while it was nice and fresh. I had planned to toss it on top of the stew at the last minute and let it lightly steam through. It would be all nice and crunchy.

Whenever I think of cabbage or toad in the hole, that tasty traditional English dish, I think of my father. I must have been around twelve years old when we were all on a holiday in Canterbury, on a cultural tour to see the cathedral. We were having lunch in a rather musty, dusty, old-fashioned café in the high street. We were intrigued by the rattling noise and the whole operation of the dumb waiter, that ingenious system of transporting food and dishes from one floor of a building to another. It originated in days gone by when, in the spacious homes of the great and the good, the kitchens and servants' quarters were housed in the basement. The dumb waiter system was a small lift at waist height, a little hatch, a hole in the wall, with shelves. You had to haul on a rope which was looped around a pully. Then, as if by magic, the food would appear, up from the kitchens. With another tug on the rope the dirty dishes, having been piled high onto the shelves, would disappear down the hatch to be dealt with by the kitchen staff below.

On this occasion the waitress was a skinny, white-faced, rather weary-looking woman, neatly dressed in her little black dress with a white lacy collar and frilly apron. Having taken our order for food, she shouted down the hatch: 'Cabbage on the toad!' Dad roared with laughter and we all giggled.

What a bizarre thing that this amusing story from my childhood should suddenly present itself while writing about this memorable trip. All because of a cabbage.

So there was John down below checking the charts, plotting our course to Plymouth and I was still calmy knitting in the cockpit. Glancing up and kind of paying attention, I noticed that the visibility was rapidly deteriorating. Ominous clouds were looming, and we seemed to be sailing into a wall of greyness. A squall was coming up. We needed to reduce sail quickly.

I tossed my knitting aside and turned off the stew. John took the helm and I raced up onto the foredeck, unhanked the jib and stuffed it into the sail bag, hauled the storm jib up out of the outrigger locker and attached it onto the forestay. We turned the boat head-on into the wind so as to be able to reduce the mainsail. It was not easy now that the wind had increased so suddenly. When we had been making the storm jib I had hoped we would never need to use it, but here we go. It was about to be christened. Within minutes the wind was screaming and we were battling head on into a fierce force 7.

My philosophy 'be delighted by the unexpected' went over the side in an instant. I was far from delighted, in fact I was terrified. This was our first encounter with bad weather. We had listened to the weather report before setting off, and this sudden change in the weather pattern had not been forecast.

Having set the sails John suggested I should try to get some sleep, which I thought was a fairly ridiculous idea. I found it impossible to stay in the bunk for more than ten minutes at a time. I was constantly worrying about him in the cockpit and wondering if I would be needed up on deck to help. It was now getting dark, and we were about twenty miles off shore, intending to avoid the strong tidal current which whips around Portland Bill.

Suddenly their seemed to be a lot of activity in the area. John called me to come up on deck. I donned my uncomfortable classic yellow oilskins, the traditional ones which the hardy Norfolk fishermen wear when setting out to sea.

Once we had pinpointed roughly where we were on the chart, off the coast of Devon, we discovered it was marked as a submarine exercise area. Lights were flashing all around us. They seemed so close – distance can be deceiving at night. It was now about midnight; torrential rain had set in. A helicopter whirred in, hovering eerily above us, flashing a blinding searchlight onto the boat several times before dropping red flares which lit up the sea all around us. The wind was increasing.

This experience was so disconcerting. We wondered if it might have been an air-sea rescue exercise – or were we being warned to buzz off out of the submarine exercise area, where perhaps some operation was underway? We never understood exactly what was happening. But shortly after the helicopter had disappeared a series of booming thuds reached us under the boat. Sound travels in an extraordinary way underwater.

The wind increased to a force 8. We put another reef in the mainsail and donned our safety harnesses. The boat was straining and waves were enveloping the deck. Every time one of us had to open the hatch to go down below for a five-minute break, water poured in through the open hatchway. The only way to rest, or 'be', was to sit on the cabin sole, jam one's legs between the galley and the chart table and brace oneself every time the boat leapt and jolted and crashed over the waves. I remember feeling glad that we were in a trimaran. Better than heeling over in a monohull. That would have been an impossible challenge in these conditions.

We had hoped to reach Plymouth, but clearly it was now questionable as to whether this was wise or indeed even possible. With great relief we finally sighted the leading lights of Start Point. As dawn broke I hoped the seas might look a little calmer, but of course that was wishful thinking. The waves were furious, short and steep. They marched on relentlessly, and I tried to tell myself that their aquamarine breaking crests were like pretty dancing fairies being blown about by the wind.

The rain had not stopped and we had been on the go since 11 a.m. the previous day. We had eaten nothing other than the odd dry biscuit. We had not slept a wink. I dumped the vegetable stew and the cabbage in the sink, and handed John a Kit-Kat and a banana.

My mother had given us an antique brass oil lamp as a parting gift and before we left I had filled it with paraffin, a very tricky job. When I was down below taking a five-minute rest, its warm glow kept my spirits up. I prayed the paraffin would not run out. Sheets of water filled the chart table every time we opened the hatch. I had grabbed a handful of clothes for each of us and had stuffed them into thick bin liners and shoved them under the forecabin bunk in the hope of having something dry to put on, if and when we ever arrived anywhere safely.

We were now completely frozen, all our clothes saturated. Our teeth were chattering and our hands were so cold that it was hard to undo a shackle and tail the sheets off the winches. Finally we decided around 8am that we were fighting a losing battle. We should put in a tack, turn back and aim for Salcombe. Navigating our way through the very narrow entrance of the harbour with such poor visibility and fluky winds would not be easy. We would have to have our wits about us, but it was the best idea as we were both now exhausted.

We somehow managed to refuel the engine with diesel – the smell always made me feel sick. That was a very difficult operation in such a turbulent sea, but we would need the motor on our approach to the harbour so it had to be done. Ominous rocky ledges were now appearing beneath the steep cliffs at the entrance to the harbour. We recognised the headland, having spent a few days there some years before, and as we rounded it and, under sail, crept closer still, the sea became a little calmer. I went up onto the foredeck to unhank the storm jib. My fingers were like ice, my hair drenched. I was shivering and completely soaked through. The saltwater was stinging my eyes. I was crying. I never told John, but I really had thought I might die that night.

We picked up a mooring buoy and tidied the boat, which was in chaos. This had been our first ordeal at sea. When undressing and discarding my sodden clothes I found I was covered in bruises. We slept until five that evening. The harbour master visited to collect his dues and asked where we had come from. We told him that we had sailed through the night from the Isle of Wight, which surprised him. Apparently not even the wise and experienced fishermen had put to sea that previous morning.

I slept well, and it was not until the following day, as I recovered, that all the negative thoughts that I had experienced on that first night at Wells-next-the-Sea resurfaced. I tried to keep my doubts and fears at bay and under wraps, not wanting to upset John. But if that sail from the island to Salcombe was what one might call a test run, a shakedown cruise, then I think the dear ship *Sweet Painted Lady*, and

John and I, had passed the test. The boat was still in one piece and so were we.

For the following twelve days gales were forecast, so we were not going anywhere. With boat life there is never any way of knowing what might happen next. Although we had other vague plans, for the moment we were stuck in Salcombe. At least it was a nice place to be stormbound.

Finally, having listened to a favourable forecast we sailed off our mooring with the genoa (foresail) set, bound for Coruña in northern Spain. At last it felt as though we were truly southward bound. Twelve miles offshore we ran into a school of porpoises, playing, leaping out of the water, their dramatic black fins piercing the surface. We set the self-steering gear, and lay on the foredeck watching the bows knife through the water. We cracked open our bonded store and celebrated with our first gin and tonic at £1 per bottle. John rested from 6pm till 10pm.

I was getting better at spotting ships and working out which on earth direction they were going. At first, of course, it was all completely confusing to me, but I always enjoyed the challenge of the night watch. On that first night after leaving Salcombe, as we were speeding along at eight knots with the wind increasing, there were three bustling streams of phosphorescence trailing away behind us. Natural magic at its best. I later learnt more about this 'sea of stars' effect and discovered it is created by the emission of light by living organisms, plankton and algae.

On my 2am to 6am watch there were times when I experienced all sorts of unexpected and wonderful things which I guess one just has to put down to exhaustion and hallucination. Once I was convinced that the sea was going uphill. I heard fire engine sirens all around me, and another time I heard bagpipes playing. That was weird, especially since I am not really fond of the sound of bagpipes. Once I thought my yellow oilskins were in fact red. The white netting appeared to be pink and green, reminding me of a shirt I had made years ago out of old sheeting. When I thought all the sails had vanished, I wondered what was going on and how we would ever get to the Mediterranean with no sails. I saw the winch handle turn into a banana and worried that it would not be of much use. Once at dawn I was convinced I saw a ship on fire on the horizon. It was of course the very first glimmer of the sunrise peeping through the low-lying clouds.

Once John was calling out to me for hours, or so I thought. And yes, once I did think perhaps I was going completely crazy when I called to John and he did not answer. I was terrified. I thought he must have fallen overboard when making a sail change. He was actually in the aft cabin busy on the toilet. He had broken our one and only golden rule and had left the cockpit without telling me. I was so upset, absolutely furious, and said I would never forgive him, but eventually of course I did.

Once while John and I were down below checking the charts, I glanced through the window. The sky seemed to look rather too grey. Whoops! No wonder. When I jumped up into the cockpit, right there was a massive container ship. Its wake indicated that it had changed course to avoid running us down. That was a lesson quickly learned. From then on we agreed that one of us must always be up on deck, come what may, and obviously and particularly when in a shipping lane.

When we eventually approached the shores of Brittany, with its white sandy beaches and pretty little clusters of farmhouses, that was another of those unforgettable moments. I was so excited to be in France. We had fought for four hours against the tide, trying to make it into the safe harbour of Camaret before nightfall. Having at last anchored, we rushed ashore for a strong coffee.

Another week of gales was forecast, so we kept busy fishing over the harbour walls for lançon (sand eels), delicious eight-inch-long, delicately flavoured fish. We explored the town, buying more wool for my knitting project, and topped up the fishing tackle box which John had given me for my birthday. There was always a 'boat job' to be completed. We decided to do anchor watch at night. That was tough. We could not afford to go into a marina, so anchoring offshore, or going into the fishing harbour if we were able to chat up a friendly fisherman, were our only options. Dragging anchor at night is a drag – literally. One has to keep a constant watch trying to assess if the boat is still roughly in the same place while it is swinging around if there is a bit of wind or if the tide is on the turn.

Unfortunately we did drag our anchor on one occasion, though not in French waters. The pointed bow of one of our outriggers smashed through the toughened-glass window of a Sunseeker Motor Sailer, much to the surprise and annoyance of the poor lady in the aft cabin who thought she had just signed up for a peaceful holiday in Poole harbour. After much discussion we gave the owner £50 to settle the bill.

Eventually we hopped on down the coast to Guilvenic, a famous fishing port. As we entered the harbour we were accompanied by about sixty boats, bringing home their catch. It was an incredible sight. We went ashore to watch the fish auction, which was fascinating. The words used didn't make much sense to us, all being spoken or 'sung' in French, and very speedily. We understood it was different from a conventional auction where the bidding starts low and gradually rises. A fish auction works the other way. It's kind of 'upside down'. The bidding starts high and falls, so you have to risk halting the bid at whatever price you think the fish are worth. It seems to me it's a more effective way of gaining a higher price. There were vast trays of fish of every description including a weird hammerhead shark and huge crates of writhing langoustines. A kindly fisherman gave us a few. Dinner was pâté au poivre followed by langoustines and salad. Mouthwateringly delicious.

Waiting for a favourable forecast for crossing the Bay of Biscay was the next big hurdle. Biscay is notorious, because of the possibility of being caught out in bad weather and blown onto its treacherous lee shore. Inevitably this hung over us, as it has done for many other cruising folk, but eventually we set off.

When we were about halfway across Biscay a small bird not much bigger than a wren collapsed into the cockpit. Completely exhausted, it tried to scramble up John's trouser leg to get some warmth and rest.

We made a cosy place for it in one of the cockpit lockers. I suggested giving it a tot of whisky, but John seemed to think that would be too much for its weakened system. I tried to identify it from my small bird book but was never quite sure. Perhaps it was an Arctic warbler or a young Greenland wheatear. Both are migrants that cover over 2,500 miles from Norway to South East Asia and from Greenland to the north coast of Spain. Sadly the dear little bird died, and we gave him a burial at sea.

On my morning watch I noticed a dark line on the horizon, at first not understanding exactly what it was. I thought it was low-lying cloud. Then, joy oh joy, I realised it was the Picos de Europa mountains of northern Spain. John's navigational skills had been spot-on. We were so excited: here we were making our first landfall. The city of Ferrol was waiting for us. We went off exploring and found a bar, gorging on delicious tapas, our appetites having finally returned. This felt like a milestone. It had taken us forty-eight hours, 310 miles at an average speed of six and a half knots. We had crossed the Bay of Biscay.

During this trip to the Med I kept an illustrated daily journal which I have referred to as I have been writing. I realise when reading it that every single day was an adventure in itself. Each day had its highlights and low points, its peaks and troughs, just like the sea.

Day by day, as we gradually sailed further south, it was getting warmer. We had left the heavy skies and grey clouds of the north behind us – and the damp clothes, thank goodness. The warmth was unfamiliar bliss. We coast-hopped all the way to Gibraltar calling in at Corme and Muros. Then on to Baiona, Cascais, Lisbon, rounding the famous Cape St Vincent to Portimão. Turning left into the Mediterranean was exciting, although it led to a slight false sense of security, since one imagines one is now in safer sheltered waters having left the Atlantic. But between the months of May and September the harsh, dry, northerly Meltemi wind often kicks in during the afternoons. The local fishermen would often gesticulate wildly as we left harbour. In my diary I had written that the words they were shouting were – in my makeshift Spanish – '*Mucho Tempo*' meaning bad weather ahead. They had probably listened to the *tempo prognosticos* and knew more than we did about the likely change in the weather. The despairing tourists retreated in their droves from the beaches and the sailors wrestled, as we often did, to make a quick sail change as the wind suddenly increased and one was suddenly enveloped in a passing squall.

We usually stuck to our plan and sailed during the day, arriving at dusk at the next port. We would rush ashore and go exploring, have a cool beer and then set off the next morning having dashed to the market to stock up with fresh goodies.

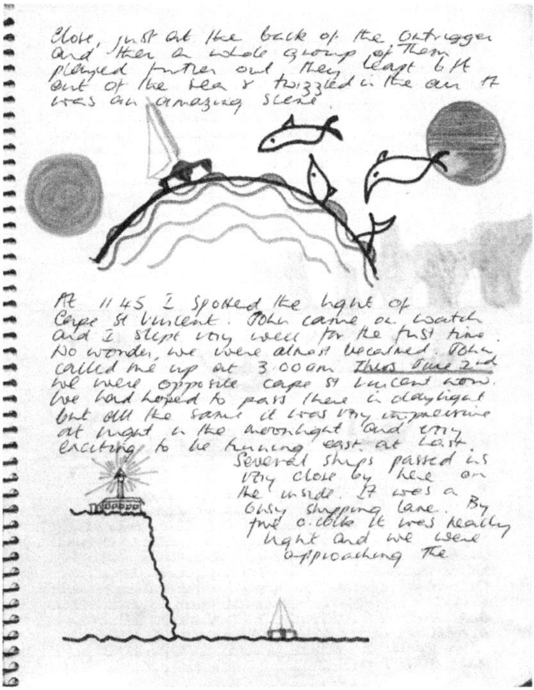

A diary illustration: rounding Cape St Vincent by moonlight in perfect weather and heading into the Mediterranean

There was always something to do on the boat. And even if there wasn't, during my watch my mind often seemed to dwell for ever on one simple thought, so the hours passed quite quickly.

One important thing we did when the weather was reasonable was to practise the 'man overboard' drill. God forbid that we would need to put it into action for real. We would throw a fender over the side and then attempt to retrieve it. There is a system. One person keeps their eye on the fender from the moment it is thrown overboard while the other, at the helm, steers the boat, directed by the one keeping the watchful eye. Hopefully this way the fender or person is safely recovered. We managed this drill successfully several times, but of course in rougher weather it would be a different story altogether. It is surprising how quickly one can lose sight of an object on the surface of the water. That's why it is so important never to take one's eye of it even for a flash of a second.

Portuguese fishermen. Heading for Portimão.
A diary illustration

We did meet a couple who had lost their child overboard and another man who had lost his dog. I remember Naomi James, the famous round-the-world single-hander, telling me how she could never get over the fact that her beloved cat had been lost at sea. If you were single-handing, of course, you would be a goner. Such thoughts and tales are not pleasant to dwell on. The water, the sea, the oceans are treacherous. There is one golden rule: 'One hand for yourself and one for the boat.' I always remind my grandchildren and my sons of this when they are off on an adventure on one of their boats. 'Hang on tight, my darlings.'

After a short stay in Gibraltar we travelled on to Malaga, Adra, Almeria, Aguilas, Torrevieja, Calpe, Jávea, San Antonio, Ibiza, Mahón (Menorca), and finally to our intended destination, Ajaccio in Corsica.

Happy hour. Drinks in the cockpit having arrived in Corsica

Way out at sea approaching Corsica we picked up the delicious scent of the maquis. This is Corsica's trademark fragrance: a delectable, heady, aromatic mixture of eucalyptus, myrtle, rosemary, lavender, thyme, juniper, mint and sage, all of which grow in the mountains and whose perfume is carried on the wind to the coast.

Once in Corsica there was more fun to be had when John's parents and some of our family flew out for holidays. I can't think quite how we all squeezed in, but we did. Tensions did not rise, nor were there any arguments. Surprising really, since we were all living in such close quarters.

A line ashore. Anchored overnight at the islands of Lavezzi on the south coast of Corsica

Occasionally when I felt the need for some space I did take myself off for a quiet walk. Once I spent the whole afternoon up on the hillside overlooking the bay where we were anchored. I sat for several hours watching ants. Absolutely fascinating. Each ant, with its head down, was busily completing its specific task, either fetching, carrying, building or feeding. And some had the job of disposing of the dead. There was nothing random about it at all, which it appears to be when one first watches. Such a complex society. Seen from outer space we must look just the same: all rushing back and forth up the motorways, scurrying hither and thither with our heads down, going about our business. Less sophisticated, and probably not as happy as the ants.

John did a single-handed trip across the Straits of Gibraltar to Ceuta.

We all sailed alongside in another friend's home-built catamaran called *Coconuts*. The skipper of *Coconuts* was himself a bit nuts. He had his pet rabbit on board with him.

Crossing the Straights of Gibraltar. John single handing Sweet Painted Lady in strong winds

Our money was running out again, but knowing we had jobs to return to, we had to face the inevitable. With a few extra stops at Alicante, Barbate and Cádiz, we finally departed from Portimão in Portugal, having stocked up with sardines and port, and did the whole trip in reverse. It was a less enticing prospect: leaving the warmth of the Med behind and turning right, heading north this time, bound for England and anticipating spending another winter on board. So bracing ourselves we decided to sail directly back to England in one hit.

Up to this point our longest period out of sight of land had been our trip across Biscay, just three days. On this return voyage we might be out in the Atlantic and out of sight of land for at least ten days. I wondered how I would feel.

We set off, and on the way home I distracted myself particularly during night watches by reflecting on all our incredible adventures. The Mediterranean with all its culture and variety had been so fascinating. There was the strangely Mexican feel of Almeria, the area where several Wild West movies had been made. I could just imagine the stagecoaches bouncing along the hill tracks and the 'stick-em-up' cowboys sauntering down the dusty streets. The glamorous film stars posing in the doorways of the local bars. Apparently there are eerie remains of some of the film sets up in the mountains.

The ever-changing scene presented frequent contrasts when we had plied our way along the coast. Alicante and Benidorm, home of the cheap package holiday, displayed the effects of tourism at its worst. High-rise buildings stretched for miles. Surely these structures will not last. They look so temporary set against the solid mass of the ancient, noble mountains.

When we had arrived late in the port of Aquilas we had found the fiesta in full swing. The music and chatter had been deafening. Families filled the bars, and the little children and babies, all dressed up to the nines, were dancing, while the grandmas and grandads tucked into vast plates of appetising-looking seafood.

Having reached Ibiza we had enjoyed a few moments of luxury. Collapsing into the comfort of plush cane chairs in San Antonio, while downing a very expensive cool beer, had provided us with some entertaining people-watching. It was a hotbed of tourists, who swarmed into the Paradise Disco, the Extasis Hotel. Fish-'n'-chips, hot dogs and the full English were being devoured on every street corner. Cash was being liberally splashed in The West End Boutique. (I wonder why the English tourists had not stayed at home?) Young, semi-naked girls paraded in hordes through the narrow streets, delighted with their latest fashionable purchases. Older ladies floated along looking elegant in their chiffon kaftans and sporting enormous sunglasses. The guys strutted their stuff exposing their hairy, bronzed chests bedecked in gold. They were on the hunt. Plenty of choice: beautiful females of all ages. How would they ever choose?

Having crossed the Strait of Gibraltar to Ceuta we had taken a bus trip to Tétouan in Morocco. Camels were being led through the chaotic street market. Wandering barefooted, dark and sad-eyed children were begging. A scribe sat diligently writing something, perhaps a legal document for some illiterate local. Live chickens, squawking, tied in bundles by their legs, were hanging upside down beside a vegetable stall. A bathroom suite was being offloaded from a bus. There was much argument, I presume over how this should be done, judging by the looks on the faces and the raised voices of the four men who were attempting it.

Wasps and flies buzzed around the raw red meat, rotting fruit and candies. Two children, sitting side-by-side, were making a pair of trousers, each sewing up the seam of a leg. Emaciated-looking donkeys with panniers transported heavy loads of bricks. Colourful spices were displayed in pyramid-shaped piles and more were stored beside the stalls in vast sacks. A blacksmith, roasting a whole sheep's head and trotters, looked troubled. Knife grinders and old men plaiting grass to make hats were chatting. Weary grannies stood in whatever shade they could find, dressed in their striped kaftans, their deeply grooved faces resembling ancient statues. The hubbub, chatter, shouting, crying, bargaining, nudging, and pushy attempts to sell us dope or cigarettes, all created a constant background noise. Buses were reversing, dust clouds were enveloping us as we wandered, becoming immersed in every detail of this unfamiliar, colourful, mysterious and captivating scene.

We held our breath when we first sighted a whale; and sailing through a pod of leaping dolphins as we approached Cádiz was extraordinary. Hauling in mackerel by the bucketload, we trailed fishing lures while sailing over the Trafalgar Shoals off the south-west coast of Spain. We'd gather up flying fish which had landed on the deck during the night. Observing the bird life, their acrobatics, their aerodynamic agility, we would try to identify them. We never knew what we might see next.

As our voyage home continued I reflected on the cruising life too. I had learnt so much on this first trip. Surviving sailing dramas is a large part of what it's all about. The only way to truly learn anything is through experience. One is bound to make a few mistakes, but on a boat one hopes one's mistakes are not too disastrous. A grave error could well cost you your boat, and even your life.

It's a case of learning the ropes, including the actual ropes themselves. Knowing how to tie the appropriate knot is vital. I eventually learnt all about the virtues of the bowline, often referred to as the king of knots, the rescue knot so easy to tie and untie if needs be, even with freezing cold wet fingers in a gale. Then there are the whys and wherefores of anchoring, letting out just the right amount of chain and rope, and if you get that wrong there is the risk of dragging anchor. Using the sextant for navigation, plotting one's course ... Learning to read the navigational leading lights when entering a port. On arrival at a large harbour there were often about ten different sequences going on all at the same time, so it was most confusing. And one had to get it right. Once we got it wrong. We had homed in on what we thought was the correct leading light on the shore and suddenly it got up and moved. It was in fact a fisherman who was relocating himself further off down the shore with his Tilley lamp in the hope of finding a better spot to cast his line.

Disentangling the boat from a fishing buoy in pitch darkness off the coast of Spain was not easy. Nor was adjusting the governor switch on the diesel engine. (I never knew what on earth that meant, although I did eventually learn how to do it.) In port we once had to find a welder to fix the broken alternator bracket, and on another occasion source a gimble for the stove to stop the stew spilling all over the place. There was so much to learn and perfect, always something to fix so as to keep dear *Sweet Painted Lady* shipshape and fit for purpose.

I could not imagine ever parting with her.

I was entirely dependent on John and his expertise and was at the mercy of so many situations which I did not fully understand or know how to deal with. But I could not afford to be petty or let some silly little niggling thing pull at my heart strings.

We did have an argument once when we were heading for Corsica. It was about my button box. For some curious reason I had taken it with me. Well, just because I loved it, I think, and I thought it might be useful to have some buttons on board. The small, circular wicker basket contained my treasured collection: beautiful buttons, mother-of-pearl, silver filigree, engraved glass Victorian ones, retro designs, all sorts. But John, being forever anxious about the weight of the boat, thought it was unnecessary. Somewhere at the bottom of the ocean there is treasure. At the height of my hissy fit I furiously hurled the little wicker basket over the side.

As we headed out into the Atlantic again on our return trip, we were soon pitching up and down, riding on the massive swell. It seemed like a giant moving cakewalk with the two different swells converging. The result was a very confused sea state. I imagined we were sailing up mountains and then falling over precipices into deep valleys, sailing across an everchanging landscape. In relation to this vast ocean we were a minuscule little piece of flotsam. *Sweet Painted Lady* had been a huge boat to build but a teeny weeny one to be bobbing about in, out there on this vast seascape. On this voyage home, food featured highly. The days were punctuated with meals. It was eat, sleep, on watch. Eat, sleep, on watch. I baked bread every day and made a huge pan of chutney with all the tomatoes I had bought on the quayside at Portimão.

A few miles offshore approaching Salcombe we had an unexpected warm welcome back to good old Blighty. We suddenly got a very strong whiff of pig shit – nowhere near as romantic as the welcome of the maquis which we had enjoyed when approaching Corsica. The weather was deteriorating, and it was getting colder every day. Back to English weather. I knew that all I wanted to be able to do was to keep dry and warm. I did not want a repeat performance of that dreadful wet and cold night when I thought I might die as we sailed from the Isle of Wight on our outward journey. I was forewarned and forearmed. So for this return journey home my dress code ran something like this:

Bottom half: woolly tights, trousers, tracksuit, oilies. Top half: vest, T-shirt, cashmere jumper, windcheater, tracksuit, Aran jumper, oilies. Head: hat, windcheater hood, towel round neck, oily hood. Hands: gloves, encased in plastic bags. Feet: socks x 3. New boots which didn't leak like my old ones used to.

I remember seeing a map of historic wrecks off the southern shore of the Isle of Wight. It offered grim evidence of the hundreds of ships which had got caught out in bad weather. So many tragic stories and lives lost. But I did not want to dwell on such things and it was exciting to be returning to the Isle of Wight once again. We had always had warm feelings about the island and, having passed the Needles, we anchored off Cowes. We spent a happy day with our friends in Wootton Creek. We dried out, and at low tide were able to scrub off the bottom of the boat. It was covered in weed which had grown more rapidly in the warmer waters of the Med. It was slowing us down and by now we were itching to get back 'home' and settle down to another winter on board. We headed for Dover and finally, on 16 September, we were back where we had started, tucked up the river at Sandwich. We shared all our stories about our five-month adventure with our friends and celebrated our safe return with a glass of port and tinned sardines. The 1,300 mile trip from Portimão had taken us twelve days.

Before too long it was back to the drawing board for John and back to whatever work I could find for me.

We knew that a goal without a plan would be just a wish. It was not long before we had made our next plan. We were going to save enough money to be able to finance a transatlantic trip the following year. We would sail across the Atlantic in *Sweet Painted Lady*.

This was our goal.

Chapter 17

Canaries calling

A good omen. Finding the Painted Lady butterflies, having arrived in the Canaries. A diary illustration

Back in Sandwich, how did we settle down again? We had to manage the cold weather for a start. It was all a bit of a shock to the system. Mornings were exhausting: just getting dressed was a mission. We had been in warm climes for five-and-a-half months, and had worn very little, often nothing at all actually, so hauling on the damp jeans, and then layering up with jumper upon jumper, took a bit of getting used to.

In the depths of winter, having smashed open the frozen hatch with the hammer (yes, that palaver all over again), we then had to slip and slide our way up the icy gangplank and negotiate the muddy narrow pathway to wherever we were going. I used to walk about a mile along the marsh bank, enjoying the haunting calls of the various sea birds. But I seemed to become acclimatised quite quickly and loved those mornings, especially on a clear, crisp day. I love all weathers, including even bad conditions. Except of course when out at sea.

Having trekked along the bank I would then pick up a bus into Ramsgate. I never took much money with me – just enough for whatever I needed to buy. I remember once having a heated argument with John because he thought I had taken too much cash to buy the tube of toothpaste that we needed. I think at the time a 7oz tube of Crest toothpaste cost about a halfpenny. Never mind. We were saving hard, and every halfpenny counted; I knew that.

John returned to working for Derek, and while he was there fortuitously met up with the yachtsman Chay Blyth, who was thinking about his next boat. He needed a very fast multihull capable of winning races, breaking records. He had spotted John, and wondered if he was one who might be willing to push the boundaries of design.

Chay is charismatic, with a refreshing sense of humour. He's a Scotsman with the fighter in his blood, an ex-paratrooper, larger than life and inspirational. He would naturally have been nothing else, having accomplished the most extraordinary feat of rowing across the Atlantic.

In 1966 he teamed up with John Ridgway and, undaunted, the two of them, with little experience of the sea, set off in their 20-ft dory, a small, high-sided boat. They crossed the Atlantic in ninety-two days. Then in 1971 Chay was the first person to sail single-handedly non-stop westwards around the world, against the prevailing winds and currents, in his 59-ft yacht *British Steel*. This extraordinary feat earned him a CBE and title of Yachtsman of the Year. By comparison, our own planned voyage across the Atlantic seemed nothing to make a fuss about. I felt so fortunate to have met him. I have often thought long and hard about what he had said about his accomplishment and about life in general: 'Discipline is of the essence.'

Evenings were often spent huddled up down below, quietly, pensively, deep in thought. We had the trip to the Med under our belt. The good times had been better than I could ever have imagined. The bad times were more terrifying than I could ever have contemplated. I think we had experienced our fair share of horrors on that first trip: gales, fog, thunder and lightning, near collisions, along with all the usual daily 'boat life' dramas, which I was now coming to understand were all just part of the territory.

There had been many unexpected moments of elation, highlights, joys, intrigues, and the privilege of having had this opportunity. The good far outweighed any of the bad. The whole experience had been much greater than the sum of its varied parts. But there was still that big question lurking: was I really looking forward to the next experience – crossing the Atlantic?

I admit that I sometimes found myself having doubts. Thinking about it was where the fear crept in. My mind would merrily play its tricks on me, paint a horrible picture, erode my confidence and cast its gloomy shadow on any vestige of positivity.

Sometimes these visions, especially at night, would run riot. This is the downside of having been blessed with a vivid imagination. I fantasised that we might get sucked into the deep-blue cavity of a whirling vortex. The sea would open up and swallow us. John would fall overboard and I would be abandoned and incapable. Then what would I do? Would I jump overboard myself? Would we run out of food, die of starvation, capsize, lose our way? There was no 'way' – only west. But what if no land ever appeared? What if the world had ended, but we did not know that it had, and everything and everybody had vanished? Less fancifully, we might be struck by lightning, run down by a ship, never seen or heard of again.

Some of these were ridiculous nightmares. Some of course were not. But ruminating endlessly and imagining every possible disaster, fantasy or otherwise, was a waste of time and energy. I had to discipline myself. I had to force myself to get up and do something practical, make a stew, knit, sing, read the Psalms, write a letter – anything to ground myself, keep my head down and get on with the next job of the day.

I returned to my work as an assistant social worker. I focused on the job, which I enjoyed, but the office hierarchy within the department at Ramsgate did amuse me. I thought it was completely unreasonable. Being on the bottom rung I had a minuscule desk which was stuck in a corner under the stairs, and I used to bang my head every time I stood up. It is as if it had been made to measure, on the principle that getting bashed and banged about would come as no surprise to me, having spent all that time on the boat. Sitting at my desk, it felt like home from home. In those days there was no such thing as a personal computer, remember. So my tiny desk was a chaotic scene of paper, paper everywhere, and nowhere to put it.

If one was on the next step up, you were allowed a desk the same size but with one small drawer on the right-hand side. Up the ladder again and it was two drawers on the right. Step up again and it was getting really exciting. Your desk had a drawer on either side. Then, if you reached the pinnacle of your career, the top-job desk was considerably larger, with three drawers on either side. Plus the bonus was, wait for it … a decent, swish, swivel chair engineered to support one's back, apparently. You'd have the best position in the room, with a view overlooking a dreary carpark.

I was told that I was rising above my station when I asked if I could possibly have a desk with a drawer, or at least a filing cabinet in which to put all my important confidential reports. But no such luck. I didn't last long there.

The highlight of the week for John and me was Friday night. We had managed to make an arrangement with a hotel in Sandwich to use their bathroom. It was a bit of a dilapidated establishment in need of a little refurbishing. The creaking staircase which led up to the third-floor bathroom was covered with a rather regal, busy-patterned, red-and-blue, threadbare old carpet.

The bathroom itself was bare, with just a huge, cast-iron bath, no heater and no bath mat. But there was the one essential: hot water. And loads of it. We used to buy a gin and tonic at the bar – that was the agreement for the services being rendered to us – take our drinks upstairs and luxuriate for hours in the bathroom. Unless one was in the bath it was quite cold, so we often used to have two baths each, spending the whole evening in the bathroom. It was the best-ever way to spend a Friday night that I can think of. I often still do that, but quietly in my own home now. My water bills are rather hefty. I will eat a mango in the bath too if I have happened to buy one. It's by far the best way to eat a mango. Just a quick tip, in case you have not yet discovered it.

Another evening occupation was to review our boat's 'to-do' list. I found it the other day written in the back of our log book. The list was endless. I had forgotten how much we had to do to prepare the boat for the next adventure.

Make new lid for water tank
Check on spinnaker
Make new awning for cockpit
Put extra reef points in mainsail
Revarnish rear cabin sole
Get better bird book
Adjust fixing for step ladder into cabin
Sound deadening for engine
Make cockpit cushion covers
Fix outrigger bilge tubes in place
Finish sail cover, i.e. extend it
Forecabin door latch
Ventilator, exhaust, fuel tank, check all
Make life ring container
Pram hood cover
New castors on day bed
Wind generator
Compass box
Spinnaker pole
Danbuoy
Get stock of better clothes pegs
Repaint boat, antifouling
Get dividers for navigation
Sewing needles for sail repair
Stock up on spare nuts and bolts
Bulb for compass
Masthead bulbs spares
Rewire electrics
Better system for refilling oil lamps
Repair depth sounder
Organise filing system
Order more charts
Get book of West Indies history
Varnish wheel and handrails
Check first-aid kit, update
Remove cooker and clean
Check fire extinguisher
Paint boat hook
Paint rear cabin hatch
Check on gas cylinders, safety stowage.
Make list of provisions required
Life raft
Emergency radio?

That, in no particular order, is only about half of the list. We had approximately eight months to complete all these important jobs and, unlike the items on my lists of today, all the tasks did eventually get ticked off before we set sail in June the following year. Wear and tear on a boat is inevitable and constant, and it is imperative to pay attention to every detail.

I had an assortment of other jobs, one of which I did enjoy: back to a bit of life modelling at Canterbury College of Art. I learnt vicariously, as it were. I was interested in listening to the tutors as they made suggestions and gave guidance to the students. I had done quite a bit of life modelling all those years ago in London at the Royal Academy, so I was used to taking my clothes off and being stared at for hours by art students. Some people might think it's an odd choice of job, and perhaps exhibitionist; if one has an interest and understanding of the arts, it's a perfectly reasonable thing to do. One is posing for students who are studying the human figure, the nude. It's a useful occupation. I enjoyed it.

After my work at the art school in Canterbury I would often go and sit in the cathedral, sometimes attend the evensong service and think of Dad and the 'cabbage on the toad' episode. That memorable café was by now long gone.

I enjoyed making a list of 'treat goodies' which we could take with us on the voyage. These were things that might hopefully keep our spirits up if we had not been able to cook for days in rough seas. What would last, what might perish? Must not forget, lots of Kit-Kats. We loved those. Might they weigh too much? Weight was always an issue on the boat. For safety reasons it was important to keep the boat as light as possible, so not too many tins were allowed.

I recently found a very interesting document dated May 1863 listing the provisions put on board the *Chepica*, the tall ship of which my father's grandfather, Richard Gales, was master or captain (it was never quite clear from the records which he was). They had apparently circled the globe, and among their provision were:

50 Belfast hams, 10 barrels of East India Pale Ale, 12 American hams in canvas, 50 prime Wiltshire cheeses in bladders, 30 cases of gin, 12 cases of brandy, 2 dozen boxes of mixed spices, 4 cases of pickles, 1 box of tobacco, 8 jars of currants.

The total cost was £116 and 5 shillings.

What an odd assortment.

Our list of provisions was not quite so exotic, but we did intend to have a few small bottles of brandy stashed away to sustain us when on night watch.

John researched the alternative routes for our transatlantic voyage, and perfected his navigational skills. We studied the stars, familiarising ourselves with the various constellations. The starry nights had been breathtaking when we were out in Biscay. There were hundreds of shooting stars and when we were near a shipping lane it was as though some of them had given up the ghost and fallen into the sea. Those lights were ships, of course. We imagined they might be even more spectacular when out in the middle of the Atlantic.

I remember my mother showing us the book about the Kon-Tiki expedition which took place in 1947, the year after I was born. The Norwegian explorer Thor Heyerdahl had crossed the Pacific in a very basic raft sailing over 8,000 miles, on a mission to prove that the Polynesians' simple but accurate means of navigation was not only an art but also a science and in their case a spiritual practice. They had not just relied on the wind but were reading the waves, the currents, and the stars in the heavens above. They had acquired a vast knowledge about the night sky and how it changes through the year as the stars rise and set. The stars were in effect their compass, their clock by which they could calculate their latitude. They were intuitive navigators.

All this is a far cry from today's less-romantic methods. Instant and constant radio contact, radar, Google Charts and computers are able to calculate one's exact position in a flash. But we had none of these on *Sweet Painted Lady*. I would not have wanted to rely on all that technology anyway. I thought it safer to depend on our wits. Well, John's wits when it came to the navigation aspect. We used a sextant to take noon sights and the *Reeds Nautical Almanac* to work out the number of degrees one had to add to account for the magnetic variation and other such incomprehensible things. John did try to explain it all to me, but it was hopeless. It is the block I have with anything faintly mathematical.

I loved Einstein's response to a letter from a high school student, something I happened to come across the other day. 'Do not worry about your difficulties in mathematics. I can assure you that mine are still greater.' How I wish I had received such a letter when I was at school. It might at least have made me laugh. In the end John wrote out, in the back of our log book, what I called the 'Idiot's Guide to Navigation' in case I did end up on my own. Step 1, step 2, step 3, step 4, etc. I could at least go through the motions and make the calculations, but had no understanding of what I was actually doing or any idea how this could possibly be indicating where we were.

The winter seemed to pass quite quickly and by the spring the bank balance was looking healthier. We were busy making last-minute plans. On 7 June, our wedding anniversary, we spent the day buying our first load of provisions for the trip. Four years previously we had spent that anniversary buying tools to build the boat.

John and Derek had been working on a design for Chay, the 53 ft trimaran Great Britain IV. I have fond and terrifyingly vivid memories of being on board for the sea trials. Tacking into Dartmouth under full sail at dawn with Chay shouting to me in the galley, impatient for his bacon sarnie.

The best parting gift of all was that it won the Round Britain and Ireland Race in July 1978. What a perfect end to this period in Sandwich, and a positive beginning for our next big adventure.

Having reached Plymouth we moored up in Millbay Docks and had twinges of excitement as we heaved four Tesco trolley loads of provisions onto the boat. We checked our two emergency 'safety packs'. Kept sealed in plastic flare packs, these comprised first aid, glucose sweets, knives, fishing gear, saltwater boil cream (oh, what joy) and a few other delicacies. Two life rings and safety lights were attached to the pack. I prayed to God we would never need to use them – I did actually get down on my knees and pray. I am funny like that, but I do believe in the power of prayer. My version of prayer.

Having been on our final English countryside summer ramble, on returning to the boat we filled the cabin with bunches of wildflowers. The sweet-smelling wild honeysuckle, briar roses and delicate grasses all transformed our home into a dear little floating country cottage.

Serendipity: as we were leaving Plymouth bound for Spain on 31st August 1978, we suddenly realised that it was the anniversary of the launch two years previously.

We were a little less apprehensive this time when crossing Biscay. We were joined by minke and pilot whales. I found the pilot whales were rather sinister with their round, blunt heads and eerie puffing. Beautifully graceful, friendly dolphins played alongside the boat, but we seemed to have become a bit blasé about seeing dolphins, as we had come across so many on our previous trip. Retracing our steps we motored up the River Tagus, passing under the huge suspension bridge to Lisbon, and visited the maritime museum.

I am ashamed to say we also went to a bull fight, which was a real live spectacle of horror. The matador, Chibanga, was gored by the bull, mangled and tossed about and eventually dragged out of the ring with four others who had previously been injured while attempting to get the bull to the ground. As I understand it, bull-dodging remains lawful, but bull fighting by the matador when the bull is killed was banned in most countries in 2011. I had not realised that the poor bulls are bred to fight: basically they are tortured. They are starved, beaten, kept in isolation, and even drugged before the fight, so that in this completely debilitated state they cannot possibly defend themselves. The bull ring in Seville is known as 'La Catedral del Toreo' and can accommodate 12,000 spectators. I will not be going there or to a bull fight ever again.

By early October we had left Lisbon bound for Las Palmas, Gran Canaria, anticipating we might be at sea for six to ten days.

An incident occurred on the second night out, when I was on watch. We had set the self-steering gear, but the boat was slewing all over the place, surfing almost continuously on the huge swell at 10 knots. We needed to reduce sail, but I had left it a bit too late. Secretly I had found it quite exhilarating, until I realised the boat was straining and felt a little out of control. As I called John up, a massive wave, a wall of water, broke over the deck and John was completely drenched. It was always much more dramatic at night, as you could not see what was coming over your shoulder. But as with some other things in life, sometimes it is best just to ignore them. 'Water off a duck's back' was one way of dealing with a rogue wave.

By the early hours the wind had eased, and with the genoa set we were slipping gently along in the trade wind magic with a favourable current.

As I sat starkers eating a bunch of grapes, my early breakfast, the sun's huge, luminous, glowing ball of fire rose from the swell seeming larger than ever. Like a puppet show, as if it were being pulled up on strings, it heralded the start of a new day, of clear blue sky, of startling, dazzlingly lucid blue sea. No dolphin sightings. No birds. No flying fish. No ships. A feeling of total isolation.

We were both becoming weary; I was hallucinating. Signposts appeared to be leading the way this time. Well, that would have been helpful: to have the odd signpost …

Somebody once asked me: 'When you go sailing, how do you know where you are, and where do you stop overnight?' I was fast learning the answers to those two questions. I trusted in John's ability to navigate, and we just had to keep going, there was no place to stop for the night.

I used to function in slow motion, thinking for hours about whether or not to go and make a cup of tea. Having decided 'Yes, good idea,' I'd then go down below and spend another half hour polishing the mug, watching the kettle boil, and eventually enjoying the cuppa up in the cockpit.

Our Roberts radio did us proud, provided we kept renewing the batteries. We were able to pick up the BBC World Service. 'This is London.' Big Ben striking. That was exciting, and it gave us an accurate time check. Through the radio we heard that the newly elected pope, John Paul I, had died of a heart attack. He was so young. He had been found dead in his bed by his personal secretary. His death made me think of my father. I wondered what Dad might have thought about us adventuring on the high seas had he been alive. Obviously I had considered my mother, but had never actually asked her what she had felt as we set off. I wish I had. I imagine she may have been worried.

More news. Terrible floods in Bengal. Rhodesia's prime minister, Ian Smith, to visit the USA to discuss the conflict in his country. Not having heard anything different we assumed the Queen was still alive and well and living at Buckingham Palace. Hearing the news was strange. We felt completely removed from that other world.

We picked up a Moroccan radio station but couldn't understand a word of what was being said.

A ship came very close one night, a little too close for comfort. I had been observing it for at least an hour. Eventually it changed course behind us and came along our starboard side, shining searchlights onto the boat. Quite scary. We were always on alert: pirates? They are out there. I was relieved when several crew came out onto the bridge deck waving and gesticulating like crazy. I guess they were just inquisitive and relieving their boredom. After all, I imagined they must have thought we were being pretty brave out there bobbing about in our tiny little 39-ft boat.

That night we had supper on deck in a pink world. The sunset was extraordinary, reflecting in the inky sea all shades of salmon pink. I tried to do an illustration every day in my journal, and I do feel these pictures capture the experience far better than I am able to with words.

I would spend ages deciding which colours to use, and would end up using every single felt tip that I had in my collection. It was true. The sea was always every possible and impossible colour. A kaleidoscope.

The period of very light airs was interesting as we flopped about on an enormous overriding swell. Two minute birds about the size of a chaffinch, with bright yellow breasts and a greenish tinge to their wings, suddenly appeared out of nowhere, came to say hello, have a rest and then flew off. A three-foot-long turtle and a slightly smaller one basked on the surface; they popped their heads up and, having satisfied their curiosity, paddled off. A bottle floated past, inhabited by a one-inch crab.

Naturally when the sea was calm there was always more time to contemplate. I used to imagine we were on a path, a road, and we were being pulled along to our next destination. This seemed to help maintain a focus. I felt I needed to create some kind of a boundary where in fact there was not one. The boat's wake provided a reminder of where we had come from, our last port of call. But as it gradually receded in my mind, and as we clocked up the miles and were able to watch our progress across the chart, the comforting thought of the safety net of a landfall emerged again.

Our moonlit dinner on deck with 'Tonight's Invent-a-Dish' menu was fun. Tuna and potato fritters would be washed down with a glass of Mateus Rosé, followed by a treat tin of lychees, the coffee and an After Eight mint. A massive cruise ship passed us that night, with its lights ablaze. What a different experience they must have been having on board, all dressed in their finery for the dinner dance, I imagine. I bet their four-course dinner was not half as good as ours.

The wind and sea state was forever changing. Suddenly we were being tossed about all over the place. When I was down below I described myself as 'feeling I was being flung about trapped in a small jam jar'. It was incredibly noisy. The violent motion made everything an effort. Every movement was a task; going to the loo, which we both seemed to need to do every fifteen minutes (nerves, I suppose), was a nightmare. No sleep. It was better to be up on deck. When dawn eventually broke,

Lights ablaze. Spotting this cruise ship was not difficult

the angry, confused sea and thundering sky reminded me of the Old Master seascapes. I had always dreaded being in one of those boats in one of those pictures, but here I was. The only consolation was that at least the sea spray and the wind was warm.

When in sight of land approaching Las Palmas, partly because we were so shattered, and because there was a lot of shipping about, we had to keep a very diligent look-out. So we decided to heave to. With storm jib up and our heavily reefed mainsail, this procedure enabled the boat to lie sideways onto the swell, giving the boat and ourselves a few hours rest.

At dawn, when we finally dropped our anchor in the harbour, we were greeted with the roar of traffic and the harsh glare of city lights. It all seemed very odd after our ten days at sea. It had been our longest passage so far.

Five days in busy, downtown Las Palmas was enough. We picked up two gas cylinders and our mail. One of the letters we received was a happy one from John's friend in Papua New Guinea. The other though, a sad one from my friend Julia. She was very ill with cancer.

Another mission was to go to the British Consulate to collect an important package. This had been arranged by my godmother, who had slightly put the wind up my poor mother by suggesting we were being very irresponsible setting to sea without a distress radio. The EPIRB (Emergency Position Indicating Radio Beacon) that awaited us for collection was an orange rectangular box with a tag on it which one was supposed to pull if disaster struck. A distress signal alarm would automatically be sounded, transmitting a signal which would hopefully bounce off a satellite up there somewhere in the heavens and we would as if by magic apparently be rescued. It was all a bit of a mystery, sounding somewhat hit and miss.

Although this was a very generous and thoughtful gesture on behalf of my godmother we had little faith that it would ever work. Every so often it would suddenly emit an ear-piercing screeching noise. Perhaps it needed new batteries? I felt much safer not thinking about it at all, since contemplating the reality that we might need to use it was way too terrifying. Best just to give it a hefty shake or bash with a hammer to stop the terrible noise and hide it away back under the bunk.

We did have a four-man life raft which was stowed in one of the side lockers in the cockpit. But quite how we might have managed to manhandle it out of this tight compartment had the unmentionable capsize occurred I was not quite sure.

Our onboard library consisted mainly of seafaring tales: the old classics of Joshua Slocum; Eric Hiscock; cruising manuals; and the more recent voyages of Clare Frances, Naomi James, and Baileys' book, *117 Days Adrift*. That dramatic survival at sea story is worth reading. Their boat, having been holed by a whale, sank very rapidly, and the couple survived in their life raft.

Our next port of call was to be Los Cristianos in Tenerife. The detailed pilot book which we used to refer to for local knowledge made things sound a bit daunting. It described the area as being open to violent and squally weather and rough seas, owing to the islands' close proximity, their heights, the ravines and gullies. Just what we needed to know as we were setting off from Las Palmas at 7.30 in the morning!

John rigged up the spinnaker lines. We were not sure if we were all set for a gentle sail. Our scrambled-egg breakfast was rudely interrupted because, as we motored out of the lee of the island, we were met wham, bam with a fierce northerly. It was as though a violent wind machine had just been turned on. The deck got a good wash, which it needed, having gathered a lot of dust from the city. John was naked, wrestling yet again with reefing the main – his sarong had been whipped away by the wind. I leapt on deck, but the boat was slewing all over the place and one of us needed to be on the helm. As I returned to the cockpit yet another wall of white water loomed up at the stern and the wave broke into the cockpit on top of me. All over again I was hating this. I was utterly miserable, and shaking.

Dreams of the country cottage instantly filled my mind. An abundant vegetable plot would be well stocked. We would be munching on hot buttered toast, relaxing beside the cosy, open log fire; the cat would be sleeping on the sunny windowsill; and a warm, dry bed and an airing cupboard full of deliciously warm fluffy towels awaited.

The good news was that we at least made incredibly good time on this leg. The snow-capped Mount Tiede loomed larger and larger. Once tucked in behind the prominent headland we had a comfortable downwind sail to Los Cristianos. John made us a much needed ham-and-tomato sandwich, and by 6pm we were safely anchored yet again. We tumbled into our bunk bed.

We spent the next ten days unwinding. We discovered that the local haberdashery shop for some curious reason sold fishing gear, so we replenished our dwindling supply.

We walked to the Playa de Américas district, and soon knew we had no desire ever to return there. This massive development, then in its infancy, seemed to be inhabited by a few lonely tourists who were wandering, with grim expressions on their faces, amid heaps of rubble and JCB diggers which were kicking up clouds of dust. They were having to contend with the hideous noise of hundreds of ugly buildings and hotels being constructed. The solitary row of dead-looking transplanted palm trees, and tattered billboards promising stunning sea views from the mingy-sized balconies, were all depressing beyond words. Not to mention the black sandy beach covered in plastic rubbish. Had I arrived there on my package holiday I think I would have demanded my money back.

But all was not lost. On our return walk to the boat we came across what must have been the only flourishing flowerbed within miles. We could not believe it. It was covered in beautiful Painted Lady butterflies.

Was that a good omen? A sign? We thought so. But we felt we needed a few more days to potter about and psych ourselves up.

We bumped into some friends in the supermarket while we were stocking up with our last-minute fresh provisions. Surprise, surprise – and yet no surprise really, since this is how it is with the cruising life. One was always encountering previous acquaintances again somewhere along the line. The American couple were artists, and after having sailed to England were back wintering in the Canaries. We bore two huge pumpkins and a kilo of tomatoes back to the boat. We had a meal with our friends on board and Becky gave me some sequin butterflies which I sewed onto my linen smock. She said they would keep us safe from any harm. I did believe her.

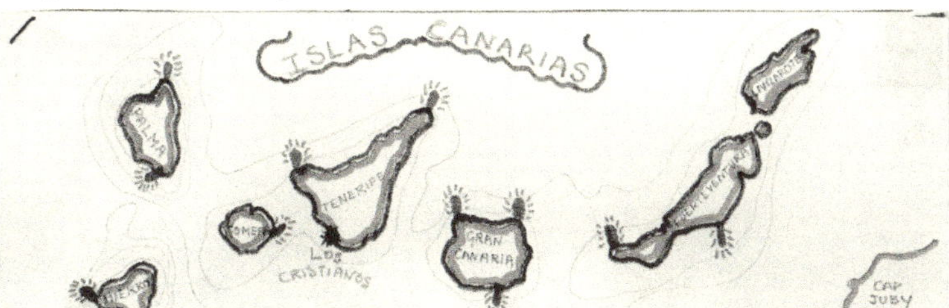

Map of the Canaries from my diary

We did a final washing of our clothes and of ourselves on the dockside, topped up our forty-gallon water tanks, and then over a glass of wine we studied the world map which we had pinned to the bulkhead. We were about to become a dot moving across that ocean for around four weeks.

Chapter 18

Starry starry night

Starkers. Out in the middle of the Atlantic there was no need to get dressed

Finally the day had come. We could not delay our departure any longer, so early on the morning of 26 October 1978 I revisited the special flowerbed and returned to the boat with a bunch of little blue flowers, having bade farewell to the butterflies.

As we motored out of the harbour we passed another couple who were off for a day's sailing. They wondered where we were heading. We called over, 'We are off across the pond – West Indies here we come!' They threw us a packet of biscuits. Chucking back a Kit Kat from our special treats cupboard I shouted, 'Take it easy, have a break, have a Kit Kat.' We were in good spirits that day. Just the right mood to see us on our way.

I had finally owned up to having a love-hate relationship with the sea. I don't think I am alone. I think quite a few cruising folk feel this way. I have a friend who says, 'Give me two hours on a boat and I'm done,' but he is not into sailing by any stretch of the imagination so that's not surprising. I myself will readily find any excuse to decline the offer of a day's sailing on a monohull. Struggling to remain upright while the boat is heeling over at a ridiculous angle is my idea of 'hell on sea'.

The multihull experience is a little different though, since multihulls do not heel over in the same way. One is of course still in constant motion even when becalmed. One is floating. Nothing is ever still or stable. So you hang on tight, remembering it's always 'one hand for yourself and one for the boat'.

All you sailors out there will have an idea of what you are in for when setting out to sea. For those of you who have never sailed I thought I would suggest how you might have a taste of at least the physical aspect of a few days out at sea.

First, if you have a spare room or one you don't really use that much, this could be the perfect opportunity. Just accept that perhaps you have been a bit of a hoarder and it's time for a mega clutter-clearing session. Chuck out everything that you had completely forgotten about anyway and do a car boot, earn a few extra pennies for a treat meal out next Friday. Or take all your unwanted bits and bobs to the charity shop round the corner. Sigh a nice big sigh of relief. Perfect. An empty room.

Dash to B&Q and buy several tins of paint, in varying shades of blue. On the way home call in at the carpet shop and pick up a suitable-sized carpet (a remnant might do), blue, to cover the floor. Get busy and slosh the blue paint everywhere, walls, ceiling, radiators, the lot. No need for any dust sheets. Having laid the carpet, chat up your friendly electrician and get him to come and install a dimmer switch and a sound system. Oh! and go to The Range if you have one close by, or Smith's, and buy 5,000 packets of glow-in-the-dark stars to stick up on the ceiling – varying sizes if poss.

Last but not least (this might be the only costly bit), buy yourself a Huku Ulu Balance Wobble Board (and one for your partner too). They are about £130 on Amazon, or the cheapie version is only £13.99. They are great for improving your core strength.You will need to be patient. It will take a little while to master the art but you'll soon get the hang of it. Don't feel daunted. You are just about all good to go.

Now the really interesting bit. With the partner of your choice enter the room and seal the door. Stand on the wobble board. You are off on your voyage across the Atlantic. At dusk you will notice the light gradually fading and by midnight you will be in pitch darkness. As the auto sound system plays 'Variations on a Theme of Seafaring', you may find yourself wondering where you are, why you are there, and what on earth you are doing.

But wait. As the stars above shine down illuminating this unfamiliar world you may feel the magic of it all. Brace yourself, remain calm and balance for the next twenty-seven days and nights on your virtual sailing simulator, your State-of-the-Art Bespoke Oceanic Wobbly Board Device. No cheating. Don't forget. At dawn the auto dimmer switch will be reactivated, and before you can say 'Jack Robinson' it will be daylight again and you will be enveloped in the eternal blueness.

Occasionally you will be handed a few light bites to sustain you. If you have some fun-loving grandchildren who need to get rid of some pent-up energy, they might enjoy sloshing the occasional bucket of cold water over you. This is all part of your immersive voyage experience. You may have random conversations with your partner, but you will need to conserve your energy at all times as this is going to be a long trip. I'm sure you'll have a great sense of achievement when you make your landfall in the West Indies. The experience might change your outlook on life forever. I'm sure it will be for the best.

Hang on tight. And don't forget that golden rule, *one hand for yourself and one for the boat*. Hope to see you over the other side in twenty-seven days or so.

Just out of interest, the flight time from Las Palmas to Guadeloupe is eighteen-and-a-quarter hours. We had anticipated that our voyage across the Atlantic might take us anything up to a month. So let's get serious and back to the voyage for real.

Just as I have just done, cruising people often lightheartedly refer to the Atlantic as 'The Pond'. That conjures up the image of a calm stretch of water, which of course could not be further from the truth. The Atlantic has low depressions bowling across the top of it and the trade winds blowing at anything up to 25 knots, unpredictable squalls in the south, summer hurricanes and seasonal tropical storms. So it's obvious one has to do one's homework and, depending upon which route one intends to take, pick the best possible window to make the crossing.

Basically there are three routes from Las Palmas: the more northerly one with less constant trade winds, making landfall in Antigua; a middle route to Guadeloupe; and a more southerly route to the Grenadines. We plumped for the middle route, knowing we were likely to experience contrary winds for a few hundred miles after leaving the Canaries, but confident that we would pick up the consistent easterly trade winds as we sailed further south.

The approximate distance is 3,032 miles or 2,635 nautical miles (or 4,879 km).

One hopes at the beginning of every voyage, or every story, that there will be a happy ending. But we can never anticipate or predict what the outcome will be. There is of course also a middle, that halfway point when one feels curious, one's hopes are raised, one is in eager anticipation of what the end might reveal. But one has a sense that there is light at the end of the tunnel.

As we set off, all I knew about the pending voyage, and of the story that I might one day tell about it, was that without a shadow of doubt we would soon be out of sight of land, possibly for a month. I felt vulnerable, daunted by the prospect of being enveloped in the complete unknown.

Beneath us, water: the sea, the Atlantic, which at its deepest point is just over five miles from surface to the ocean bed. Above us, sky: the heavens, this unquantifiable, infinite space spinning out over us and all around us for ever, for ever, for ever and for ever …

How would I cope? What on earth would we do all day? Four-hour watches on and off for perhaps a month? Our sleep patterns, body clocks all over the place? Would we have arguments? Would we die? What would happen if one of us was ill? Would the days merge into one? Would I think I was going mad?

There was no turning back. We were on our way.

As well as the essential ship's log book in which we wrote details of the wind strength, sail changes and distance covered, we marked our position on the chart twice a day. That was always an exciting moment. To see that we had made progress, however small. We were heading in the right direction. West.

My daily journal also recorded our progress, and along with my scanty felt-tip drawings it described significant events, thoughts and feelings. It is interesting to read it today. Some of the details are quite funny, some not so amusing. Many I had not even remembered or thought of from that day to this. Now, having read it, I feel I have sailed the Atlantic twice. I have been very emotional, and sometimes when writing I have found myself in tears. It has been almost as challenging and exhausting as the voyage itself.

We had five sails, the mainsail, spinnaker, genoa, jib and storm jib. Keen to use every zephyr of wind available so as to clock up the best possible daily mileage, depending on the weather conditions, we made fairly regular sail changes. If we were not changing sails we were constantly tweaking them so as to maximise our speed. We were out there on the ocean, on *Sweet Painted Lady*, sailing with her to the West Indies. Sailing safely and surviving.

Daily activities in between the four-hour watches were surprisingly numerous and quite varied considering there was nothing out there except the two of us, our boat, the Atlantic Ocean, long drawn out days and starry night after starry starry night.

Sleep was the priority, but it didn't always work. I guess we must have got used to the motion and we must have slept, but I can't imagine quite how. I am older now, of course, and seem to need everything to be 'just so' before I can get to sleep. I suppose exhaustion was a good thing in that we must have reached a point of collapse and finally were able to just crash out.

Cooking featured highly. Days and nights were punctuated with food. What's next on the menu? On our first night out we had a dinner date and I made Coq-au-Tin plus Vin. A meal with a difference. It was disgusting and we agreed that we would not be buying tinned chicken ever again. I baked bread every day and we usually scoffed the whole loaf immediately as its delicious smell was irresistible. I sewed a patchwork, and carried on knitting my famous rainbow jumper which I had started the year before on our trip to the Med.

We had deck gym-fit sessions. After a few days we both had the desperate urge to stretch our legs, as in the normal 'stretch your legs the walking way' that one does in everyday life on land. That was quite fun.

Every morning and evening I tried to capture the seascape, skyscape or nightscape with my felt tips. Each one seemed more spectacular than the last. The sea was always different. Sometimes the oily-looking surface was completely unbroken and the vast, overriding, heaving swell reminded me of the rolling Devonshire countryside which we had left behind. A tanker on the horizon having disappeared below the swell would then slowly reappear again. At night in these conditions, as the bows of the outriggers sliced through the water, the sparkling phosphorescence would bubble up around the hulls. It was truly magical and unbelievable, an image that is etched in my mind for ever.

Riding the mid Atlantic swell at sunrise. A diary sketch

At dawn the sunrise and the day moved on minute by minute into the blue, blue, blue, blue, blue forever blueness. Then at dusk we would take our seats for happy hour, the 'Sunset Theatre Show'. Wow, the colours! Gradually all shades of darkness merged to create the night, and we were enveloped in the magnificent heaven above. I often cried, overwhelmed and in awe of the magnificent mystery, simplicity and complexity of it all.

On the windless, dull, greyer-than-battleship-grey days I found it hard to keep my feelings of depression at bay. Those days of gloom were not so good, but I would hear my mother's words: 'This too will pass.' She was right. Eventually the greyness and my mood would lift.

There was always housework to be done. The brass oil lamp had to be polished. The Tilley lamp which we hung in the backstay at night had to be refilled with paraffin each day, a tricky operation. Cupboards had to be kept shipshape, with no tins rolling around, as in rough weather they would clatter and bang about and make it even more impossible to get any rest. I even did the dusting. It seemed to be dusty even out at sea – very strange. The air seemed full of minuscule insects, tiny little green things a bit like baby grasshoppers. Where had they come from? Had we brought them with us? Were they all hatching out? Or did they live out here? If so, where? So many mysteries.

Boatwork too never ceased. It's what Sea Gypsies call 'boat life'. Jobs were continual, always something to be mended, adjusted, rejigged, repainted, reconsidered.

Reading, writing and arithmetic. Often at night, by torchlight in the cockpit, I would be reading or writing my journal or poetry, stringing a few words together somehow, but definitely no arithmetic other than my attempt at calculating our position with John's clever 'idiot's guide to navigation'.

The occasional game of Scrabble was fun. John scored well when he landed his Q10 on a triple-letter score. My 'figs' and 'this' and 'that' were not so impressive.

There were nature lessons, birdwatching and whatever research we were able to do with our minimal onboard library. Saltwater showers were invigorating, or towing behind the boat on a rope, a saltwater Jacuzzi. But that was a wise pastime only in good weather with calm waters.

Christmas list making, and more list making, and then even more list making and then hopefully some more sleep – all these activities were a way of creating some kind of a structure for each day. The days needed to have pattern and shape to them, otherwise days and nights turned into a blur and we felt we were losing all sense of time. I spent a lot of time 'wondering', but I was never bored by my ponderings.

We had gained a very interesting travelling companion: a Remora. I wonder if you know anything about this curious fish? I certainly didn't. We had noticed, before we left the Canaries, that there appeared to be a strange grey thing about eight inches long attached to the skeg of one of the outriggers. It turned out to be a hitchhiking fish. The Remora has an adhesive pad on its head which enables it to stick to any surface, including another fish, a shark, a whale, a turtle or indeed a ship. There are many legends attached to these weird creatures, some of which say that they impede the progress of sailing vessels (that would be all we needed). They were often illustrated on Greek and Roman vases and have been referred to as far back as Columbus in 1494 as being the 'ship holder'. We felt honoured though that 'Remmie' had chosen to travel with us. He was company. He had reattached himself to the main hull at the stern, so we could keep an eye on him.

We had estimated that we would need to average 135 miles per day if we were to complete the 2,700-nautical-mile crossing in around twenty days. On days when the log read only around 104 miles we would feel despondent and disgruntled about progress. Those were the days we had to get a grip, take control of our feelings and not lose heart. It was hard to apply the mantra 'it's all about the journey, not about arriving…' That didn't always work for me. In truth I simply wanted to get to the other side and see land again.

And yet the many days with a typical force-4 trade wind were utterly magical and I did not want to be anywhere else, doing anything else. We would set up the self-steering gear, which meant we did not need to be on the helm. On easy days such as this I would work on the article I had been asked to write for the *Eastern Daily Press* newspaper. I decided that, whether they liked it or not, I would write a cheery piece, not all gloom and doom and drama. I wondered if they would accept it. I had heard that the press usually prefers the story to include a near disaster, a calamity of some sort or other, especially when it comes to sailing across an ocean in a home-built boat.

We sometimes amused ourselves – or I would more accurately say tortured ourselves by reading *The Ship Captain's Medical Guide*. It was full of hundreds of horrific pictures of every disease or ailment one could possibly, but not likely, have. There were skin conditions, septic saltwater boils, tooth rot, gum inflammation, ulcers, armpit rash, lacerations, eyelid fungus, putrid penis discharge, varicose veins, worms – the lot. Once having opened it, if we had an itch or a scratch or a tiny little pink spot on the sole of one foot we would become completely paranoid, obsessed and convinced that we had identified the problem. Then it was out with whatever magic cream from the first aid kit we could lay our hands on, shut the dreaded book, and best forget about it.

By the time we had reached latitude 25 it was noticeably hotter. We knew, having read the pilot book, that it was likely we would experience calms, and sure enough we did. These latitudes 25 and 35 are referred to as the 'horse latitudes', a term originating from the days when sailing ships becalmed for long periods sometimes had to jettison their cargoes of livestock in order to conserve their water supply. What a grim thought – having to hurl cattle over the side.

For seven days the boat flopped and slopped about from one outrigger to the next on the glass-calm sea and we went nowhere. I thought, what if this is the end of the world? It has actually happened. The world has ended.

There was nothing but utter silence. It is not something I feel able to describe; it has to be experienced. All I can say is, it felt holy. Private, vast, empty, yet brim-full all at the same time.

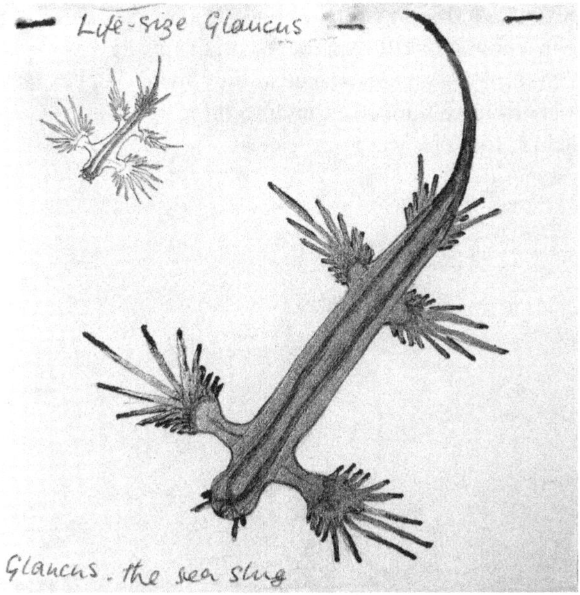

A drawing of Glaucus the sea slug, the remarkable little creature which we fished up in a bucket from the ocean

Faced with this situation, especially during the night, I found it almost more scary than when we were caught out in the bad weather. There was nothing to do sailing-wise. We lost all sense of direction, intention, motivation. It was very disorientating.

During the day, with all this time on our hands, we became fascinated by the surface of the water and wished we had a microscope on board. We fished up bucketfuls of water and examined the contents. Glaucus, the sea slug, was the most fascinating little creature, about half an inch long, a bit like a newt. Its delicate silver body resembled a beautiful piece of jewellery, with navy-blue painted edges to its sweet, dainty little flipper feet. It apparently swims upside down on the ocean's surface and consequently has evolved with an inverted colour scheme. From down below it appears silvery, so it is at less risk of being spotted as a dainty morsal by a big fish. Quite remarkable.

Several large tuna had gathered around the boat. It seemed they might even be sheltering in the shade between the main hull and the outriggers. Their stunning, streamlined bodies can knife through the water with immense skill. Apparently their fins have special grooves in them, minimising any resistance as they swim. Supper ? There is no way we could have jumped in and used the spear gun. Killed them? Eaten them? No. They were our friends.

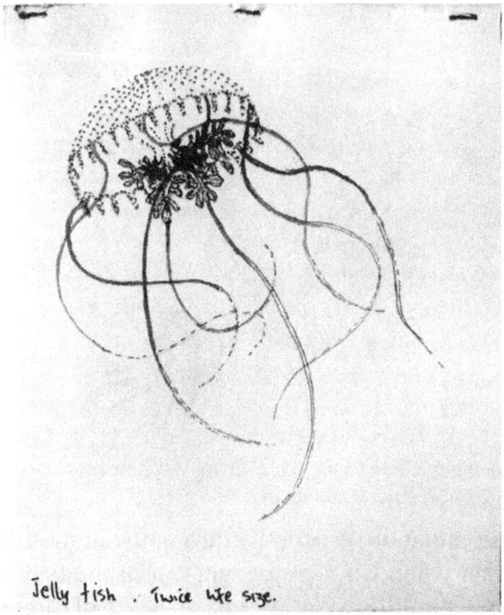

Jelly fish. Twice life size sketch of this beautiful little parachute creature with its spotted pink lace frill and delicate maroon trailing tentacles

A very small but favourable current meant we moved about one sixteenth of an inch on the chart over the seven days. We basked in the sunsets, just us in a sea of gold. If only we were not trying to get somewhere. On nights such as these I felt we were truly in heaven.

We carried only twenty gallons of diesel and were down to our last jerry can, which we needed to save for our arrival; so the option of motoring for any length of time to make our way out of the doldrums was not something we could consider. We did motor for an hour or so on some days, more to boost our morale than anything else. We made the mistake of reading one of Eric Hiscock's accounts, in which his voyage from the Canaries to Barbados took forty-four days. We prayed it would not be the same for us.

We also had to take stock of our water situation. Our forty-gallon water tank was all we had, and we worried that we might run out if we were becalmed for much longer. We decanted enough for four drinks each day and that was our ration. We did not allow ourselves a drop more. Of course, we hoped it might rain, and we were all set with a system for gathering any drop ... but we were not in luck. We used salt water for cooking rice, vegetables and grains, and for washing the dishes.

Becalmed, seven days of life in limbo

I found the period of calm particularly challenging at night. I visualised us within a sphere, enclosed by a wall of stars, a bit like a planetarium, but of course it was not like that at all because there were no walls. I tried to capture my feelings in a drawing surrounding myself in all I knew. I felt afraid. I felt I was melting. I could not erase the nightmare thoughts from my mind. I guess I was tired.

By the sixth day of doldrums I wrote in my journal that I thought I might be cracking up, but that I must somehow keep it to myself. I sat in the cockpit desperate for John to wake as we were no longer in the heavenly gold world but in a grey, thick fog. I had worked out that if we drifted about twenty miles a day, still with 2,000 miles to go, we faced another 100 days of this – by which time I would definitely be a complete basket case. The fog must have been a forerunner to a changing weather pattern, because by the following evening there were two large confusing converging swells – no wind at all. The boat crashed and banged and leapt around on the top of the heaving swell. This was yet another extremely uncomfortable hell.

The Fifth of November: Guy Fawkes' day. It was a shame I'd forgotten to take along any sparklers, but we had our natural spectacular phosphorescence display to look forward to, if and when some wind kicked in. What could be better than natural sparklers? We had been at sea for eleven days. Perhaps we would soon be able to say we were halfway. The wind did finally kick in: up with the spinnaker, and we were off again. Thank goodness – joy, oh joy!

Then came further excitement: sails on the horizon. We altered course to go over and give the boat a wave. What a remarkable coincidence. This motley crew had set sail from Las Palmas the day before us and, guess what, John knew one of the nine crew on board. Their catamaran design had cramped sleeping arrangement in the two hulls, but other than that no comfortable communal space down below. The open cockpit provided no shelter from the sun or weather. All the crew looked pretty miserable. We later heard that on making their landfall they all jumped ship and apparently vowed never to go to sea ever again in their lives.

Gathering together an inexperienced crew in order to finance such a voyage is the way some folk did it in those days, but a bit risky as this case showed. In such close quarters one is tested to the hilt, tensions can arise, and group dynamics can challenge even the wisest of skippers. Tempers become frayed and there can be mutiny. We wished them well as the striking black hull with its unusual yellow sails disappeared over the horizon. It was a romantic picture, but in truth it did not seem to have been the enchanted experience that the crew had envisaged.

Uplifted by the good progress we were making (now averaging 150 miles a day) I found myself on my morning watch reading the Psalms: all the ones I knew and had remembered from school. A dragonfly landed on the page of my prayerbook. Its beautiful lacework wings had brought him all this way from somewhere. Where? Why?

On another occasion a Painted Lady butterfly suddenly fluttered out from between the cavity of the self-steering wind vane. She had travelled with us from the Canaries we presumed. Sadly she died. That took my breath away. I wrote in my journal that I was missing the birds' dawn chorus and wondered if there was a sea-life dawn chorus beneath us every morning. I expect there may well have been.

I identified the beautiful white-tailed tropical birds. They seemed to appear from nowhere, especially on days when in light airs we were flying the spinnaker. When in calm waters it was fascinating to watch the flying fish. They didn't appear to move their wing-like fins. They just 'spivved' through the air like lightning, diving into the waves or landing on the deck. Poor things – what a shock they must have had, but what a spectacle they were.

When we appeared on the chart as a dot right slap bang in the middle of the Atlantic it was a significant and magnificent milestone. Our log read 1,350. We were halfway. Cause for celebration. I was on watch, and when I peered down into the saloon I saw John sitting at the table looking a little studious and impish. What could he be doing? He was having a truly creative moment making blue-and-pink paper chains out of loo paper. How bonkers can you get – but my journal proves this is true. Having hung up the decorations I drew a picture of the cabin and we celebrated with a bottle of Mateus Rosé.

With steadier winds we were now making continuous progress, clocking up on average the anticipated 150 miles a day, and it was more exciting than you could possibly imagine when we picked up Radio St Kitts-Nevis.

Our barometer had for some reason broken, which I was quite pleased about, since I was happier not knowing that a low-pressure system was likely to be coming our way. Ignorance was bliss. Now that we were on the homeward straight, as it were, with the West Indies looming, the tension seemed to ease slightly; but of course we were not there yet.

With 850 miles still to go suddenly we hit squally weather. Uncertainty. Endurance. Exhaustion. The wind whistled in the rigging. Recurring thoughts of, is this just a ridiculous endurance test all over again? A poor joke? Why on earth are we putting ourselves through this hell? What a crazy idea this is.

A sinister sunset with ominous rain clouds seemed to form vast cityscapes in the sky all around us. The fast-moving, foreboding clouds were lit every so often by the full moon which lurked behind the blackness. We huddled inside peering through the rain-splattered windows. The weather deteriorated. John donned his safety harness

Full moon mid Atlantic

and went up on deck to reduce sail. Up with the storm jib again. We were both covered in bruises, having been bashed and banged and battered about. Continually having to brace oneself was exhausting.

The very odd thing was that, once we had got used to the sea state, and the motion, and had overcome the fear, it was all quite spectacular – the foaming crests breaking all around us, the light, the colours, the noise, the sensations, the power of it all. Nothing else but the elements and our vulnerability. Realising our insignificance for me was a curious merging of feeling humbled yet exhilarated.

Two days and nights of that weather was sufficient. Shattered once again, we tried to get proper rest so that we would be on the ball for making our landfall in a week or so. We picked up several local radio stations including those of Trinidad, Barbados and Antigua, and then to our dismay but of course utter delight and thrill we heard Radio Guadeloupe. All these stations were busy selling Christmas. 'Get all your top-quality gifts at Downtown Jamie's store.' I wondered what their top-quality gifts might be.

Watching the ever-changing silvery patterns of the weird dawn sky I found the pink and mauve cotton-wool-like clouds almost comical. They did not look real. I felt I was watching a theatre set taking shape. We could not believe that the day was fast approaching when we might be able to say: 'Tomorrow we will arrive.' Could it be true?

What a surprise. A Super Tanker

The following night was one to remember. The unfamiliar sight of a massive supertanker. John called me up on deck. It seemed to be bearing down on us and passed very, very near across our bows. Way too close for comfort, we thought. Suddenly, like a gigantic fun-fair illumination, the ship flashed three lights on and off – a signal that they had seen our tiny little masthead light and had probably picked us up on their radar. We flashed them back with our not very powerful torch, tacking to change our course and pass behind their stern. It would apparently take a tanker of that size several miles to stop or even slow down. Sailing boats do get run down by large ships. Enough said. It was kind of exciting, but absolutely terrifying. I felt sick.

Reeds Nautical Almanac provides a comprehensive guide to ships' signalling systems, which we did study from time to time; but in the heat of the moment, slightly panicked and confused in the darkness, it was not always easy to remember and identify which sequence of lights meant what.

A magical sailing day. Slipping peacefully along and watching the hull pierce the calm water, a dream had come true that day.

Talking of sickness, mercifully neither of us suffered from seasickness at any stage. Any nausea or funny tummy that I had was due to either my nervousness and fear or something not very nice that I had cooked.

We were greeted at daylight with a perfect light breeze – so up went the spinnaker again in order to take maximum advantage of the light airs. Oh yes, no country cottage for us. We were off on a high again, imagining before long we would be sailing off into the Pacific. Our dramatic mood swings matched those of the changing weather. Inevitably that was all part of the voyage experience.

Very gingerly we laid the Guadeloupe chart out on the table. As we ate our pumpkin stew, with apple crumble for pudding (a Saturday treats lunch), it was hard to believe that we might be making our landfall the following day.

Radio St Kitts was enjoying its Sunday. The non-stop hymns and psalms were fabulous, and I sat up in the bunk all morning singing along to my favourites. 'The day thou gavest, Lord, is ended …'

I love the third verse:

As o'er each continent and island
The dawn leads on another day,
The voice of prayer is never silent,
Nor dies the strain of praise away.

I had taken my prayerbook with me, the one my father had given me for my confirmation. I read the words he had written on the front page.

Miranda Symington
on her Confirmation Day
7th March 1959

I have it here in front of me now. Funny to think it has sailed the Atlantic too.

Funny also to think of the odd random moments when I found myself thinking about my father. I would suddenly hear his voice so clearly: 'Get up you lazy sluggards, lazing in bed all day.' He often used to say this to us when we were teenagers still lounging in our beds at lunchtime. I hope on this occasion he would not have thought I was being lazy. I hoped he might have thought I had earned the right to rest in my bunk bed, and that he would have been happy to hear me singing my hymns while on this amazing adventure.

John's navigational skills were spot on. We picked up the Barbados, Antigua Martinique and Guadeloupe radio beacons and then SIGHTED LAND! A vague, misty outline, still a way off, but definitely out there on the far horizon. Yes, it was land. No, we were not imagining it. Yes – it was the island of La Désirade, which lies just off Guadeloupe.

We then had a hard decision to make because we knew, having studied the charts, that the approach to Pointe-à-Pitre, a harbour city in Guadeloupe, was pinpricked with reefs all over the place and to enter the port at nightfall would not be wise. So we made a plan. We would stop for the night between the two very small islands of Petite Terre, which the pilot chart described as being a secure and safe anchorage, before heading on to Pointe-à-Pitre the following day. These two islands lie close together, with a small channel running between them with reefs at either end. The Atlantic current funnels and rushes through between them.

As we approached and saw the huge breaking waves crashing up against the reef, our fears grew. We wondered, is this really a good idea? The spray created a rather beautiful misty haze. We hastily mulled over again whether we should not risk it. The alternative was to head off back out to sea and just sail about back and forth during the night, wait till dawn and then head for Guadeloupe.

So near and yet so far. Exhausted, excited, impatient, desperate now to come to some sort of rest we headed for what appeared to be a small break in the reef. The depth sounder read 6 ft, as the huge swell and breakers slewed the boat round very close to the edge of the reef. We surfed and slid through, and within half an hour we were anchored in twelve feet of crystal-clear waters with the ocean bed visible beneath us. Land, greenery, and signs of civilisation.

A small powerboat was anchored on the sandy shore. A few people stood beside it, beckoning us over. John leapt into the water and was immediately whisked away by the extremely strong current, but he struggled his way back to the boat to get the flippers. I was not confident that I would be able to swim against the current, but John insisted that I would be fine. So I donned my flippers too, plunged in, and flapped and flipped and swam like crazy over to the shore.

The two French families immediately plied us with iced rum punches, and invited us to join them for their barbecue of freshly caught fish, and every other kind of delicious goodie. Being French it was no ordinary picnic.

Very wobbly legged, dizzy, faint, beaming and glowing we were in shock, and it was hard to convey to them how much we appreciated their warm welcome.

They admired the boat and wanted to know where we had bought it. 'We built it ourselves in England.' They couldn't and wouldn't believe us.

They were curious as to where we had come from.

'We have just sailed across the Atlantic. We have been at sea for twenty-seven days.' They couldn't and wouldn't believe that either.

It is a strange thing but I can honestly hardly believe it myself.

Chapter 19

Caribbean adventures

Landfall at last. John and me safely anchored off in Antigua in 1978

Our welcome was indeed amazing. Just as it was getting dark, the French party swung by in their speedboat and offloaded the remains of their picnic with us. I must say one could hardly call them remains, let alone the remains of a picnic. It was as if a gourmet floating restaurant had magically appeared out of the blue. There was no bill and no ten percent to be added either. What a lovely gesture. Ice for starters – what a luxury! We had not seen ice for nearly a month, and the weather was now very hot. Cooled beers. Three bottles of extremely expensive chilled wine, French loaves, yummy cheeses and a huge, delicious, cooled watermelon.

I have just checked my jottings in the log book and I see that, when we went ashore and the French party learned that we had just sailed the Atlantic, they thrust a grilled lobster into our hands too. I had forgotten that. Lobster happens to be my absolute favourite treat. John used to say how he loved to watch me eat a lobster, as he could not imagine how anybody could possibly get any more enjoyment from devouring one. I'd suck on its claws, picking every morsel out of the shell, savouring every mouthful. So you can imagine I was in heaven. Poor lobster. If only he knew how much I was appreciating him.

Our French friends bade us farewell, congratulating us again as they disappeared in the fading light bound for Guadeloupe's harbour of Pointe-à-Pitre.

Night had fallen. Everything was unfamiliar, including the sounds and scents. We had returned to the land of the living, this other world.

The violent sound of breaking waves crashing on the reef was a little disconcerting. So was the occasional splosh of a diving pelican, the flashing of the little lighthouse marking the islands, and the delicious aromas emitting from the hot earth and rocks.

Point a Pitre, Guadeloupe. Our landfall in the Caribbean. And as if by magic our blue world had turned to one of green

We could collapse... or could we? Well, ever so slightly. But, of course, back at our anchorage again the very wisest thing to do was to keep a lookout. We knew that; we did not want to fall at the last hurdle, take any chances. We might risk being unaware that we were dragging our anchor, and end up shipwrecked on the reef. So we settled for one more very diligent night on watch, but a very special one. We had made our landfall, or just about. We were in the Caribbean.

The following morning we hauled up the 45-lb C.Q.R. (a quick-release) anchor in the early hours and sailed over to Pointe-à-Pitre. Having anchored again we rushed ashore, our priority being to send telegrams to my mother in England and John's parents in South Africa.

We leapt onto a bus which we hoped was heading downtown. The rather lackadaisical-looking driver hurtled crazily round the hairpin bends, hooting almost constantly, for no apparent reason so it seemed. The impact of the abrupt jerking movement of the bus, especially when the driver suddenly jammed on the brakes, was another thing we were not used to. So were the unforgiving jolting sensations of wheels on the harsh and potholed surface of the road. All this was so different from floating almost airborne on the water as we had been for nearly a month. Such a dramatic contrast.

There was so much to adjust to all of a sudden: the noise and clatter and chatter of humanity. Very loud, jangly, tinky-tonk steel band music was blaring out of the windows. The bus was crammed with locals of all shapes and sizes. Their baskets were crammed with flowers, pineapples, christophenes, onions. Netted sacks bulged with sweet potatoes and pumpkins. Massive pale green watermelons, some cut open exposing their beautiful pink crisp innards and their dark seeds, dripped their refreshing juices as they were handed round the bus to keep the little ones cool. There were chickens, dogs, birds in cages, beautiful bright-eyed children with intricate braided hairdos, babes in arms … and us on board, amid the hubbub, feeling unbalanced, dizzy, rocking all over the place, in shock.

When we got off the bus the land seemed to be moving under our feet. I tripped and fell flat on my face. No damage, luckily. It takes quite a while to get one's 'land legs' back.

Post Office Telegram Services, 22nd November 1978
To: Mrs Symington, High Barn, Stanhoe,
King's Lynn, Norfolk, England

FANTASTIC VOYAGE LOTS OF LOVE FROM
THE CARIBBEAN AND SWEET PAINTED LADY.

In hindsight that seems a rather minimal message to have sent to my dear mother, who no doubt had been waiting anxiously to hear of our safe arrival. But I expect it was because every letter of the alphabet cost a fortune, and we were already keeping a watchful eye on our tight budget.

It has been a very interesting experience writing about the voyage, reliving it. I have found it difficult to believe that I was really there. I feel as though I have told you a story, a made-up story about a couple who built a boat and sailed it across the Atlantic Ocean.

I have already mentioned that when I was seven and at my first boarding school, one of the ways in which I thought I might get attention was to hatch a clever plan that involved telling a convincing lie. I no longer need to tell lies, like Matilda in the famous poem by Hilaire Belloc. So, yes, I have to tell myself, I was there sailing across the Atlantic in the boat we built together. It's not an imaginary story. It's all true.

I think there is a simple explanation as to why I find it hard to believe. It's just that I am a lot older now and can't quite contemplate doing such a thing. I am certainly not about to batten down the hatches, don my slippers and snooze the rest of my life away. My body, mind, and spirit are still raring to go, but I, like many older folk, do not have that same level of energy, physical strength or stamina that I had when I was younger.

I have been so fortunate to have had this opportunity. It was a shared experience. One in which we relied upon each other in different ways for different things.

At the same time we each experienced it in our own unique way. The solitude. That aloneness with nature and one's thoughts. Experiencing each moment with all one's senses in a state of heightened awareness. The quiet, the calms, and suddenly the foaming raging sea. That constant changing mood of wind and sea, and having to deal with my own fluctuating moods as well. Embracing it all and having to take on board the serious responsibility of what we had undertaken individually and together.

Being disciplined enough to keep my mind focused is what kept me going. I had to maintain clarity of vision in moments when I was scared and hating it and felt like giving up. I knew I had no choice, other than jumping over the side. An inner strength, common I guess to all wanderers and explorers, seemed to develop. It was an experience which I wish everyone could have, humbling and truly sacred: one which has strengthened my faith.

I wondered if I would ever be able to return to living ashore. I feared that life might seem diluted and humdrum, have no meaning. I wanted to maintain the intensity, the internalised tingling feelings of my very own vital, fearful, exhilarating and grateful sense of aliveness.

I have been asked so many times what we did for money when we had arrived. Yes, well, as we know, it does not grow on trees. The Caribbean is a little bit 'manyana-ish'. I do not like to make generalisations, but I feel it's fair to say that on some of the less-developed islands not a lot appears to get done beyond the day-to-day basics required to keep the place functioning, the wheels turning. There does not appear to be any sense of urgency. When things eventually do get done, they often have to be redone within a few weeks because they were not done properly in the first place.

Something that struck me immediately was how slowly people seemed to talk and walk. A delightful state of lethargy seemed to prevail. It is, I feel sure, partly due to the heat, and liberal use no doubt of certain substances, but it is part of what is so captivating about the Caribbean.

Anchored in St Barts. Just back from shopping

We had been told by various friends – old timers who had been cruising around for years – that once we arrived in the Caribbean we would have no difficulty picking up paid work, so we never doubted that this would be the case. Having built our own boat this was a good enough advertisement that we could master most things boat-wise. And, after all, we were a young and reliable, hardworking English couple. They would see us coming. We had no doubts and were confident that we would soon be employed, perhaps by a charter company.

My mother enjoying her holiday in the West Indies on board Sweet Painted Lady, anchored in Jos van Dyke in the British Virgin Islands

We felt we deserved a little break, however, so before we went in search of work we went off exploring some of the islands. Our first Caribbean Christmas was spent in Antigua. I swam ashore to freeze a bowl of brandy butter in the deep freeze of a kind hotelier. The Christmas pudding was decorated with coconut palm leaves. We enjoyed a full-scale traditional roast turkey meal with friends. An inflatable Father Christmas stood watch from his lofty position, having been hoisted to the top of the mast. I twined Christmas lights around the rigging. It was strange to be hot at Christmas time.

Our cruise down island to St Vincent was one of the most interesting.

We climbed La Soufrière, the Mount of Suffering. Its peaks rise to over 4,000 feet. As we gazed in awe, whisps and sulphurous fumes silently wafted from the gaping crater of the volcano and the wind howled around us. Two weeks later, on 13 April 1979, La Soufrière erupted, wiping out the entire southern hillside. Twenty thousand people were evacuated and the island was covered in fine ash which fell like snow as the mushrooming clouds filled the sky. I felt inspired to try to capture my memories and feelings in this poem:

Grumbling rumbling earth,
Tired in your heart
Of all you have had to bear.
Scarred through time
In wild frustration
You erupt and scream.
Let loose your fury
Stun us with your power
And send us running
From your path of desolation.
We stumbled up your jagged ridges,
We gazed into your lungs,
We watched you breathe.
We wondered at your heart.
We followed you
Deep into your burning core.
We marvelled at your ancient grace.
You have stood and watched
Through time so long;
Now you have had your word.

When cruising one meets so many interesting people from all walks of life. The common denominator is the boat itself, which has an almost hypnotic way of binding you together immediately. There is a mutual respect and understanding between boat people, however crazy and strange, rich or poor, experienced or not.

Bob, a Frenchman, had adopted a little boy from the island of Dominica. Patrick was twelve, and his one ambition in life was to become the skipper of a yacht. Having met Bob previously he had believed that Bob would take him on as mate on his boat; and so he waited on the end of the little wooden jetty for three weeks every single day, his bag packed and ready to go. Bob did return, and with the permission of his grandmother, Patrick joined Bob on his cruise, which took him down island. Their intention was to cross the Atlantic and cruise around the Mediterranean. I often wonder what happened to them.

When we had been about to leave the Canaries we had met a young man who was living aboard his tiny boat with his two scallywag children. They used to spend all day running barefoot up the mast, in training I thought perhaps for scaling the palm trees in order to pinch a coconut. They would swing out over the water on the rigging, scamper all over the deck like little rug rats. They were true sea Gypsies. The dad was a skinny, raggedy-looking guy who apparently was intending to cross the pond too. He didn't seem to have much of an idea about sailing (I can talk, as nor did I), but also not a clue about navigation. He asked John if he thought he would arrive safely in the Caribbean if he just headed right, or west. John politely pointed out that there were a few things he might need to take into consideration and promptly gave him a crash course in navigation, similar to the one he had given me. I often wonder what on earth his story was, and what those two little boys are up to these days.

The official hurricane season falls between early June and the end of November. On 29 August 1979, a depression developed in the Cape Verde Islands, and by 1 September it was described as a potentially damaging, intense tropical cyclone. We listened to the radio and picked up the nervous tone in the voice of the broadcaster as the storm was being tracked steadily west reaching wind speeds of up to 130 mph, carving a path of destruction. Along with many others we stocked up on provisions, left the marina in Red Hook where we had been moored up, and sought our hurricane anchorage in a sheltered inlet in the lee of the island. Having hidden ourselves away deep in a mangrove swamp, we then used every line we had on board to lash the boat to the twisted trunks. We must have looked a bit like Gulliver: tethered, immobilised, captured, but we hoped adequately secured. We waited.

The full force of Hurricane Frederic hit the Virgin Islands on 12 September and continued to Puerto Rico and Cuba, finally hitting the United States Gulf Coast and causing terrible damage there. Once it had passed, it was several days before we finally decided it was safe to emerge from the mangrove swamp and return to our mooring in the harbour. As expected, we were met by a scene of chaotic devastation.

The aftermath was scary. Palm trees had been ripped out from concrete, torn up by their roots. Overturned and wrecked boats littered the boatyard. Lampposts had been twisted into spectacular, weird sculptural works of art, and the numerous flimsy buildings with their corrugated roofing had been blown to smithereens. Piles of unrecognisable debris littered the streets. Wandering amid all this were many shattered, desperate-looking people, salvaging what they could. Miraculously there had been no fatalities. We helped as best we could with the mop-up operation in the marina. Yet another boat-life experience. Our dear *Sweet Painted Lady* had suffered no damage.

In the December of that same year, 1979, I flew to Miami to meet my mother. We had paid for her to come and join us for a holiday on the boat. She arrived all excited, armed with her oil paints, sketchpads and canvases in the hope of capturing her 'Caribbean holiday of a lifetime'. She was always so frustrated when she was painting, complaining that the light was so astonishing and that her paints were not vivid enough to do justice to the vibrant scenes she was trying to reproduce. It is true, the Caribbean light is remarkable. Everything seems more clearly defined, in focus, intense, uplifted.

My mother had brought an amusing newspaper article with her about an Italian explorer who was intending to cross the Atlantic on the top of a Volkswagen car which he had filled with expanded polyurethane foam. He had previously been around the world on a Lambretta scooter, had crossed the Sahara strapped to a kite, and had explored in Alaska. He had no radio, not a clue how to sail, and thought he might be at sea for around four months, having apparently abandoned his long-suffering wife and five children. I wonder what on earth happened to him, too.

Other more serious cruising folk might be heading further south for Panama and the Pacific, circumnavigating the world. Charter boats of all shapes and sizes wined and dined their guests by moonlight on the deck and provided the occasional amusement as they sipped their gin and tonics and piña coladas. Sound travels well over water, and we were often amused by the overheard conversations which, after a few drinks, might turn into more than heated discussions. The odd crew member jumping overboard and screaming abuse at the skipper provided real live theatrical entertainment at its best.

We basked in the heat, enjoyed the Caribbean experience and had fun making a tape recording to send home to the family of snippets and sounds from our watery world.

The banana plantations spread deep into the hillsides, and hot mountain roads enticed one round their twisting corners. Bamboo was hewn with the glistening blades of machetes to construct very simple housing. Everything that grew and that was not poisonous was either eaten, boiled to make tea or a medicinal potion, roasted, used as compost, or smoked.

Occasionally the romantic lights of a huge cruise ship decorated the horizon. But Charlotte Amalie, the port capital of the US Virgin Islands situated on St Thomas, would become swamped with tourists who had been disgorged from the ship in order to stretch their legs. It was then virtually impossible to move along the narrow streets. I remember being asked by a lady whom I met in a shop there which island she was on. She seemed to have no idea or be particularly interested in the place itself, and she quietly whispered under her breath: 'Don't let my husband hear, but I haven't a clue where we are and I can't wait to get back home.'

On 30 March 1979 the 656-foot-long, Dutch-built cruise ship the *Angelina Lauro*, which was docked in the port, was completely gutted by fire. It had apparently started in the galley. Most of the 740 passengers were fortunately ashore at the time, and there was no loss of life. The gutted, charred hull of the ship was a dramatic and sad sight as it smouldered in the harbour, where it stayed for several months until September. Then, while it was being towed to Taiwan by a German salvage company, it slipped beneath the surface as it started taking on water. It had been a beautiful ship. What a dismal end to its forty years of life on the high seas.

The coral reefs, before they had become endangered, spread in splendour around the Tobago Cays, and the rainbow-coloured fish and sea life of all description never ceased to amaze and intrigue me. I never got to grips with diving with a tank, but I got enough pleasure just from snorkelling.

Coral collection. An illustration from my journal

Carnivals were a way of life. Steel bands played almost incessantly and, while the little babies slept into the night curled up in their mothers' arms, other children danced the night away. It was hot, hot, hot, every day. The colours vibrant, the light astonishing. I realised that the Caribbean needs the sun. On the occasional overcast day the atmosphere would change and hang heavily. The place seemed tired, dusty, worn out, out of sorts with its very self. On such days one shamefully could hear oneself thinking, not another shitty day in paradise …

We continued our adventuring and sailed south to Dominica, Martinique, St Lucia, St Vincent, Bequia, Canouan, Carriacou, Tobago Cays, and then retraced our steps back to Antigua. Then we went north to Nevis, St Kitts, St Eustatius, St Barts, St Maarten and Anguilla, and finally as our money was running out we headed for St Thomas.

Each island had its own feel, its own character, its own history and its own highlight. One of those highlights for me was when we sailed to the very small and quiet island of Anguilla. At twilight we went ashore for a beach wander and forage. I loved gathering shells, twigs, flotsam and jetsam and making little mobiles, trinkety bits with which to decorate the boat.

And on this occasion there she was: a tree bedecked with thousands of fireflies. They appeared to be dancing among the foliage. These remarkable soft-bodied, winged beetles emit light from their abdomens to attract a mate. Their other name is 'lightning bug'. The males usually start up the conversation, and if a female is attracted she flashes him back. Sometimes the *femmes fatales*, as they are aptly called, lure an unsuspecting male into their den and devour him alive. I am glad I knew less about their habits at the time. It was one of many magical highlights. The firefly tree.

But it was back to work. We were not simply on a jolly short lived holiday. Living afloat and cruising is a way of life. We worked as we went along. Luck came our way. Perhaps it was the coin which we had stepped under the mast. The Polynesian god Tangaroa was looking down on us. Almost within a day of arriving back in Red Hook, St Thomas, we both landed jobs with a charter company, La Vida.

John pretty well managed the company and spent a lot of time going to the rescue of some of the charter boats whose crews didn't have much of an idea how to sail. It seemed that they thought it was not dissimilar to being behind the wheel of their car. John would go roaring off in one of the chase boats and frequently had to revive the dysfunctional outboard, unblock a loo, fix the barbecue, deliver more beer and rum, retrieve an anchor which had got stuck on a coral reef or pacify hysterical females who had freaked out at the sight of a giant cockroach scuttling out of sight down the side of their bunk.

My job was to clean and de-cockroach the boats and provision them. This usually involved hauling numerous crates of beer on board, filling the ice box, stashing away vast quantities of rum and piña colada mix and tossing the odd bit of food into the fridge. The perks of the job were that, when they departed, we were given all that they had not consumed, which often meant we needed to do no shopping for weeks.

A day off from work at La Vida Charters. On the dock at Red Hook, St Thomas, BVI

There were some other amusing tasks too. A very loud American from Florida, having regaled us with stories of his ex-wife's crazy antics, having dived on a reef had retrieved a huge piece of brain coral. He requested that I package it up and send it to the said ex-wife. He thought it would be a fitting parting gift to her, since he considered she had absolutely no brain cells whatsoever and this might help. I lugged it to the post office, having bubble wrapped it and concealed it in several old beer boxes. It weighed a ton and cost a fortune to post. I wonder if she ever received it and what her response would have been. However insulting this gesture was intended to be, I would have been thrilled to receive a huge piece of brain coral. It was so beautiful and intricate.

We were glad to be working again. We regained a sense of order and determination to save up for the next leg, although we had no idea at this stage what that next leg would be.

We acquired two cats, Alice and Socrates. They loved going out with us in the evening, after we had finished work, for a row in the dinghy. Alice fell off the boat several times, so we made a little carpeted ramp for them both which we lowered into the water off the back of the outrigger in case they ever slipped up again.

I had heard from my friend Julia, with whom I had shared the flat in London, that her cancer had taken hold and she was now very ill. I decided that I would like to go and see her. I flew to Toronto where she was now living. It was a sad trip. I was with her in hospital where she died two days after I had arrived, but I was so pleased that I had got there in time and had been able to be with her. Coincidentally, Kendall was now remarried and living in Toronto. He was kind, looked after me, drove me to and from the hospital and helped me with an incredibly complicated auto-alarm doorbell system at Julia's flat where I stayed for a week while we made all the various arrangements with the funeral parlour. That was one of the very weirdest interludes.

The bleak, soulless Canadian funeral parlour reminded me of a Travel Lodge-style motel. It was situated on a highway that was in the middle of nowhere with non-stop passing, roaring traffic. A vast tarmacked car park stretched out in front, with no sign of a living tree or green plant of any kind. In the parlour itself, too, there was not a plant in sight, not even a plastic one. The whole place was completely devoid of anything comforting for the recently bereaved. The syrupy-sweet, semi-religious piped music did not cut the mustard either. The atmosphere of the whole place sent shivers down my spine.

Off the corridor with its tastefully designed star studded midnight blue carpet were numerous parlours into which the mourners were ushered. Cheap white nylon drapes hung round the walls and over the windows. There she was, Julia, propped up in her coffin in the corner of the room and so heavily made up as to be hardly recognisable as the person I had known. Some kind person had no doubt carefully chosen a wig, applied the makeup, dressed her up for her final departure. Her outfit seemed to me most inappropriate. I cannot imagine Julia ever choosing to wear a blue suede suit and thigh-high boots.

We all kind of 'cocktail partied' around the open coffin for a while. Then, when it was closed, we ignored poor Julia and carried on that way for a few hours. It was too bizarre for words. Finally I was able to make a quick dash to the airport. I was so pleased to be returning to the normality of life afloat, my very own little island, like a snail with its home on its back. I was so sorry that Julia had never visited us on our boat as we had planned.

The recurring theme with boat life is that not a lot ever seems to go according to plan. We were working hard, saving hard and had a vague idea that we might take the boat out of the water, store her safely on land and do an overland trip somewhere. We sat many an evening in the cabin discussing ideas with friends over conch fritter dinners.

18 Lynn News & Advertiser, Tuesday, February 19, 1980

Dream voyage to the Caribbean

A WEST Norfolk couple who built a 40' trimaran in their back garden have made a successful Atlantic crossing and are now living and working in the Virgin Islands.

John and Miranda Shuttleworth spent 8 months building the good ship Sweet Painted Lady in the garden of their home at High Barn, Stanhoe.

They completed the project in the summer of 1976 and transported the boat — not without difficulty — to Wells.

'Unique'

The couple made a trip to the Canaries the following year and set sail for the Caribbean last October.

Miranda takes up the story: "Crossing an ocean in a small boat is a unique experience that I wish every one of us could have. The solitude of vast distances, that aloneness with nature and oneself, the quiet, the calms and suddenly the raging sea.

"The serious responsibility of what one is doing, just the two of us and our little boat. The constant changing mood of wind and sea and of ourselves.

"The beauty of the leaping dolphins, the quiet inquisitive turtles and the occasional winging of birds around us. All these our voyaging companions.

'Coral reefs spread in splendour around the Tobago bays . . . Yes, this is paradise.'

"During our crossing of the Atlantic I kept a daily diary which has been very interesting to look back on. We were proud of our 25-day crossing. It was very slow but nothing mattered except that we had arrived safely and exactly where we hoped to be.

"The island of Guadaloupe and surrounding islands of Petite Terre and Marie Galante emerged out of the blue haze at dusk on the evening of November 20.

"It seemed a miracle had occurred. A dream voyage filed away behind us and we related to the land of the living once again.

"Christmas was spent in Antiqua. I swam ashore to freeze a bowl of brandy butter in a kind hotelier's deep freeze and a full-scale traditional meal was enjoyed by many friends.

"Christmas pudding was decorated with coconut palm leaves and Father Christmas watched from his position up the mast.

"Banana plantations spread deep into the hillside, hot mountain roads entice one round their twisting corners. Bamboo is hewn with glistening blades of machetes to construct very simple housing, everything that grows and is not poisonous is eaten, boiled to make tea, roasted or smoked.

"Coral reefs spread in splendour around the Tobago bays and the rainbow colours of the fish never cease to amaze. Yes, this is paradise. The sun shines. It is always hot, hot, hot.

But life is a reality and as always, when cruising, money runs out sooner or later. Ours was not a two-year with enough funds and stores on board to finance an extended holiday. Ours is rather a way of life and so we work as we go.

Crew

"We are now living and working in the Virgin Islands. A string of islands each with crystal bays lies out here for us to explore. We are glad to be working again — a sense of order and determination to save up for the next leg of our voyage, whichever leg that will be, is what we need.

"Sweet Painted Lady sails well. We love her and we shall soon be planning a short cruise down the islands with our two new crew, Alice and Socrates, our Caribbean kittens.

A newspaper article written for the Norfolk Lynn News and Advertiser

By the early spring of 1980 we had become quite excited about the possibility of this overland trip and a period of reprieve from boat life. However, an unexpected proposal was made to John. Chay Blyth confirmed that he had secured the funding from Brittany Ferries to build a racing trimaran for the first ever two-handed trans-Atlantic yacht race. He asked John to design it. First, could he return to England for a meeting? And would he return to England to oversee the building of the boat? Naturally, without any deliberation, the answer was 'yes'. But what would this mean in the long run? A change of plan, no doubt.

During the following few weeks we were consumed with endless discussions as to how to manage this, what exactly to do, when, where and how. And all the while I was not happy. I had been experiencing excruciating pains, and I knew I must be sensible and see a doctor. We speedboated our way to the island of St John, where a specialist clinic was held once a week. I was thinking that I, too, might be about to be delighted by the unexpected. But no, the tests indicated that I was not pregnant. We roared back in the boat, crashing over the waves, and I remember crying and feeling sad, cross and disappointed. The agonising pains returned that night. A few days later, a further test confirmed that which in my bones I had known all along. When a woman listens to her body she knows these things. I was expecting a baby. Of course, I was over the moon.

We were to become parents, and John had been commissioned to design a boat for a world-famous yachtsman. A different future was on the horizon. A new chapter for us both.

We tentatively considered selling the boat. As we sat in the yacht broker's office discussing the options I was in tears, feeling a complete traitor. We knew this was not the moment for any rash decision, so we put that idea on the back burner and booked a flight back to England for an initial meeting with Chay and for me to register with a doctor.

We packed up the boat, secured her safely in the Red Hook Marina on St Thomas, and made arrangements with our friends who had promised to keep a close eye on her for us. It was heart-breaking to be leaving. But at the same time we were caught up in a whirlwind of excitement as we set off back home.

We arrived in England in late March and headed to the Cornish village of Pensilva, close to Chay's home and convenient for meetings. The weather was still cold, so living in a damp caravan in the depths of an even damper Bodmin Moor, pregnant and with no creature comforts, was the next challenge. I reminded myself that I had always been able to adapt. I remember the bed was extremely uncomfortable, typical of those cronky old fold-down beds in old-fashioned caravans. There was a two gas-ring cooker but no bath – I don't recall what we did for bathing. I made one friend while I was attending the childbirth classes in Liskeard, but other than that it was a somewhat isolated period. We both had our heads down, me quietly growing my baby and John growing his boat.

I lived in my pink, floaty Caribbean skirt and little pink-blue-and-white-checked smock top, and never took off my comfy leather Zora sandals. As winter was fast approaching I remember Chay one day asking John why he didn't just go and buy me a proper pair of shoes. But I was quite happy still in Caribbean mode wearing my sandals.

I finally called the shots and with my due date of early October we agreed that we needed somewhere a little more comfortable in which to live and welcome our baby. We moved to a cliff-top bungalow in Looe, and for the first time in ages we enjoyed hot running water, baths and a comfortable bed. What bliss.

I have never seen anyone move as fast as Chay when, in the middle of a last-minute tea-time meeting with John about the boat, my waters broke.

On 10 October 1980, Orion James was born, miraculously safe and sound, in Plymouth hospital.

My intention was to have a natural childbirth, which at the time was considered to be an irresponsible decision and a bit wacky. Earlier in my pregnancy we had been shown around the labour suite at the hospital, which to me appeared more reminiscent of a torture chamber. We were shown the birthing table, then a pair of metal forceps, the strops into which one's legs would be placed and held splayed if an assisted birth was deemed necessary. I found all the instruments, gadgets and knives so alarming.

I spent a lot of time researching the French obstetrician Frédérick Leboyer, whose controversial gentle birthing technique, radical at the time, years later has become fully accepted. His inspirational book *Birth without Violence* was published in 1974. We came very close to deciding to go to his hospital in France and having the baby there. In the end events overtook us. The consultant was indignant, believing he knew best, when we told him that the head of the baby was not engaged and that my baby was lying in a breech position. I could feel and even see the shape of the baby's head pressing up against my rib cage. In this position the cord was around his neck. In the end it was necessary to deliver him safe and sound by emergency Caesarean section.

I was not allowed to see my baby until several hours after the delivery. He was in an incubator in a ward with about twenty other newborns, and my deepest fear was that they might bring me the wrong baby. I had once heard that this had happened. I was only allowed to hold him for a few minutes at a time. I used to go and gaze at him in his little incubator.

I felt desperate, and on 12 October, having signed the necessary papers, much to the disapproval of the doctor who had said I could not even stand up after the operation, I drew myself up, marched in agony twice, up and down the corridor of the hospital to prove that I could walk perfectly well, and discharged myself. We bundled Orion into his Moses basket and drove back to our cosy little home on the cliff top. In those days it was unheard of for a woman to be discharged so early following a Caesarean delivery.

I was learning on the hoof as all new mothers do, loving every moment being with my baby boy while John was concentrating on the building of the 65-foot Brittany Ferries trimaran. As I said before, most boat-building projects take twice as long as one thinks they will and cost twice as much too, but this huge project had to be on target, and it all seemed to be moving along according to the plan. Meanwhile our plan was to be at the finish of the race in Rhode Island in June.

So in late March 1981 we decided to fly back to the boat and sail her with Orion, now aged six months, from the US Virgin Islands through the Bahamas to America. The trip took around three weeks, sailing from St Thomas to the tiny island of Culebra, then island-hopping to Puerto Rico and San Salvador, the Bahamian island where Christopher Columbus is said to have landed. En route we caught a 5lb barracuda with fiercely sharp teeth. Alice was fascinated, and enjoyed devouring the head for her dinner while we enjoyed grilling the rest for our supper.

We sailed on to Nassau, Cat Island, Stirrup Cay, Grand Bahama and finally to West Palm Beach, Florida.

The trip had not been without various fiascos – as to be expected, since in addition to Alice and Socrates we now had our tiny little crew member on board and as well as doing my four-hour stints on watch, I was also now on breastfeeding watch. We created a cosy hammock-style crib for Orion in the forecabin. No cradle rocking was needed. He was just lulled to sleep by the constant motion of the boat and seemed hypnotised by our fluttering Union Jack flag which was attached to the backstay. He lived in Huggies nappies, and lived on mashed bananas, and did well to survive the mosquitos.

Although it was a very short trip in comparison to Biscay or the Atlantic, strangely I had not provisioned the boat adequately. Stocks ran very low. My befuddled baby brain was preoccupied with something much more important, and, when I went shopping before we left the Virgins, all I seemed to have stocked up on was Huggies nappies. I remember when we were down to one onion I used half of it for spicing up one meal. For the next meal I cut the remaining half in two and used one of those. Next meal I cut the remaining quarter-onion in half again, etc, etc, etc. It was reminiscent of wartime rationing. Finally, having got bored with onion-spiced rice, when we were unable to find a shop on the next island we asked a hotel manager if we could possibly buy some food from them. He took pity on us – a babe in arms can work wonders – and he gleefully led us into the kitchen, whereupon he opened the doors of a massive walk-in cooling area jammed with giant fridges and freezers.

Shelves were piled high with every delicacy imaginable. 'Just help yourselves,' he said as he wandered off. He refused any payment or even a drink. How very kind. We had been saved.

We had heeded what we thought were the wise words of various friends who had recently sailed through the Bahamas. They suggested we avoid the more southerly islands, hence our long hop from the Virgins up to San Salvador. The southern islands, they said, were the hotbed for drug running, murders and pirates. When we reached San Salvador we met other friends who suggested the exact opposite, and told us to move on as soon as we could.

Alarm bells did ring when we took a walk up a dusty track at Hawks Nest Creek on Cat Island. Among the swampy mangroves and dense foliage we came across what was obviously a landing strip for a light aircraft. It had been mysteriously carved out through the jungly undergrowth. We followed signs to a 'bar', but that was a big mistake. You could hear a pin drop as the very tall, broad-shouldered, dodgy-looking guy bedecked in gold chains glared suspiciously at us when we asked if we might buy a beer. Two massive ferocious dogs barked and snarled at us. I turned to John. 'I don't think we need to be here. Let's go – *now*.' We left, not bothering to finish our beers.

So we never knew what the true story was about the islands; one never does. But it is certainly true that drug-running is in operation, and pirates do exist, and unfortunately if one happens to be in the wrong place at the wrong time one might get bumped off.

The Bahamas are an extraordinarily beautiful cruising ground. The shallow waters and reefs around the islands mean one's navigation has to be spot on, which John's always was. It was a curious feeling to be speeding along in such shallow, crystal-clear waters, often with no more than twelve feet beneath us.

The Intracoastal Waterway begins in the Gulf of Mexico and runs all the way up the east coast for 3,000 miles. Having entered it at West Palm Beach we plied our way for over 500 miles north to Charleston, South Carolina. We were never tempted to swim as the water was murky, nothing like the beautiful clear waters we had left behind. Often the rather ugly head of a manatee (also known as a sea cow) would pop up beside the boat.

At midday on 12 April we passed the Kennedy Space Center at Cape Canaveral where in the early hours of that same morning 600,000 people had been dotted all along the coast and beaches to watch the Columbia Space Shuttle being launched on the first of its twenty-eight missions. It took to the skies almost exactly twenty years after the first manned space flight of Yuri Gagarin. We could not believe we had missed witnessing such a moment of history, but it was not to be.

Negotiating the many bridges of the waterway was my least favourite thing in all the world – especially the bridges where the operator would lift the bridge to what he had estimated would give adequate clearance in order for us to pass underneath it with our 40-foot mast. Often as we approached it seemed there could not possibly be enough clearance. I used to hold my breath and disappear down below in hysterical panic, which made poor, long-suffering John very irritated. We did later hear of a boat that was badly damaged when the bridge clipped the top of the mast, so perhaps my hysteria was not so unreasonable.

Realising we were running behind schedule to meet the end of the race, just for a change having secured the boat in a marina, we took a bus, northwards from Charleston to Rhode Island. The one-hundred and three boats in the Observer double-handed trans-Atlantic race left Plymouth on 6 June. Britain's favourite was Robin Knox-Johnston on his catamaran *Sea Falcon*. But on Saturday 20 June, after fourteen days, thirteen hours and fifty-eight minutes, Chay Blyth and Rob James crossed the finish line in *Brittany Ferries GB*, winning the race.

Going out on the spectator boat to greet Chay and Rob was incredibly exciting. The sea was boiling, white with spray and the foaming wakes streaming out from behind the hundreds of spectator boats of all shapes and sizes. Lots of corks were flying about that day.

Very tragically, some years later when Rob was sailing his 60-foot trimaran from Cowes to Plymouth he fell overboard off the coast of Devon and died. He was only thirty-six years old.

Following the boat's success, I had a feeling that there was going to be a turning of the tide.

Chapter 20

Terra firma

A lazy morning in bed with my boys

Life was suddenly moving on in an unforeseen direction, and it seemed we could not swim against its tide. After the record-breaking race win of the trimaran *Brittany Ferries GB*, John had enquiries for further designs, and his career took off. He went on to become one of the world's leading multihull designers.

As well as it being an interesting and adventurous lifestyle, in some ways living afloat can sometimes feel restrictive and exhausting, especially with a little one on board. And we were a family now. So having sailed our final leg up to Virginia on *Sweet Painted Lady* we left her secure in the marina at the Naval Station Norfolk VA. At this juncture life seemed a bit topsy turvy. We had endless discussions as to how, and if, we could fit the somewhat spartan and nomadic boating lifestyle that we loved and had become used to into the changing jigsaw puzzle that we were now facing.

I shed more tears on the sad day when finally, after much deliberation with gritted teeth, we contacted a yacht broker and put the boat up for sale. Although we welcomed this new chapter, the thought of returning to dry land and turning our backs on the cruising life was tinged with sadness. Having made the decision to sell *Sweet Painted Lady* I lived for a while with a terrible sense of betrayal. Would we ever put another boat afloat?

On returning to England we initially went to stay with my mother again in Norfolk and John quickly set up a makeshift office in one of the bedrooms. The county has always seemed to me rather reminiscent of an island. Bordered on the north and east by its spectacular, heavenly coastline, it is out on a limb. Once one has arrived, there is really nowhere else to go other than to head off into the Wash and the North Sea, as we had done in the boat. Patient and welcoming as my mother was, living alongside each other was not the easiest thing for any of the three of us. We decided it was time to settle in our own home somewhere else.

Much as we loved Norfolk, after a few months we found a wonderful little cottage to rent on the water's edge beside the River Luck at Gurnard Marsh on the Isle of Wight. We were happy to be returning to the island which had made such an impression on us on our initial cruise south.

It seems I have often gravitated towards islands. They have always featured in curious and various ways in my life. As a child I remember choosing the smallest room in the house as my bedroom, perhaps because it felt womb-like and I felt safe within the confines of its walls. It felt like being on my very own little island. My refuge. My sanctuary. Being marooned at boarding school I could liken to living on a desert island.

But more recently I have come to appreciate the security that the inevitable boundaries of an island naturally create. There is only so far one can go in any one direction. In a way the boat represented an island too, and having explored most of the Caribbean islands we now found ourselves returning to yet another: the lyrically beautiful part of the South of England that Queen Victoria loved and called simply 'The Island'.

The transition from the boating life to life ashore was made easier since the idyllic position of our new home, albeit only temporary, was right on the edge of the Solent. We were still living close to the elements. The cottage was perched on a small promontory but so near to the crumbling sea wall that in rough weather the waves would break right over the garden. During the occasional fierce winter storm, the sea spray would come lashing down the chimney, virtually extinguishing our open fire.

An encounter with another island had begun.

Orion, who was now aged two, was used to the water and spent most of his days wearing his Viking helmet happily playing knee-deep in the river. He floated out to sea his little boats, which we had made from driftwood gathered from the shore.

We had managed to cram the entire contents of the boat into a container roughly 4 ft x 3 ft, and had it shipped back to England. When it arrived, having emptied it we transformed the wooden crate into a perfect playhouse for Orion and his friends.

Nine months passed and *Sweet Painted Lady* had not sold, so it was 'decisions, decisions' all over again. We arranged for a professional delivery skipper to sail her back across the Atlantic, but on the very day he was due to depart from Norfolk, Virginia, the broker called us and said he had a buyer. We understood that a fireman from New York had bought her, repainted her white and renamed her *Celebration*.

More tears. We never saw her again. To this day I am still in search of her.

There was a silver lining: having sold the boat, we were able to put down the deposit on a house which we had miraculously found after searching for well over a year. When I first set eyes on it I was immediately reminded of High Barn. It had the same feeling about it and, just like High Barn, had a beautiful willow tree growing in the middle of the garden. We were so pleased and lucky to have found it, and I was excited that at last I could put down my own roots and make my very own home ashore.

The vendors had received several offers on the house, but kindly accepted our slightly lower one. They liked the idea that our family would be able to enjoy the beautiful forest location. Orion was so excited and handed over his contribution, his little bag of hard-earned pocket money. Mostly pennies.

The cottage bordering Parkhurst Forest, up on the hill of Mark's

Corner, was just a mile from the sea at Gurnard. It was perfect for us, ideal for growing lots of vegetables in the large garden. And after a year, once we had settled down, it was ideal for growing our family as well.

I was overjoyed when on 14 November 1985, safe and sound, Sky Robert was born.

I was so fortunate to have Mary Cronk as my midwife. She happened to live locally and had spent a lot of time with her husband sailing on their small boat. We had plenty in common, so in addition to my birthing plan we had a great deal to chat about whenever she visited us.

Mary was an independent midwife, known both nationally and internationally as having a radical and compassionate approach. She inspired two generations of midwives, was an expert on breech births, and was awarded an MBE for services to midwifery. She naturally understood that I was a little nervous, having experienced the emergency in my previous pregnancy. I had planned well and hoped to be able to have the baby at home, under her expert guidance, straightforward and cosy in front of the huge log fire in our sitting room. But at the last minute I lost my nerve and we dashed to the hospital, just a few miles down the road. Mary respected my decision and, as we bounced along the very bumpy road in her little mini, my contractions came to an abrupt halt. But within half an hour of arriving at the hospital Sky was born. I was home with my beautiful little baby within five hours.

Sky's birth was a very easy one, a wonderful experience. As I was cutting the umbilical cord I remember so well exclaiming: 'Wow. I would love to be able to give birth every single day.'

Growing up at the White Cottage was a great opportunity for our two boys to be free range. The forest was essentially their back garden. They knew all the criss-crossing paths and we had amusing names for the many meeting places: 'Bench Corner'; 'Primrose River Valley'; 'Dark Woods'; 'Humps and Bumps'; 'Silvern Lane'; and 'The Tarzan Swing'. They loved all the hide-aways and dens which we were always building. We had afternoon and evening picnics, Halloween parties and the occasional camping out on a summer's evening among the daisies in the beautiful open field in the middle of the forest. We ferried everything we needed in a wheelbarrow, and would set up camp, light a fire and sit round and cook 'dampers'. As the boys got older, biking at 'Humps and Bumps' was one of their favourite pastimes. All these adventures we loved, shared and enjoyed.

Barrow boy. Sky aged two with the fruits of our labours, vegetables all grown in our garden at the White Cottage

The photograph albums bulge with memories of those days. One of my favourites is a picture of Sky in the wheelbarrow virtually buried beneath all the vegetables which we had grown and just picked for supper. Another shows Orion in the garden floating in the large paddling pool on board his raft. He had ingeniously made it from bits and bobs he had found in the garage and garden.

There was so much exploring to do on the island as well: walks on the downs, or sledging with friends in the winter, night hikes, festivals and fayres, camping at Newtown Creek, pirate parties on the shore. And as we were never far from one beach or another, the car was usually loaded up with everything watersports-wise, all set for the next Saturday's 'boys and their toys' expedition. Surf boards, water skis, kites, bats and balls, life jackets, buckets and spades, blow-up plastic boats were all chucked into the car and our Mirror dinghy on its trailer would often be towing behind .

We had many wonderful holidays abroad too, in South Africa, America, Canada, France, Spain, Portugal and Bulgaria. The most memorable one was when we drove down through France, over the

Afloat. Orion aged six. Off on his voyage across the paddling pool in his ingenious design. An old tin bath and tyre all topped off with a colourful umbrella

Pyrenees, diagonally across Spain to Portugal in our pale-blue Citroën 2CV. Orion, then six years old, would not be parted from his huge bag of favourite toys; Sky was just getting the hang of putting his feet to the ground, and was only content if he was supported in his little wheelie-walker contraption. So that was jammed into the car along with hundreds of nappies which I stuffed into all the possible crevices, along with everything else under the sun needed for a family of four heading for a six-week sailing holiday on a catamaran.

We all survived the journey, the holiday, each other and the mosquitos.

The catamaran had been loaned to us by a kind client of John's. It was John's design. We found ourselves hankering after another boat and, now that our appetite had been whetted once again, it would not be damped down.

Preparing for our Portuguese road trip. Me with Sky in my arms and Orion. How will we all squeeze into the 2CV? But we managed

Family life was fairly chaotic. With our two young boys five years apart, like most families we found ourselves juggling a hundred things, trying to please all the people all the time, which of course was impossible. With John's parents in South Africa and my mother in Norfolk we were going it solo, with no hands-on grandparents conveniently round the corner to call on when we were desperate for a moment's reprieve. Daddy was upstairs in his design office with his head down earning the money, while Mummy was downstairs wading through the toys and running her somewhat different show.

Meals were a bit of a smorgasbord, since John usually needed a hearty meal while I was often attempting to stick to some kind of stupid diet which was not working; one child liked a certain food which the other one didn't. Sky loved Emmental cheese but would only eat the bits with the holes in, so he often left the table saying he was hungry. Catering for all these different tastes nearly drove me crazy.

I sometimes insisted on a moment of calm when everyone seemed content with whatever was on their respective plates and I would quote my dear father. One of his favourite sayings was: 'Look at the picture rail.'

When we were children, having gathered all the fruit and veg from the garden, and after mother had laboured over making yet another delicious meal (cooking was not her favourite occupation) my father would insist that we paused, looked up at the picture rail, appreciated all the tastes, and give thanks for our food and to our mother for having prepared it so beautifully. I always thank my taste buds. I think they are pretty astonishing – our brains being able to identify and differentiate all the scrumptious flavours and textures. At school and sometimes at home we would say grace too: 'For what we are about to receive may the Lord make us truly grateful.' I liked saying grace. Nowadays it's 'Blessings on the meal' or 'Bon appétit'.

Happy holidays. Sky and me in Portugal at a beachside restaurant

Up to this point I had not had time to explore my own interest in the arts, nor had I the least idea what if anything I might want to pursue, but without the physical space in which to experiment I felt a bit stifled and frustrated. The kitchen table was not an adequate or suitable work space. So one day I made an executive decision and took it upon myself to divide the huge playroom into two rooms. We built a stud wall and, joy oh joy, I had my first little studio area. I could not find an answer to John's question as to what I was going to use the room for. I just knew I needed some kind of a work bench, and I managed to convince myself that it was OK to take some physical space for myself.

The boys and their friends hiding in the swimming pool lockers

Often when the children were finally tucked up asleep, although exhausted I would get a new lease of life. Having some creative fun, I'd just play around a bit like my own children at playschool, using paints, papers, glue, fabrics and other people's odd cast-offs. I would rush to every possible jumble sale on Saturdays. I hauled treasure from old wayside skips: bundles of discarded tangled electrical cables, rusty tins, broken glass. And when I spied a little gem lying in the gutter having picked it up I would let out a shriek of delight. I gathered beach glass and driftwood, barnacle-encrusted pieces of metal, bricks and stones, and I gradually accumulated an array of all sorts of materials, just anything that I came across in my path to drag back and eventually use in my creative den.

I found it fascinating to ponder over all my finds. I was always intrigued about their past life. I made 'found object' collages, cards, boxart, picture frames, sculptures, things for the garden, wall hangings, macramé and mobiles. I found all this tinkering away was a therapeutic pastime. I began to sell a few pieces along the way.

I also made some very original clothes for the children. On a mufti day the boys' trousers were often admired by mothers at the school gate. I had bought old rugby jumpers from jumble sales, my favourite being a green-and-red-striped one. I chopped the sleeves off and then sewed them up the middle to form the crutch. It's a bit complicated to explain, but the two sleeves had now become the two legs. With elastic round the waist, in a flash there was a brilliant, fun, designer pair of trews. Such trendy little boys I thought. But in all truth I think they were a bit embarrassed at all the comments and questions as to where I had bought them. They probably might have preferred to be wearing a normal pair of jeans from Matalan.

A family collage

While John was upstairs working on every possible permutation for the design of his latest commissioned multihull, his head throbbing with the most complicated mathematical calculations, I was happily and busily looking after the children – and when there was time having fun doing 'my arty thing' downstairs. I was spontaneously following my nose, having all sorts of ideas and cobbling things together any old how in a slightly random way. I was attempting though to make something out of nothing. The Italians have a phrase for this which I love: *l'arte di arrangiarsi*.

I have never succeeded in acquiring any specific skill. My ideas tend to run away with themselves, and then somewhat overenthusiastically and impatiently I just bodge things together. The other day I was wondering if there was such a thing as a degree in bodging; perhaps I would award myself one. It is an interesting word, so misunderstood I think. It originates from the days when highly skilled woodturners, itinerant folk, lived in the woods of the Chiltern hills. Having felled the trees they artfully turned the legs for chairs made out of the beech wood where they were living.

So, if you are ever temped to call yourself a bodger, as I have done, remember you are in fact a highly skilled person as opposed to somebody who just chucks things together. Making a bodge job of something is actually a skill. I like to think of it that way anyway. I don't think my father would have been very impressed by my round-about thinking. But I have decided for my own amusement I might as well be proud of my bodging skills.

We were very busy during the boys' early school days with all the usual sports days, school plays, Christmas fayres, carol concerts, and trying to keep on top of homework, helping them with their reading and having friends round to tea after school. Holidays were always best, and it was during those weeks that we usually found ourselves discussing the possibility of the next boat. Could we fulfil the long-held dream of sailing with our boys into the Pacific, perhaps even around the world?

John started working on the design for a larger boat, a catamaran. We had learnt so much from our six years living onboard, and his design incorporated many of our ideas which would potentially provide a much more comfortable and realistic home if we were ever to go cruising again. It would also double up as a suitable boat for chartering, for fishing trips, even a means of transporting people from island to island. It would be a kind of all-round work boat or even a ferry of some kind. All these options were possible means by which one could also make some money.

I was preoccupied with the boys and a little distracted at times with working on my various random arty creations. I was having thoughts that I might like to start some kind of training in the therapeutic use of the arts and then by chance in 1990 I happened upon an interesting-sounding course: 'The Living Art Training'. I signed up and was determined to commit to this year-long programme. It meant I would be in London away from the family one weekend each month. This was a big decision, a giant step. One which I did not take lightly.

Meanwhile, a Devonshire boatyard started building the catamaran. When the shell was finished, although the interior was far from complete, we sailed her from Devon to the island and found a berth in the Island Harbour Marina on the east side of the River Medina. We named the boat *Zazen*, which translates literally as 'seated meditation', a meditative discipline that is a typical practice of the Zen Buddhist tradition.

This was a painful and strange time. John and I had to face the fact that, while the boat was taking shape, simultaneously our relationship had been collapsing.

We muddled along for a while but in the end were defeated. The testing challenge of trying to understand, unravel and accept the complex dynamics within our relationship was exhausting. There are always two sides to every story, but from my perspective, very briefly, I had to accept that I felt I had lived for too long in John's shadow; I knew it was time for me to sing my own song. I would have to go it alone and '*take courage, risk the flight, for you are done with holding onto, dark side of the moon, there is no rush*'.

The above words are a few lines of a poem from a collection of twelve which I wrote during that dark period. The poems were eventually set to music and recorded on my CD *The Journey of Trust*.

I wish all those years ago I had known of the Serenity Prayer: *'God, grant me the serenity to accept the things I cannot change; courage to change the things I can; and the wisdom to know the difference.'* Those words might have been of some comfort.

During those first dreadful months of our separation, Orion and Sky spent time with both John and I, toing and froing between the White Cottage home where I was still living and the unfinished boat *Zazen* where John was living aboard in the Marina. The lives of all of us had been turned upside down.

But one must take responsibility for one's actions. So, to be more accurate: I felt we had turned our lives and the lives of our children upside down.

Chapter 21

Singlehanding

Pop up poppy hiding in the rocks in the Sierra Nevada.
The flower that changed my name in 1993

I had never managed to pluck up enough courage to sail *Sweet Painted Lady* single-handedly, although I did come close to it once when we were living in the Virgin Islands. I really wanted to sail from St Thomas across to one of my favourite bays on Jos Van Dyke. I thought I could do it, provided John was alongside in a rescue boat in case things went pear-shaped, but I chickened out at the last moment. Not having achieved it I cannot say what that experience might have felt like; but now, finding myself alone as a single parent, I felt that I was single-handing. At times I felt I needed a rescue boat.

John and I had spent nearly twenty years together, and had shared many amazing adventures. In a sense, through them I felt we had grown up alongside each other and grown together. In the end, sadly, we had also grown apart and agreed that it was time to go our separate ways. It was mercifully an amicable parting.

The decree absolute was finally granted in November 1994 on the grounds of irretrievable breakdown. It has taken me a long time to realise that going through a divorce is a form of bereavement. I felt responsible that our separation was inevitably going to have an impact on the lives of our two boys, who were eleven and six at the time. Knowing this, I also felt irresponsible.

My concern was for their wellbeing, and I had to fight off my feelings of guilt, shame, fear, failure, inadequacy, uncertainty, despair and loneliness and every horrible feeling that comes with such a trauma.

During the worst days, when I was having panic attacks, I felt I was having a breakdown. I was not sure how or if I could handle all the mixed feelings. I had all sorts of little sayings jotted down in my handbag notebook.

'Forgiveness is giving up all hope of a better past.' I thought long and hard about this. I had to forgive myself, and forgive John.

It was at this stage that I threw out a lifeline to myself. I sought help in the form of a therapist. She helped me to believe in myself again, and over time I gradually regained confidence. She suggested that, rather than seeing myself as having a breakdown, I could turn it on its head and celebrate. I was in fact 'having a breakthrough'. I thought this approach to my situation was a positive and reassuring one.

But I found it difficult to accept that I had not always been discerning – that some of my decisions and actions had not always been the wisest. But dwelling in hindsight was useless. The past was the past, and all I could do was hope to learn from my mistakes. I came to believe that we are only ever doing the very best we know how to at the time. How can one do more than that? I had to believe that I had done the best I possibly could trying to salvage our marriage. I had certainly not given up on it easily.

With counselling help and the mediation services we negotiated a financial settlement. It was another very sad day when our family home was sold. The driver of the huge pantechnicon saved the day by suggesting that I drive my little Citroën 2CV into the removal van rather than chugging along in it behind him all the way up to Norfolk. That was such a great idea, and did make me laugh. The gigantic vehicle was already crammed full with the contents of our home, so I then filled my car with all the remaining bits and bobs, carefully drove it up the ramp and then jammed in all the garden paraphernalia around it. The final thing to fit in was our black-and-white cat, Four Paws. The poor nervous creature was clearly upset and weed all over the kind driver's bedding.

My master plan had been a well thought out one – well, as best it could be under the circumstances. I had applied to the Norwich School of Art to do a three-year visual studies degree and had been offered a place. It seemed I had come full circle, returning to the art school in which my parents' paths had crossed all those years ago. I wondered, in a very light-hearted way, whether I might be so lucky, that history might repeat itself and that I might have a similar fortuitous meeting.

I had always been intrigued by my mother's description of the mosaic floor in the entrance foyer of the art school (presumably installed in 1889 when the building was constructed to house the Norwich Technical Institute). Twenty bees surrounding the castle and lion emblem seemed to symbolise industriousness. One of the lecturers speculated that perhaps bees were meant to represent collective rather than individual endeavour, and could even provide a model of society in which all workers play an equal part. Who knows? Recent research has concluded that bees are able to make the best possible decisions for their overall wellbeing. Having done so they can then function in positive and effective ways, having their own best interest at heart. How clever of them. More switched on than us poor floundering human beings .

Every time I entered the school I always paused, admired the beautiful bee mosaic, and thought of my Mother and Father having met there, grateful that after all those years my mother had made the very wise decision to marry my father.

Back in Norfolk I was closer at hand and able to help look after my mother, who was not getting any younger. We had all agreed that she was now too vulnerable to be living alone at High Barn. I would see Orion and Sky as often as I possibly could – every weekend, I had hoped, and during their school holidays. They were living with John, who had moved to London with his new wife, having sold the catamaran, *Zazen*, to an Australian, who with his family had sailed the boat to Oz.

I had rented an attic room, a bedsit in Norwich. It was rather dark, strangely near yet another noisy roundabout. I had to share the kitchen with the peculiar young landlord who kept his huge, ferocious dog in a cage in the utility area. It would bark incessantly whenever I was in the kitchen cooking my supper. So, I gave up using his kitchen in the end and just ate salads.

In the words of the old saying that John Lennon quoted in a song lyric, *'Life is what happens to you while you are busy making other plans.'*

In July 1996, very shortly after my return to Norfolk and before I had actually started my degree, my mother became ill very suddenly, and died of E.coli food poisoning. This was a terrible time. The family gathered and we knew she would have preferred to have passed away in her beautiful garden in which she often used to sleep out in her truckle bed under the stars, beside the apple tree. So, we brought her home from the hospital and laid her coffin under her beloved beech tree. She had written a beautiful poem about this tree and she rested there for a night before the funeral. Brewy, her golden retriever to whom she was devoted, laid for several days on her empty bed grieving for her.

Following my mother's death my sister Anabel decided to buy High Barn, where she lived for a further twenty-five years until recently moving on. We were all so lucky as a family being able to spend many more years visiting the beautiful place in which all three of us had grown up, and where we could continue to enjoy camping weekends, arts gatherings and all kinds of festivities. Much water has passed under the bridge now. Both my sisters still live in Norfolk and each has two children and between them nine grandchildren.

My marriage had failed, our family home had been sold, my children were living with their father, my mother had died. That following year, 1997, was yet another of loss, sadness, adjustment and uncertainty.

During that summer I used to frequent Norwich Cathedral. On the one occasion when I was late entering for the service I was immediately aware of a very sombre atmosphere. Many of the congregation were sniffing and crying. I couldn't think why. The woman beside me whispered: 'Princess Diana has been killed in a car crash in Paris.' The outpouring of grief that followed was extraordinary. The world felt the loss of the fairy tale and of the princess herself.

At the time I know I felt I had been living through a never-ending period of drama and crisis. I think I had been going through my own identity crisis too, following our divorce, not really knowing who I was any more, and not even having a clear sense of what name I wished to be known by.

I have always thought it is so important to be comfortable with one's name. To really like it. After all, it is the first thing that people learn about you. You don't go to a cocktail party in your little black dress, stand there and introduce yourself as 'Blank'. Nor are you likely to attend an important conference wearing your latest bespoke suit with the name tag attached to the lanyard around your neck reading: 'Mr Blank. Project Manager.'

You see your name multitudinous times on every dreaded bill, for a start. You use it in all correspondence, sign it on your cheques (if they still exist). Your name is on your birth certificate, on your death certificate, and of course on your gravestone too. It lives on with you long after you are gone. So in my view, while you are still in the land of the living, it's nice to feel good about your name.

I was surprised when I was running creative arts workshops, when doing an exercise around names, how many people said they hated their name and had always fancied a different one to the one their parents had chosen for them. So, for fun sometimes, for the duration of the course I would suggest they choose what they considered to be a perfect name for themselves. Jane became Blanche, Thelma became Trinity, and Fiona became Foxie – and everyone was happy.

I was christened Miranda April and I always liked the Miranda bit, but I was not, as I have said earlier, fond of my second name of April. I love my maiden name of Symington and of course I will forever be a 'Symington'. My marriage to Kendall meant that I became a 'Carey'; then with my marriage to John I became a 'Shuttleworth'. So, after all those years of various permutations, when finding myself a single woman again, I was wondering, who on earth am I now then?

With support from my therapist, one specific aspect in the process of rebuilding and healing myself was to discover my true name. A name which once and for all I would identify with and one which I would like to be known by ... So I took myself off to Spain on a mission in search of it.

I was heading for Cortijo Romero, a holistic healing centre outside the small village of Órgiva in the foothills of the Sierra Nevada mountains. In previous years I had attended several interesting courses there. I loved this place. It had become my second home. The courses were very varied, each with a different focus, ranging from arts, creativity and self expression, wellbeing for the body and mind, yoga, creative writing, relaxation, rebirthing transformation, meditation and much more.

As I set off for Spain that week I knew that Nigel, an inspiring man, a great character and the then owner of Cortijo Romero, was to lead the group. The title of his course: 'Cast Out the Old, Invite In the New', had struck a chord. It sounded perfect.

We walked, talked, wrote and swam, meditated, painted, ate and laughed. One of the planned excursions was a long hike up the arid, dusty riverbed into the foothills of the Sierra Nevada. It was extremely hot. Not a drop of water was flowing. No plants were growing.

Nigel had suggested that all twelve of us in the group walk slowly in silence, taking time to let ourselves know exactly what it was in our lives that we wished to change or cast out. He suggested that, when we had done so, we should envisage something new that we would like to invite into our lives. I don't quite know why or how, but I knew in my bones that this day was about to be a very special one. One which would mark a turning point in my life.

I wandered along the riverbed overcome with emotion, a little fearful, tearful. As I walked I gathered a few old, dry sticks, some twisted twigs, a prickly branch, a handful of spiky dried grass, scraps of paper, a page of an old newspaper, a rusty tin can, a torn plastic bag... all these things which randomly had caught my eye. At that point I remember thinking perhaps I would preserve them somehow, take them home with me and turn them into one of my found object box art works of art. I sat and rested on a rock for a while and was suddenly struck with horror at the sight of my pathetic collection. I seemed to know that all these bits and bobs represented the unwanted, unloved aspects of myself, all the confusion and doubt that I was at last ready and willing to dump once and for all. I must put this miserable collection aside, I told myself, leave it here. Let go of the negativity of the past and look to the future afresh.

As I got up and turned to continue my walk up the valley I suddenly noticed a tiny little pale red poppy growing in the middle of the dry, grey, shaley, almost undistinguishable path. It was no bigger than a pound coin. How could it possibly have existed in these semi-desert conditions, isolated with no protection, no shade, no water? It had not been trampled on, either. It was clearly not thriving, but it had not given up the will to live. It had survived.

As I cupped my hands around it I burst into tears.

I collected some large stones and placed them carefully around this beautiful little flower. I sat beside it for a good hour and finally, having photographed it I calmed myself and, although I wanted to stay longer I tore myself away, and re-joined the other walkers further up the valley.

On returning to the centre a few hours later we shared our various experiences. I explained to Nigel that my new name had been revealed to me. I told him that from now on my name would be Miranda Poppy. We laughed, as this did sound a little ridiculous. Miranda and Poppy did not exactly fit poetically alongside each other. Nor did they roll at all musically off the tongue. Nigel had the answer. The Spanish name for a poppy, he told me was *amapola*.

An orchard lay beyond the buildings, and Nigel had laid out rugs among the wild poppies and lemon trees. Having magically arranged for food and drink to be brought out, he then quietly announced that this was to be my christening party. Of course by now, with such a propensity for weeping, I was in tears yet again.

As I danced my way through Málaga airport on my homeward journey I was feeling ecstatic to have found my name at last, one which I am so happy to be known by. People often comment on it and enquire about its origin. 'Well, yes, there is a bit of a long-winded story attached to my name, but the abbreviated version is that *amapola* is the Spanish for poppy – but, no, I am not Spanish.' At which they look bemused. They sometimes ask yet more questions and I have to make the excuse that I haven't time to elaborate. So this is the price I sometimes have to pay for being so bothered about my name. I don't regret it for a moment. After all this time, this is who I feel I am: Miranda Amapola.

I felt that I had been guided. My true name had been miraculously

Returning home. Keeping cool in Malaga airport. It was so hot that day but I was very happy to be returning home, having discovered my true name at last

gifted to me through nature and this helped to convince me to take the next important step. The first thing that I did on returning home was to officially change my name by deed poll.

But still without a proper home I felt all at sea, betwixt and between, not knowing in a practical sense quite what to do. With my sons in London, my mother having died, I knew I would have to make a new plan. I was enjoying the degree course, but I needed to turn the page. I had been living back in Norfolk for a little over a year and I wanted above all to provide a home for Orion and Sky as soon as I could.

Every night my eyes were drawn to a very special postcard which I had propped up on the table beside my bed. I would fall asleep pondering the beautiful image of Tennyson Down. I had set my heart on returning to the Isle of Wight, the lyrical island which I had previously sailed around, walked around, flown over in a light aircraft, and along the hilly backbone of which I had trekked. It was not long before I had found a little stone cottage in the village of Niton, on the southernmost tip of the island just to the west of Ventnor.

Niton nestles at the foot of the downs and has perfect access to numerous footpaths and bridleways. It is fascinating to read about its ancient history of smuggling. One can still wander through the tunnels which were used by the pirates for shifting their booty across the island way back then.

Some previously invested money together with an inheritance after my dear mother died enabled me to buy my own property. The cottage which I bought backed onto a field where the sheep peacefully grazed. I would sit out every night in the tiny little back garden overjoyed to have my own home again – but sometimes it was not quite so peaceful. It seemed that the only way the farmer could round up his sheep in the evenings was to curse and swear at them, his angry voice resounding across the fields for hours on end. He was in stiff competition with my resident blackbird whose sweet serenade at dusk I did prefer.

I set to work renovating the cottage. All my furniture and belongings which had been in storage in Norfolk were shipped back to the island yet again, and within weeks of moving in both boys came back to live with me. They settled back into their island schools. Having sorted out the Niton cottage, I spent the following four years juggling my single-parent life, picking up on all sorts of work and attempting at last to provide some sense of stability for us all.

Variety was certainly the spice of life during this period. In between doing the school runs I fitted in a morning shift at a sailing centre where one of my jobs was to prepare the spuds for lunch. I chucked tons of them into one of those vast, industrial-style potato-peeling machines. Having switched it on I would have to block my ears as the rumble, tumble churning noise was so deafening. I refilled the horrible Tupperware containers with cornflakes and Sugar Puffs, laid the tables, swept up the crumbs from the night before, had a quick whisk round with the Henry Hoover, folded napkins and beat a quick retreat, sometimes taking a moment to pause by the riverside before heading back home.

The boys and I had fun planning some exciting holidays. We went on the trip of a lifetime to America. As well as taking all the usual tourist excursions we had all sorts of fun adventures. We bought roller blades and bombed it around New York's Central Park where we came across a man taking an alligator for a walk on a lead. We then met a lady with a pig dressed up with a white frilly bib around its neck. An elaborately dressed blonde lady with a very loud voice delighted in showing us her pet, an albino rabbit. She had painted its toenails red and was proudly taking it for an afternoon stroll on its diamenté-encrusted red leather lead.

Sky had set his heart on buying the very latest gadget, an egg-shaped, hand-held, pocket-sized, digital virtual pet, a Japanese Tamagotchi. We scoured the shops and eventually found one at the famous Macy's store. They were the very latest craze and were selling out fast. This demanding little toy whose cartoon image would appear on the screen completely dominated our lives for the first few days. It had to have its nappy changed, be put down for a rest at regular intervals, be fed or it might die, be kept warm or it might temporarily give up the ghost. Miraculously, if you attended to its every need, once grown to adulthood it could marry and have babies. Frustrating beyond belief, it was completely bonkers – and only a short-lived fad, I was pleased to discover.

Just recently, having done some research, I see that if you are fortunate enough to still own your original version of this little treasure (which possibly cost you around £8 back in the late nineties), it is estimated now to be worth £3,500. I must tell Sky. If you believe in miracles, it might even still be alive and would be willing to pay for another trip to New York.

Before returning home to England, we visited friends in Maine and I was determined to visit one more very special place which I had heard about: Pacem in Terris; Peace on Earth. This little oasis happened to be not far off our route from Maine back to New York, so we caught a bus and arrived out of the blue to a warm welcome by the Dutch artist, sculptor and writer Frederick Franck.

One day he and his wife had discovered a derelict old watermill by the Wawayanda River in Warwick, NY, that was for sale. They decided to buy it and transform the space into a peace garden, a sacred space conducive to contemplation, recollection, meditation and prayer. They lovingly restored it with their own hands, and with help from volunteers. It was financed entirely by contributions from those who felt in sympathy with their vision. It became an extraordinarily beautiful place. Meandering paths wind their way through wild gardens, the original walls of the watermill have been preserved, and a simple auditorium has been built where exhibitions, concerts, talks, services and marriages can all take place.

There were other holidays, too, but that was a special one, culminating in our visit to such a beautiful and rejuvenating place. Maybe I was trying to compensate in some way for all the upheaval and loss that I imagine my boys were experiencing, and also now living apart from their father. As I tried to rebuild some kind of a life for us, together in our new Niton cottage home, I was always hoping and praying that they might at least be feeling a little more settled.

I gradually transformed one of the downstairs rooms into a studio. I got on with my art again, making driftwood mirrors, frames, assemblages, anything that came to mind. I felt more inspired after my year at art school and had come away with new ideas.

Orion's seventeenth birthday was looming and he politely hinted one day that perhaps a party might be on the cards; could he commandeer my studio as the disco dive for the night? I agreed to this, but had little idea what else was in store. The entire contents of the fishpond in the back garden were emptied, and it was filled instead with ice and bottles of beer (the goldfish had been thoughtfully rehoused in a large bucket for the duration).

I was cleverly lulled into a false sense of security having been told it was to be a 'proper' party, that the dress code was DJs, and that all his friends were very civil and polite. I had no doubt about that, but under the influence and with a shortage of females it was not long before a jealous fight was brewing over one of the very pretty miniskirted girls. I saw a few lads off down the lane and told them in no uncertain terms they could continue their fight elsewhere but not in my home, thank you. I wandered round gathering up glasses and tipped the contents down the sink – better that way than down their throats. John did a fly past to wish Orion a happy birthday and disappeared off for dinner. One lad ended up a little worse for wear in the garden pond while four others ended up together groaning in the bath in the early hours. I served them hot chocolate when they finally fell into various beds.

Despite it all, it was one of those parties which has gone down in history as one of the best. They all survived to tell the tale and recently at the wedding of one of these friends, the best man referred to it in his amusing speech.

I had renamed the cottage at the top of Pan Lane 'Scallop Shell Cottage'. I liked the pretty, age-old image of the scallop shell, which is used as a sign of direction along the Camino, pointing pilgrims towards their destination of the cathedral city of Santiago de Compostela. The symbol of the scallop shell is worn by pilgrims and placed outside the houses of those who are offering a bed for the night for the weary walkers of the way. It provided assurance to the pilgrims that they were on the right track. I felt at last that I was on the right track again, so it seemed a fitting name for our new home.

Orion was soon off to uni, first to Oxford Brookes to study architecture, then transferring to Nottingham Trent where he studied product design and met beautiful Vanessa, who later became his wife. Sky was in his final year at Cowes High School.

I made this driftwood and found object piece as advertising for an exhibition at St James's, Piccadilly.

When I was reflecting on this period of my life I decided to list all the things I had been up to during those four years while living in the cottage at Niton. I surprised myself that I must have been very busy.

I continued with my art

I wrote articles for the magazines Resurgence and Human Potential.

I studied at the Institute for Arts in Therapy and Education.

I recorded a CD of my poems, The Journey of Trust.

I attended the Gabrielle Roth 5Rhythms dance workshops.

I initiated the social, anything-goes, 'Wednesday group meetings'.

I studied practical philosophy with the School of Economic Science.

I had several exhibitions locally and on the mainland.

I trained in reminiscence therapy at Age Exchange in London.

I tutored a women's group run by the Workers Educational Association.

I ran art workshops for the NHS and a craft group for Quay Arts.

I developed and ran 'Treat Yourself' groups for women.

I cooked for sixty people in a campsite for my German musician friend

I spent many hours hauling up driftwood from the beaches.

I rented out my house for short-stay holiday guestsI attended craft fairs selling jewellery cards and decorative guitars.

I hiked along the coastal paths most weekends.

I acted in a Noël Coward revue, Cowardy Custard, at the Apollo Theatre in Newport.

I worked as a care assistant at an NHS unit for clients with profound disabilities.

I was a part-time waitress.

I designed the stage set for the school play, The Tempest.

I helped some friends decorate their son's coffin.

I completed the foundation year of counselling at the Metanoia.

I managed to persuade Sky, fun though it might have been, that it was not a good idea to go on night hikes around the village extracting the cat's eyes from the middle of the road for his unique collection.

I was the Christmas tree fairy at the High Barn Christmas Fair. I sat in my decorated grotto dressed in all my glitter and finery. I invited people to come in and make their wish. As I waved my wand I told one rather glamorous holidaymaker that, having made her wish, if she promised to keep it secret, she might be lucky – it might come true. I met her a year later in the local butcher's shop. Much to my surprise she recognised me as the Christmas tree fairy and told me with delight that her wish had been granted. She had moved house to Norfolk.

I signed up to the Island Artists Open Studios, showing my home, studio and garden to visitors. I have difficulty with the description 'artist'. It jangles me. I find it stressful and difficult trying to describe my work and explain what I do, what I don't do, what I make. I prefer just to think of myself as having come from a creative background. Creativity is in the genes.

But I have to say that, in the end, doing Open Studios was an eye opening experience for me. Having prepared the house, garden and studio as best I could, labelling every artwork and providing careful directions for the mini guided tour, I stood back and allowed those who visited to freely experience my living and working space however they wished. I found it was a pleasure to share my creativity. Without the need to explain anything, the description of 'artist' was conveniently smothered and could temporarily, at least, be forgotten about. What a relief.

Anabel, Antonia and I drew up a proposal for '*The Three Sisters Art Exhibition*'. We had thought it might be an interesting idea to exhibit alongside each other, since the mediums in which we work are very different, but having finally written our profiles we ran out of steam and it has never happened. Perhaps there is still time to resurrect the idea.

I ran several Millennium Resolution Creative Arts Workshops using, as a focus, the inspiring words drawn up by the non-denominational world churches. The words held such promise for a brighter future.

Let there be respect for the Earth
Peace for its people
Love in our lives
Delight in the good
Forgiveness for past wrongs
And from now on a new start

Many people participated in the workshops, but sadly over the past twenty-three years the world seems far from experiencing the peace that we had hoped for.

One of my decorative guitars displayed in Harrods' window as part of their Christmas 'Winter Wonderland' theme

Unlike our small 'boat-life' library my 'land-life' library was extensive and included every self-help book I could lay my hands on. One of my favourites, *'Don't push the river (it flows by itself)'* by Barry Stevens is still a joy to read. From the sticking plaster approach, claiming an overnight quick-fix, to the more well researched theoretical books describing the complex process of emotional healing, I avidly read all these, gleaned what I could, and tried to put some of what I found helpful into practice.

I realise that after throwing myself headlong into all these various working and recreational activities I was gradually gaining more experience. The significant connection between them all was that, while I was interacting with people of all ages, I was also recognising the therapeutic value of the arts in all its forms. This became my passion.

A happy lunch at my Gurnard home

Amid all this work I was wondering about so many things. I was doing my best to be that 'ever-loving Mum', and I was also contemplating yet another move back to the village of Gurnard.

In the summer of 2001, having spent four years in Niton and having eventually found a buyer for Scallop Shell Cottage, we upped sticks yet again. At the time of this move both my sons were now naturally breaking away and forging ahead with their own lives. As the young often wisely do they went off on their worldwide travels and I had to adjust to the reality of the empty nest.

I settled into my tiny Gurnard cottage, only a short walk from the sea. I have heard that, apart from the death of a loved one or a divorce, moving house is high on the list of traumatic experiences. So I have promised myself that I will not be moving ever again. It certainly was an upheaval and one that I would not relish going through again. I wonder if I will manage to keep my own promise.

Chapter 22

The bell that rang true

Roughing it in Cornwall outside the shepherd's hut with the sheep, Itch, Titch, Munch, Mushroom and Puffball

I had spent the best part of eight years on my own, and now it was time to take stock. Although I had become perfectly used to my own company and felt able to spend time alone, was I intending to settle for just that? Possibly with the risk of ending up a sad old lady drifting about for the rest of my life in a rather solitary fashion? This didn't present much of a pretty picture. I knew in my heart of hearts there was something missing. After all, at the age of fifty-six I was still in my youth and had lots I thought I would like to share. So, I decided to be proactive and jump-start myself.

In days gone by, one possible way of meeting a man was to surreptitiously drop one's pure cotton handkerchief in the hope that a well-mannered gentleman passing by might pick it up for one and say, 'How do you do?' And from there on in, it would be love ever after. I don't use cotton handkerchiefs, so I resorted to the modern method and contacted a dating agency.

Funnily enough, looking back to 2002 that method now seems an equally old-fashioned way compared to the sites of today. Having written my neat little letter I popped it into the postbox around the corner. I had described myself, listing my preferences, and stated that I did not fancy meeting up with a smoker, a dog lover or a gentleman who lived on the other side of the world. The deal was that, having paid my £45 (I sent a cheque in the post, which also seems an ancient method of payment), I was then given the details of three 'possibles' whom I could contact at my own leisure. This I duly did.

The first admitted he was a chain smoker; the second told me he was a breeder of bull terriers, it was one of his hobbies. I wondered what other hobbies he might have had. The third gentleman lived in an even more far-flung place than the other side of the world. He was in heaven. His sister who answered the phone told me that her brother had died a month past. Well, poor man, that was sad for him and his sister of course, but a fat lot of use to me.

I called the agency, complained, felt it would be reasonable to have my hard-earned money refunded for services not rendered. They were reluctant to oblige but suggested that they could happily provide me with the names of three more gentlemen. I thought I might as well give it one more try.

I was given three more names, one of which was Richard. I imagined that a long-distance relationship would be hard to maintain, so the fact that Richard lived in Portsmouth, just across the water, bode well.

We agreed to meet at the ferry terminal in Ryde. It was surprising that I recognised him at all, since he had described himself as tall and dark haired. I hoped he might be handsome too. He was not particularly tall and had very little grey hair – in fact he was balding. That was lucky though, since I seem rather attracted to bald-headed gentlemen. Strange how balding gentlemen always seem so embarrassed by their lack of hair. I can't understand it. It crossed my mind if in his excitement of coming to meet me he had forgotten to don his black toupée.

Being modest he had not described himself as very handsome, but indeed he was: a James Dean lookalike, a real dish. He had a kind face, a lovely smile and I had a good feeling about him from the moment we had our first spontaneous hug on this, our very first meeting.

We had shared several telephone conversations before meeting up; I liked the sound of his voice. That was very important to me. I am not fond of voices that seem to sound like 'cheesegraters', 'watered-down milk' or 'metal on metal', or when a person's words seem to disappear down their throat, or flutter away like a bird on the wing almost before they have even uttered them.

During one of our phone chats, Rich told me that as a volunteer he had helped build the tall ship *Tenacious*. I was sitting up on my bed at the time we were having this conversation. From my bedroom window I have a wonderful view of the Solent. As we were speaking, magically as if on a movie set a tall ship slipped into view and sailed past towards Portsmouth. I found that rather serendipitous. Later that day he enquired of the ship's voyage plan and, sure enough, it was confirmed that the vessel was indeed *Tenacious* and she was due back in port that very day. I have always thought this was one of those inexplicably strange coincidences.

On the first day that we met we walked from Ryde to Seaview. Having had some lunch we jumped on the number eight bus clutching our cups of tea served in not-very-nice polystyrene cups. I said I thought it was very significant that we were riding on that route, because in Japanese culture the number eight is sacred. Its two interlocking circles are the symbol of eternity, representing the concept of limitlessness and signal abundance. Poor Rich looked puzzled.

I continued to relate how in the angelic realm number eight meant you would be protected and guided and encouraged on your journey through life. Protected by your soulmate, together you would then have infinite energy – and anyway, in Japan eight is the lucky number. Rich appeared even more confused by this time, wondering what sort of basket-case he might be about to get hitched up with. He politely told me that we were not Japanese, nor were we in Japan. We were in England, to which I replied that I knew we were. He squeezed my hand a little tighter; we got the giggles and spilled the rest of our tea.

We continued to chatter away, and before he left he tried to kiss me underneath an ancient oak tree beside the rather romantic fairy-tale Appley Tower on Ryde Sands. A bit like a teenager I told him he was being far too fast. Kissing would have to wait, and holding hands was perfectly exciting enough for the time being. I had fallen for him though. We met again the following week. I knew I had struck gold.

Rich's nickname at school, given to him by the teachers, was 'Smiler', and his parents used to call him 'Beamer'. Both names were so fitting, as more often than not he did have a smile on his face. Even if he didn't feel particularly cheerful, he would always say it was worth trying to put one on. He was a cup-half-full person, always positive and always grateful. His parents had been bombed out in Portsmouth three times during the war, and he vividly recalled as a child rushing into the Anderson bomb shelter at the bottom of their garden and watching the bombs falling on the church just up the road. As I have often heard, young children, not really understanding what was happening, found the falling of bombs all quite exciting.

As a young man Rich joined the Merchant Navy. After several years at sea he decided he wanted to spend more time back home with his childhood sweetheart. They married. He left the Navy and joined the police force. Sandy and he had four sons, the first of whom died at the age of four. This tragedy was something Rich could never come to terms with. I remember him telling me he was granted one day off following the death of his beloved little first-born child. No compassionate leave, no counselling; no support whatsoever in those days. I cannot imagine the agony of such a loss. It was something he never wished to talk about.

After he had lived through such a stressful time, no wonder his only way to carry on was with a stiff upper lip, his emotions kept under lock and key. He had to support his grieving wife in her collapsed state, keep her going, put on his brave face while caring and providing for his family.

Rich was a gentleman, and a very gentle man. He was never self-important, demanding, rude or unkind, but patient, reliable and selfless. He maintained there was always a simple solution to everything if one just waited, and trusted that it would emerge. He never wanted to waste a moment arguing or sulking. One of his favourite sayings was: 'It will all come right, you see.' I found his attitude calming and refreshing. His actions matched his words.

On my first visit to his home overlooking Langstone Harbour I had noticed a little piece of paper tucked in behind the glass pane of one of his kitchen cabinets. The words read:

BEING KIND

Gentle thoughts and kindly ways,
Help us through the troubled days,
Hands outstretched to others' needs,
Helpful words and friendly deeds,
Not great things? Well, never mind,
Life's best art is 'being kind'.

This summed Rich up. Whatever was going on he was always kind.

After a little discussion we agreed that the perfect solution would be to spend our time between his home in Portsmouth and my home on the Isle of Wight. After all, I had promised myself that I would never be moving house again. Both of us would be able to enjoy each other's homes and different environments. We each had our family close by and we accepted that to a certain extent we had grown used to living solo, and would need our own space for periods of time. We admitted that in our slightly older age we had both become creatures of habit and would not find it easy, perhaps might even find it impossible, to contemplate living full time with another person.

Rich had been a real, live, old-fashioned Hampshire bobby on the beat. He told me that, although he had been offered promotion many times, he had never wanted to rise up the ladder within the police. During the sixties he had been deployed on the picket lines during the miners' strike, he'd served in Northern Ireland during the Troubles, and he'd chased trains following the Great Train Robbery of August 1963.

More recently in 2001 he had assisted farmers during the terrible outbreak of foot and mouth disease and had witnessed thousands of cows being disposed of on Hampshire farms. He had enjoyed the hands-on stuff of catching robbers who were up to no good. He had faced everything from finding dead shepherds in fields, pacifying desperate parents of wayward youths living on the rough housing estates in Portsmouth, to helping old ladies assemble their Zimmer frames. He used to keep us entertained for hours with his stories. He still kept his truncheon under the bed just in case.

As a policeman he was essentially a keeper of the peace. He could enter a pub on a Friday night and with one shrill blow on his whistle draw many a drunken brawl to an abrupt close in an instant. The hurling of chairs would cease immediately, and having grabbed his handcuffs he would lead the culprits away, his job completed.

It was always the same mayhem downtown on Friday and Saturday nights, and I later discovered that these were the nights on which he never ever willingly wished to set foot outside his own front door. Having retired he preferred to stay in the peace and quiet of his own home.

It took me a while to get my head around why the altogether different concept of resolving conflict was such a challenge for him. I always presumed it was partially as a result of his training as an officer, but also due to his upbringing during the end of the stark war years which must have had a huge influence on his approach to life. One just had to get on with life, grin and bear it, and certainly never complain or be self-indulgent in any way. He tended to apply this philosophy to the way in which he lived his own personal life.

On the odd occasion when I was rattling his cage about something, he was usually more comfortable sweeping it under the carpet, ignoring it, in the belief that whatever the issue was it would soon be forgotten about. Which of course it usually was. He was self contained and a very private person. Keeping his emotions largely under wraps was one of his ways of coping. One of my endearing nicknames for him was, 'My clever water skipper'. This ingenious little bug traps air in the hairs of its thin legs allowing it to move easily and walk on water. Like the water skipper Rich had mastered the art of skating on the surface when he felt the need to.

My approach has always been a little different because I like to try to understand the reason why discord arises. But I know well that I can be a bit like a dog with a bone, rabbiting on about something and becoming distressed, especially when I am unable to settle my disturbed emotions. But we grew to understand and accept how different we were in some respects. Perhaps my ruminating story about 'The Artist and the Policeman' may come to light one day...

In the police force every officer is officially known to his colleagues by a number. Rich was 529. 'Five to nine'. He prided himself on being punctual. He had never been at work a moment later than nine in the morning, but mostly he was there five minutes earlier. 'Five to nine' was such a fitting number for him and 'Never late' another of his amusingly appropriate nicknames.

His training had obviously been one where discipline and vigilance were of the essence, and he was always prepared for every eventuality. Forward planning was his forte, and I frequently laughed when he was so adamant that everything had to be 'factored in'. His precise and accurate details of the day's events when on duty had all been recorded in his tiny pocketbook. Today these little pocketbooks are interesting historical documents.

Rich had carefully structured and ordered his life and had a well thought-out plan in place, one in which he had decided to retire early and enjoy life with his dear wife, go travelling and see more of the world. He'd spend time restoring and driving his various classic cars and leading a quiet life after all the hectic years of being a dedicated dad and living with the daily dramas encountered as a policeman. These were all part of his dream. His plan was cut short abruptly when his wife, who had suffered all her life from asthma, died very suddenly.

Two years after his wife's death, our paths having collided, he picked himself up and we made plans for a future together.

He was very diligent with money and religiously kept an accurate account of every penny he spent. He scrimped and saved and checked his bills, working out what money was available for unanticipated extras, birthday present money, Christmas, dentist, and his annual treat of a new pair of shoes. He would then transfer any excess funds at the end of the month into the 'Holiday Money' column.

He had that rather old-fashioned habit of parsimoniously piling up his coins in little towers on the sideboard in his kitchen, just like the old boys used to in the pub, checking they had just enough coppers for the next pint. Unlike them, though, he rarely went to the pub or drank, but he maintained, just as my father always used to say, that if you looked after the pence then the pounds would look after themselves. That way he would be able to afford lots of well-earned holidays.

Our first trip together was a magical and romantic trip to Mull and Iona in his sparkling new VW camper van. Casting our eyes to the skies we spotted a pair of eagles ceaselessly circling. Sitting quietly by the shore we watched otters on the rocks playing among the seaweed. We climbed Ben Nevis and witnessed the marriage of a gay couple when we reached the summit.

We had a fabulous trip on *Tenacious*, sailing out of Nice to Corsica and Monaco. The Jubilee Sailing Trust has two ships: one is *Tenacious*, the other is the *Lord Nelson*. Each paying crew member was buddied up with a physically disabled passenger to assist and keep an eye out for.

A young girl who had been paralysed in a car accident was hoisted up the mast in her wheelchair. A man whose fingers had been badly burned in a chip fryer accident was aided in climbing the rigging all the way up to the crow's nest. A partially sighted gentleman took the helm and steered the ship into the port of Monte Carlo. We all did our daily watches at various stations on the ship and were allocated specific jobs as crew. Rich and I wrote a funny little sea shanty describing all the crew and guests and we performed it on the deck at sunset on our last night aboard as we sailed back into port.

We went hiking in the Picos de Europa of Northern Spain, and I remember so clearly the day that I searched for a telephone box in the mountain village to which we had hiked so that I could call Orion and find out his degree results. He had gained a first-class honours in product design at Nottingham Trent University. I remember shouting for joy. We were so pleased for him, and celebrated with a bottle of San Miguel.

We had decided we would like to have a blessing ceremony, so by way of a pre-blessing honeymoon Rich planned a wonderful trip to Venice. We set off in the spring of 2006 driving through France to Switzerland,

Austria and Italy, finally arriving in Venice after having driven up the famous Stelvio Pass, one of the highest mountain passes of Europe at 2,759 metres, with its numerous hairpin bends.

This had been one of Rich's long-held dreams, and it was all undertaken in his renovated grey, classic-car MGB coupé. The engine overheated halfway up the pass and I was instructed to direct the cooling air from a miniature handheld fan into the glove compartment. Not sure exactly how that would have helped, but I complied, and we made it to the snow-capped top. I remember writing in huge letters in the snow, 'THANK YOU WORLD'. We were on such an amazing adventure together, as high as kites, having reached the top of the Stelvio and feeling as though we were literally on top of the world.

We'd initially had a bit of a ding-dong when I'd arrived in Portsmouth all set for the trip with a huge suitcase of clothes which Rich told me I could under no circumstances take with me. There was simply not any room for pretty dresses. So after a few cross words I calmed down and selected a dress or two; we crammed a smaller suitcase, the two-man tent and all the camping gear into the tiny boot and set off.

We travelled to Toronto, New Zealand, Switzerland, and had many great camping holidays in England too. We both loved hiking and exploring the coastline of the West Country. I know that I always made a point of thanking Rich profusely, but I hope he really knew how sincere and appreciative I truly was. Never did I dream that I would have so many wonderful holidays with him when we first met.

In New Zealand in 2011 we sat on the wall outside the cathedral in Christchurch on the very evening before the 6.3 magnitude earthquake struck, partially destroying that very cathedral. We were lucky. Imagine what could have happened had we been there a few hours later.

When in Toronto I noticed a lady passing by in a wheelchair. She was very beautiful, serene. She was wearing a dazzling white T-shirt and, printed in turquoise within a circle of brightly coloured spring flowers, were the words 'Perennial Optimist'. Ever since I have always tried to dress cheerfully. The memory of this chance encounter often pops into my mind. I wonder what her story was?

When we were in Hong Kong I was fascinated by the camaraderie and ingenuity of the many people who provide a large section of the live-in domestic workforce, employed by the rich and famous as housemaids, cooks, gardeners and cleaners. While in employment they have no homes of their own as such, so on their days off they sometimes congregate on the large expanses under the busy motorways. They set up their individual little camps, creating boundaries by building walls out of cardboard boxes, laying down rugs, ferrying camping stoves, food and flowers, 'playing house' together and inviting each other over to their temporary home to share food. It was quite an extraordinary sight. At first I thought I was watching a sit-down demonstration, but I was told that these people had not been allowed to gather in the parks for some reason. So, determined not to be beaten, they had found whatever space they could in which to break bread.

I have always wondered if there is any truth in the idea that it is possible to determine personality types through analysis of handwriting, or whether it's just all a kind of pseudoscience. Apparently, there's not a lot of evidence to support the theory, but it is interesting. I mean, my handwriting is appalling, no style, not uniform – the words usually gallop across the page rather wildly, possibly reflecting my rather random approach to things. It was hinted at in something that I happened to read somewhere that this inconsistency could indicate an ADHD trait, but I don't think I am going to speculate on that idea right now.

Rich, on the other hand, did have very uniform writing. It was always the same: small, perfect, neat and tidy, evenly placed on the page and more importantly legible, which mine often is not. I used to tease him that I needed a magnifying glass in order to read it. He said his writing had developed that way from the days when he had to record events so neatly in his 3-inch by 4-inch pocketbook.

It was on the day that I opened one of his very neatly written unexpected letters that I remember wondering why I couldn't write like him. But of more significance was the content of his letter.

Unbeknown to me, during one of our camping trips in Cornwall, Rich had heard from my niece that they were thinking of selling their beautiful little shepherd's hut which was kept on their eight-acre smallholding, not far from Penzance overlooking Mount's Bay. He had decided that he might like to buy it. What did I think? He had often talked about what he called his fantasy, of how he would love to just live out his twilight years with me in the quiet of the countryside. But the possibility of selling up and buying a house in the depths of his beloved Hampshire was indeed a fantasy, since house prices had soared over the recent years.

Apart from my initial total surprise, my response was: 'Of course, yes.' This could be our idyllic countryside love nest. What a wonderful opportunity. Rich was thrilled that I liked the idea, and we began making

Rich and me taking a break during our Shepherds' hut days on the land at Balwest near Penzance

plans. I had up to then been continuing with my reminiscence work in many of the island's care homes, but Rich had been concerned that I often seemed depressed, and would sometimes fall in the doorway after work in tears, distraught after witnessing the lonely bleakness of some of these poor people's lives. He had suggested I give it a break or retire altogether, since I was no spring chicken myself and in fact was older than some of the residents. I rather reluctantly agreed, feeling guilty that I would be abandoning many people with whom I had bonded, but accepting that perhaps it was time to call it a day.

Synchronicity played its part almost immediately. Orion was now looking for a place to live in Gurnard, so I suggested that he take over my cottage and I would disappear into the depths of Cornwall with Rich for a while.

It all worked out perfectly, but there was work to be done. First came clearing the decks in my house of all its bits and bobs. There was a lot of sorting to do, getting it habitable, clean and fresh for Orion and his girlfriend. But I rolled my sleeves up, shoved a lot of stuff into my studio at the bottom of the garden, loaded my car to the gunnels with my version of essentials and bombed off down the A30 to Cornwall.

Rich met me down at 'the land' with his car loaded too, but with all the more relevant essentials which he knew we would need in order to lick into shape the somewhat forlorn-looking little shepherd's hut. Ever the master of forward planning, he had thoughtfully gathered together all the sensible and useful things: tools, jacks, tarps, saws, shovels, spades, torches, drills, stepladders, roofing materials, storage boxes, hinges and paints.

Having arrived on a beautiful spring day with the summer months stretching ahead, the family welcomed us with a dinner of sausage stew bought from the local farm and we all sat around a huge fire under the stars.

A traditional shepherd's hut – one dating back to the golden, olden days when I was a child, and one in which a real live shepherd would have spent nights attending to his sheep and their lambs – would have had a simple layout. There would be a door at one end, a bed at the other, a stove of some kind for cooking. Probably a bucket for emergencies too. All would have been mounted on a sturdy metal chassis with small, traditional, cast-iron wheels so that it could be easily moved from field to field. The modern versions today are all the rage with anyone who has a piece of land on which to put one, and are used as extra bedrooms, offices, B&Bs or 'chill parlours' for the young. They are often trendily and elegantly decorated and mysteriously rigged up to all mod cons so one can live as if one is cosily and comfortably still at home.

Our shepherd's hut, or 'the wagon' as it was called, was none of these things. It had been built by a 'craftsman' who kind of knew his stuff, but it was also a bit of a hotchpotch. It had been mounted on an old caravan chassis, had a fitted bed at one end, a cupboard and a small galley area with a two-burner stove. It measured 10 ft x 7 ft approximately: roughly the same size of the main cabin of our boat *Sweet Painted Lady*. There was just about enough room for the two of us, but not really room to swing a cat. Although we could not enlarge on the space itself, there was a lot of potential for improvement.

We soon got things sorted inside. We installed a Pipsqueak wood-burning stove. The firebox was not much bigger than my two clasped hands, so I had to chop miniature kindling sticks so that they could just fit through the tiny door. We fitted dainty little corner cupboards and shelves, rearranged things so that there was extra storage under the bed, fixed the leaking windows, refitted the stable door, made pretty cushions and patchwork curtains. I had gathered some very special large pieces of driftwood from my favourite Isle of Wight beach with which we built an outdoor kitchen area alongside one end of the wagon. It all came together in no time.

But of course there was no such thing as running water, electricity, or a toilet. We drew water from a standpipe across the field, and sat by romantic candlelight every night, or lit a fire outside. We kept a bucket under the bed for emergencies, finding the 'bucket and chuck it' method perfectly satisfactory, or we stumbled across the fields to the compost loo.

I was never happier. This was the simple life. I was out in the fresh air every single day, come rain or shine.

Cornwall is often referred to as the wettest county in England with significantly more rainfall than the national average. I read in some smart holiday magazine that with the constant wet air, no matter what you do, how hard you try, and how much money you are prepared to spend on extra insulation your bijou holiday home will almost certainly always be damp. I am afraid I found that rather amusing. Having spent a shedload of money one might still be living in a damp mansion. But Cornwall, the surfer's paradise, has the bluest waters, and it is said that Kynance Cove can be compared to the most beautiful of New Zealand's beaches, so I guess one had to turn a blind eye to that one inevitability.

On 'days off' we explored this wonderful coastline, hiking with our picnic along the South West Coast Path, seeking out magical little cafés on beaches for snack lunches when we felt we deserved a treat. On 'days on' we worked on the land, digging, planting, pruning, clearing brambles, mowing pathways, repairing roofs, creating dead hedges, gathering boulders for stone wall repairs, fixing gates. We were never short of jobs. We called ourselves 'the land girls' . Living the good life on a smallholding was nothing but constant hard work, rewarding but relentless. It enabled a very good night's sleep at the end of the day.

My niece's family had grown to include two young children so I often helped out with child care. Other friends would come from time to time and lend a hand with jobs and I would make giant cauldrons of soup to feed the hungry troops. That was one of my favourite jobs. I would search in the cupboard for whatever was to hand and concoct my famous 'anything in the cupboard' soups. Perhaps an onion, a leek, some marmalade, some chickpeas, a handful of spinach, some noodles, a stock cube, a little seasoning... Having gulped it down, everyone always seemed re energised, raring to go again and ready to complete the afternoon jobs.

Another of my favourite pastimes was attending to my niece's five Jacob sheep. I christened them Itch, Titch, Munch, Mushroom and Puffball. These names suited them down to the ground, describing their size, habits, colour and characteristics. When they hung around the wagon in the corner of the field with its fabulous view out to sea, busily munching and keeping the grass just about under control, the scene reminded me of one of my favourite pictures by Jean-François

Millet, which I saw in the Musée d'Orsay in Paris: 'Shepherdess with her Flock'. Sadly, one of the sheep died, having become infected with the horrible parasitic blowfly, and Rich and I had to dig its grave. We excavated a massive hole, deep enough, we hoped, that the resident fox would not sniff it out. But it didn't work, and within a few days the whole thing was unearthed. The stench wafting across the field was appalling.

I never thought I would have the opportunity to learn all about the extraordinary life cycle of a blowfly, nor about the numerous varieties of sheep and merits of their various fleeces. One of my favourite books was *Know your Sheep*. It made very intriguing bedtime reading. My niece used to laugh as she jumped on her bike and chased off through the lanes to find an escapee sheep.'It's all normal for Cornwall' she'd say, and we'd crack on with whatever job had been lined up next.

Rich, from time to time, would head back to Portsmouth to check things out back home and leave me to my quiet life. I quite enjoyed these periods as it meant I could spread myself out a little in the wagon. Instead of my morning cuddles with him I had visitations from my great-niece little Lilly Bonita. She was four at the time, and she would come trotting across the field on many a morning wearing her red polka dot wellies, clutching a bunch of wildflowers which she had picked on the way. Or she would arrive with a note from her mum tucked into her little willow basket, which was full of fresh and sometimes rotten eggs. She would scramble into bed for story time with 'Manda'.

One day she came dressed in her most recent favourite jumble sale numbers, a pink cashmere jumper, all full of holes, with her new smart black leggings. I loved finding a fitting name for her each time she visited. That morning as she snuggled down with me, she became little Miss Marsha Cashmere. Her skin was so marshmallowy, cashmery soft. Another day, as she surprised me with a delivery of morning post wearing her polka dot wellies, she became Little Miss Polka Dot Post Lady.

Yes, many memories of the Cornish shepherd's hut life. Memories of living knee deep in mud and endless days of donning my Wellington boots. It rained, rained, and rained, sometimes for days. And if it did not rain there was often a damp sea fret, the mist enveloping the land, and I began to wonder where I was and why exactly I was there in the first place. Occasionally, on days such as these, I retreated to my damp bed and perhaps for reassurance, I think, I would write a list of what I was enjoying about my spartan Gypsy life. I found one of those lists the other day.

WHAT AM I ENJOYING? WHY AM I HERE?

1. Simplicity. The sense of satisfaction gained from the effort required to fulfil the essentials. Getting water from the tap across the field. Boiling water for outdoor washing of dishes and clothes. Gathering and chopping wood for the fire and wood burner.

2. Candlelight. It is beautiful, subtle, soft, and enriches any scene. I never want electric lights ever again. Too harsh.

3. The pitter-pattering of rain on the tin roof.

4. Fresh air and all weathers. Mastering this. Functioning in extreme conditions, especially when wet, windy, foggy, muddy, damp and cold.

5. Silence.

6. Media fasting. No need for TV and I have no internet. No desire for it. It all disturbs my mind. Occasional radio, but batteries proving too expensive and get damp anyway and don't work.

7. Having a simple purpose. Feeling and being useful on the land.

8. Time to reflect and wonder... and wonder... and wonder...

9. Realising that this simple lifestyle satisfies the vagabond in me, the Gypsy, the rebel, the Luddite.

10. Enjoying the trial-and-error approach required for managing many of the jobs here. Make do and mend. Heath Robinson will more than do.

11. Enjoying being around the innocence of young children. Perhaps I have never really grown up myself?

12. Not minding if some of my friends can't quite understand it when I say I am living 'in heaven' down here. It's heaven to me and that's all that matters.

13. Being incognito. I look deplorable most of the time as though I have been drawn through a hedge backwards, but who cares? I am often scrambling through a hedge backwards so it's not surprising what I look like. There's no pressure or need to look like anything, for anybody, at any time.

14. Sitting out under the heavens.

15. Listening out for the hooting barn owl.

On the odd occasion when I did feel the need for dumping my muddy boots, and putting on a clean pair of trousers (although they were usually damp), I'd catch the bus to the end-of-the-train-line town of Penzance. It is said that Penzance is one of the poorest towns in Cornwall, one in which many people get washed up like flotsam and jetsam, and having got off the train there they are not likely to return from whence they came.

It's true I saw many lonely and desperate-looking people, sadly many of them young, wandering aimlessly, often munching on a famous Cornish pasty. But I enjoyed my days poking around there and would often return with yet another little decorative treasure with which to enhance the wagon.

Living the simple life, a minimalist life, in a shepherd's hut, with no mod cons, had at the outset been a bit of an experiment for me, just another interesting experience. But having spent all those years afloat in such a small space I never doubted my capacity to deal with what others might have considered a completely ridiculous way to spend two years of my life, especially at my ripe old age of sixty-five. I often thought of my mother as I huddled round my little Pipsqueak stove at night. I think she felt fulfilled by every aspect of the outdoor life and living so closely alongside nature; she often said she should have been a Gypsy. I think she might have been very content living in this way.

I discovered that a toothbrush, a hairbrush and a well oiled saw were all I really needed. The odd pot and pan came in handy too, and with an assortment of rather raggle-taggle scruffy old clothes, wellington boots, some clean underwear and a very sharp knife, I was happy. I did in fact have two knives, which I would not have been without for a moment.

Knives I have always thought of as artworks. A well balanced, perfectly sharpened knife is a joy to use. I find them beautiful but somewhat threatening when being used irresponsibly, as in the case of the stroppy chefs I had encountered, or the poor, mad Spanish Antonio.

The memory of watching my mother sharpen the bone-handled carving knife on the granite kitchen step at High Barn is etched so vividly in my mind. It was always a happy occasion, since we were all awaiting the moment when the delicious shoulder of lamb would magically appear from the Aga and the freshly sharpened knife would slice its way with ease through the succulent, sweet-smelling meat spilling its juices into the huge serving platter. I treasure my four silver fish knives, one of the family heirlooms. The blades are engraved with the most beautifully intricate feathery leaf design, including a detailed image of a woven fish basket with two fish lying beside it. I like to give thanks for such artistry every time I use them.

The Knife Angel is a stunning 27-foot tall contemporary sculpture created by Alfie Bradley at the British Ironworks Centre based in Oswestry. It is made from 100,000 knives handed in during a weapons amnesty in an attempt to reduce crime on the streets. The knives are all perfectly aligned, forming the very effective feathery wings of the angel. It was built to highlight the negative effects of violent behaviour. I have wondered if one of the knives which my friend's son had handed in was among them.

Every little boy will forever no doubt treasure the memory of the day on which he was given his first Swiss Army knife, and proudly trucked off to Scout camp with it safely secreted in his knapsack, useful for all sorts when at camp. And a sharp knife was indeed one of the essential items in the emergency grab bag on the boat, as it was in the shepherd's hut.

For some curious reason I seem to have had more than a few close shaves with knives, which have not always been pleasant.

In the Caribbean, when I had trespassed into a local's jungle plantation of palm trees hoping to find a fallen coconut, I was met face to face with a rageful man brandishing a gleaming machete. Shame on me... serves me jolly well right. I beat a quick retreat as he chased me off down the road screaming. I was quick to learn my lesson there. There were no precautionary notices pinned to the tree either: 'Danger. Falling Coconut Zone'. I understand that on average 150 people die every year from being hit on the head by a falling coconut, so I was lucky to escape on two accounts that day.

On another occasion following a residential weekend workshop at which I had been employed as the cook, as the weekend drew to a close, I offered bed and breakfast at my home for the last night to one of the participants. He needed to catch a very early morning ferry the next day and my house was close by the ferry terminal. On arriving at the White Cottage, after I had shown him his bedroom, he reappeared wanting a cup of tea before he turned in. He suddenly drew from his jacket a massive kitchen knife. With full force he jabbed its blade into my beautiful circular coffee table (the one around which my mother had carved a delicate design) leaving the huge knife standing firmly erect. He said he wanted to kill his mother.

I asked him where he had got the knife from, and then with horror realised that he had stolen it from the kitchen in which I had been working. I suggested he travelled on to wherever he had planned to go next and that he deposited the knife with me. Wild eyed, he insisted on taking it with him to London. Not wanting to labour the point I did not suggest it again. I calmy bundled him into my car, survived the short trip and sighed a big sigh of relief, having put him on the late night ferry. That incident was more than an unpleasant surprise.

Then there was the sad case of a disastrous internet date with a poor gentleman – I can't really call him a gentleman, though. The 'dark horse' would be a more accurate description. Being so gullible or plain stupid I had been enticed with the suggestion of a trip to Florence, which didn't go at all well. He didn't want to go to the Uffizi gallery, said he didn't do highbrow, arty stuff. Didn't want to go to a service in the Duomo, said he didn't do religion. Didn't want to sample the famous dishes of bistecca alla fiorentina and tagliolini with truffles, said he didn't do truffles (I did try this delicious Florentine dish later. It was jam-packed with delicious truffles fresh from the forests of Tuscany). However, we both seemed determined to overcome the initial disappointment of this first trip, and a camping excursion to northern Spain was next on the cards.

Having taken the ferry across to Bilbao we drove along the coast. His driving was appalling but I managed to keep my mouth shut. After passing Santander we stopped at a delightful place which I had visited before, called San Vincente de la Barquera. He seemed to be quite cheery at this point. The tent we pitched turned out to be not even a one-man affair but one of those little kids' kind of play tents, with about enough room for an eight-year-old and his pet guinea pig. I did wonder where exactly I was going to be sleeping. He suddenly disappeared, telling me he was going to suss out the best fish restaurant in town.

When he finally returned it was by now chucking it down with rain. Oh no, not again, recollections of years gone by standing on that famous doorstep waiting for John. As it continued to pour and pour, I jammed all my things back into my small rucksack in an attempt to keep them dry and we retreated into his car. By now, for whatever reason, his mood had changed dramatically. He seemed distressed and agitated. He started up the engine and we roared off at great speed. He turned down a dark side-street in the town and I thought we might be heading for the restaurant. But no. He suddenly stopped the car. Rain was lashing on the windscreen. He sighed, turned to me face to face, took hold of my head, his large hands covering my ears. Did he not want me to hear what he was about to say? Well, I did hear, and I was terrified. 'I could quite happily slit your throat right now!' Of course, I could not help wondering if he had a massive knife stuffed into the huge pockets of his ill-fitting jacket. I did not hang around long enough to discover whether that was so.

I leapt out of the car and, having had the good sense, (perhaps the sixth sense) to grab my rucksack containing all my valuables, I rushed off into the town. I knew just about enough Spanish to be able to ask if a bus was likely to come along. When one did, I jumped onto it not caring where it was going so long as it was going somewhere. Arriving in a village in the mountains about an hour later I came across 'Casas Rurales' where I spent two nights recovering. I eventually made my own way back home, assuming the man must be suffering from some sort of a financial mid-life crisis, not in a good space at all; and I was pleased never to see or hear of him again.

Going to the old-fashioned circus as it was in those golden days was always a mix of light-hearted fun and absolute terror. Particularly hair-raising was the knife-throwing spectacle. A scantily clad, incredibly brave and gorgeous girl would stand with her body pressed firmly against the large, slightly tilted circular disc which was a bit like a huge dartboard. The hunky knife thrower, hopefully skilled at his art, would then hurl his glistening-bladed knives at the disc, creating an outline around her body. It was utterly terrifying. As light relief this act would often be followed by the grand entrance of an elephant, who would be led in and guided to sit back on an eight-inch red-velvet stool. Then the clown would arrive, fooling around with a water hose, and tumble about in his old broken-down banger trying to get it started with a crank handle. But I always found it difficult to sleep after we had seen the knife throwers at the circus.

Any knife which I have ever owned never seems to remain very sharp, possibly because I often end up using them for something other than specific use in the kitchen. I might trim the tough stalks of freshly cut flowers as I am arranging them in a vase, or be tempted to use one to prise open a jar of out-of-date olives, scrape glue off the kitchen floor, trim my hair or even carve a snowman. So a few years ago when Orion asked me what I would like for my birthday I did mention that a sharp kitchen knife would be useful.

Orion would have thoughtfully spent hours researching knives, I know, making a wise choice for his hopeless mother who he knows would be likely to misuse it given half a chance. So why should I expect him to waste his hard-earned money? I called him and told him that I had been thinking about it and I would really rather he gave me a candle for my birthday; but he must have forgotten that I had made this suggestion, because when the day came I unwrapped my present and it was the most beautiful knife. A Mercer, high-carbon, no-stain, German steel, six-inch blade. I treasure it. I look after it. I will never use it for anything other than that for which it is intended, and each time I do use it I think of him. He kindly resharpens it for me whenever it seems a little blunt.

So I must put the subject of knives to bed now and reflect on what a wonderful summer Rich and I had enjoyed. One in which we had also spent a magical camping holiday in Sussex. On returning to our cosy shepherd's hut one day, while I was busily chopping veg for the evening's soup with my favourite knife, my thoughts were moving on towards Christmas.

I wondered if Orion would like to come and spend the festive season with us down in Cornwall. I suggested I could make up some kind of a bed for him in one of the other huts on the land in the adjoining field. Although he knew it was no luxury pad he thought it sounded like a fun experience. I was surprised and delighted that he leapt at the idea.

That Christmas for me was one of the 'shepherd's hut-era highlights'. We all squeezed into the wagon in the evenings, huddling around the Pipsqueak stove. I had pushed the boat out and bought new batteries for my little radio. Christmas carols were playing. The little table was laden, and we all tucked in to all sorts of traditional Christmas goodies served on miniature plates. We sipped mulled wine from tiny liqueur glasses and the wagon was decorated with holly and nightlights. This scene was a Christmas card in the making.

A Christmas Eve carol service held at a nearby farm competed as the highlight. All the animals were gathered in the huge barn: donkeys, sheep, cows, horses, rabbits, pigs, chickens, ducks, geese, dogs and the farmyard cat. And a real, live baby Jesus who had come into this world a few weeks previously had been wrapped in his blanket and was laid on soft straw in his manger. Singing carols with the background cacophony of the animal choir was just unforgettable. All we needed was some snow to complete the idyllic old-world picturesque event, but there was none in this particular year.

The day after Boxing Day, Orion wanted to get back to his work on the island and was able to give Rich a lift back to Portsmouth. As they were leaving, Orion gave me a huge hug and he told me that it was the best Christmas he had ever spent. He had loved every minute of it. He also told me that he and his girlfriend, Vanessa, had at last found a suitable house to rent and therefore my home would soon be standing empty again.

I had developed an almost permanent cough which I seemed unable to shift. This was possibly because I had spent those two very damp winters living in the wagon. I had been wondering, after this happy Christmas, whether it was wise to sit out the bleak months of January, February and March which were just around the corner. Perhaps it was fortuitous that my home would soon be available again. I wondered what the best plan might be. Rich and I could always return to the wagon for the odd week or two in the spring when the weather would be picking up again.

I got back into my routine and busied myself with all the various jobs on the land. I was surprised when after a few days Rich rang saying he wanted to ride down on his motorbike, but that it would be only a fleeting visit. I wondered why, after all the effort of such a long journey on his bike, but he insisted and said he'd explain when he arrived.

I planned a yummy welcome meal, laid a huge fire outside the wagon, bought him several bottles of his favourite cider and some Guinness. He called me again as he was setting off from Portsmouth, said he would stop overnight at a B&B and would arrive the following day. I was always nervous when he was out on his bike. I had not enjoyed the one time I rode on it with him. As we were whizzing around the lanes, approaching a steep hill somewhere in the depths of Hampshire, we had to halt at a junction. Rich seemed unable to keep the bike stable, not being used to having my extra weight on the back I think. The bike tipped over and we both fell off into the middle of the road. I didn't go on it again after that. Lost my nerve completely.

Rich arrived safely down in Cornwall, and all was well. We had yet another lovely evening round the fire, sipping our warmed cider and reminiscing about our family Christmas and the magical animal carol service. It was not until we had snuggled down in bed that he explained to me the reason for his fleeting visit. He had wanted to tell me face to face that he had been diagnosed with CLL, and that he needed to return for further blood tests within two days. In my ignorance I did not even know anything about CLL. But he explained that it was a form of leukaemia. Chronic Lymphocytic Leukaemia.What a bombshell.

I had noticed during the recent months that he had often said he felt 'strangely tired'. I had been worrying on and off why this was. We had no idea what lay ahead, except that perhaps this diagnosis would mean that our shepherd's hut days might have to draw to a close.

Rich was anxious to get back home, so positive as ever he leapt onto his bike the following day and rode back to Portsmouth. I decided I would drive back too as I wanted to accompany him to the hospital and find out more details of the prognosis. That is the bit one dreads. His was a late diagnosis, which was good in the sense that he did not have to live for years and years with the knowledge of the illness hanging over him, which as best I understand it can be the case with CLL but not so good in that at this stage we had no idea if the cancer was beyond the stage of effective treatment.

Having had our first meeting with the oncologist, Rich decided his time was up – that whatever time was left he would enjoy. He was adamant that he did not wish to spend his final years having treatment. The consultant was brutally honest and told us that without treatment he might survive for a further three months, but only if the wind was in his favour.

It was a terrible day. Having heard this shocking news, we drove down to the beach at Southsea and went for a long walk. We sat on the shingle bank and cried. Later that night Rich decided he would like to talk to his consultant after all. Was he having second thoughts, I wondered? Perhaps there was still hope if he reversed his decision. I quickly learnt that Rich's illness was in a sense mine as well, since it had so suddenly taken over our life. There had been a life before his diagnosis, and a completely different one following it. We both felt we had been halted in our tracks.

I returned to Cornwall for a brief visit, tidied the wagon, discarded all my filthy old ragged clothes, donating them to the compost pile. I bade farewell to Lilly Bonita and the family and to my four remaining beloved sheep, packed my sharp knife, my hairbrush, toothbrush and wellies and, teary eyed, sped back to be with Rich.

As best we could we kept life jogging along. In between his hospital appointments he would come over to the island when he felt up to it and we would enjoy our favourite island strolls and cosy up at home. These worrying days were punctuated by a dramatic event in the late summer of 2014. It was also an exciting time. My first grandchild was expected in September.

In July 2006 Rich and I had enjoyed our blessing ceremony in the ancient little church at Bonchurch. By way of marking this special day the boys had given Rich and me a chiminea, and I had decided on the night of 23 August to light it. We loved sitting out beside it, usually in the late evening as we were doing on this occasion. Unlike the huge blaze-ups we used to have beside the shepherd's hut down on the land in Cornwall, we had to be careful, since my garden is small and narrow and sparks could fly high. But we were always very diligent – or so we thought.

It had been a very dry summer and I had enjoyed a busy day gardening and clearing all the Russian vine which had grown rampantly and almost entirely hidden one of the garden sheds from view. I had bagged up all the trimmings and had ferried them through to the front garden ready to take to the dump the following day. All that remained was a thick, duvet-like layer of twigs on the roof of the shed.

Rich had retired to bed and I sat alone by the fire for a while pondering the imminent arrival of this little baby, a wondrous addition to our family. I was so excited that I was about to become a grandmother and was praying all would go smoothly. I was also intrigued thinking about the passage this being was about to undertake, soon to be entering this world: but as yet still within the safe haven of his mother's womb.

Gazing into the bowels of the chiminea I became transfixed by the glowing embers. I could imagine all sorts of characters living in the caverns between the smouldering logs. Mystery worlds seemed to suddenly open up in the belly of the fire; stories of their imaginary lives in this underworld were running riot in my mind. I remember realising how much I loved this rich, fiery orange colour, having never been fond of it before for some odd reason.

During the week I had also been refreshing my memories of the whole magical birth process. I had seen an interesting, and quite amusing, visual explanation about that essential aspect, the dilation of the cervix in order for a safe passage and natural birth. From a mere centimetre, the size of your average blueberry, to a two-centimetre size of a cherry, to a four-centimetre slice of lime, to a six-centimetre chocolate chip cookie, to an eight-centimetre orange slice, and finally to a ten-centimetre bagel when fully dilated. While watching the sparks fly from the ceramic chimney I suddenly realised that its opening was almost exactly ten centimetres. Goodness. This young woman, my daughter-in-law Vanessa, was about to breathe her way through her labour and when, fully dilated, as if through the chiminea opening, her baby would make his entrance. How incredible.

With positive thoughts, having checked the final glowing embers of the fire, I went to bed. For some very odd reason as I was getting out of bed at around 2am to go to the loo, I glanced out of the window and, NO! To my horror the garden was ablaze. A huge fire was raging.

I screamed to Rich. Hearing my words, but not really registering, he turned over, kind of groaned and muttered: 'What on earth have you done now?' There was no time for an argument or any discussion. I rushed downstairs. The electrical cable providing lights in my garden had got damaged in the fire so all the lights in the house had tripped out. In the dark, having grabbed my torch, I called the ambulance (I mean fire brigade – you see even now, after nearly nine years, even thinking about it sends me into a panic). They seemed to take for ever to come. But eventually two fire engines and four firemen turned up. I stood whimpering, paralysed, shaking in the corner of the kitchen watching through the French doors into the garden, unable to believe what was happening.

In the midst of my terror, it was odd but I remember thinking how hunky the men were, like all the policemen, the AA men, the lifeboat men. All these amazing volunteers who come to the rescue always seem to be such good-looking guys. They are always also so kind.

With their heavy boots, four of them came clomping through the front door, dragging the huge heavy hoses straight through the kitchen, sitting room, conservatory and out into the blazing garden which by now was entirely engulfed in flames. The fences on either side were burning. The fire had caught one of the sheds in which I had stored all the things you naturally keep in a shed. All were highly inflammable.

Paint, gas bottles, petrol for the outboard motor, resin… it was fireworks, snap, crackle, pop, but not in the least bit funny, and then even worse, when suddenly all the glass in the windows blew out.

29 August: report in the Isle of Wight County Press newspaper. 'The Isle of Wight Fire and Rescue Service firefighters were called to a shed fire in the early hours of Saturday, August 23rd. Two fire engines from Newport attended the property at The Avenue, Gurnard, shortly before 3am. They spent around half an hour extinguishing the flames.'

A baptism of fire. Time seems to stand still at a time of crisis, and it certainly seemed many more minutes than thirty that the fire was being fought. Every second seemed like an hour as I watched it destroy my garden, my plants, my artworks, my sheds, my woodpile, my beautiful driftwood chair which Rich had lovingly made me for my birthday earlier that year. Finally, once the fire brigade had managed to reassure me that the fire had been fully extinguished, they left. I felt completely incapacitated. In complete shock I broke down and wailed.

During September I worked very closely with my insurance company, the NFU Mutual Norwich, providing a detailed inventory of every item which was destroyed. I cannot praise them highly enough, and also Rainbow International restoration and clearance, who began clearing the site. They were kind and sensitive, which made all the difference as the scene was one of complete devastation.

The aftermath of the fire in my garden caused by sparks from a Chiminea. A scene of complete devastation

I called an artist friend who works with textiles. I had a feeling she would find beauty in the weird shapes and colours, distortions, and curious, twisted, unrecognisable objects. And perhaps she might be able to seek some inspiration for her work. She took a lot of photographs, as I did too for insurance purposes. This was necessary. It was surprising to me that, despite having lost so much and having lived through the trauma, I could still find such beauty in the rich, black velvety layers of charcoal, ash, shattered glass and debris.

It is heartening now to see how nine years later, with that terrible event in the past, like a phoenix rising from those ashes, or a kind of alchemical transformation, my little garden has recovered. I am able once again to enjoy it. The trees have grown, and on a sunny day the dappled light makes it feel quite magical. I love being in my garden, I love being out in the air. It seems that birds of all kinds enjoy the place too. I love watching everything squeak back to life in the spring and then fall silent and rest during the winter months. Mucking about, raking, digging, planting, observing, pottering, I am often accompanied by my resident robin. I find it therapeutic. I chatter

With a little tender loving care and renewed enthusiasm over the past six years, my garden has sprung back to life

away to myself and to the plants and bushes and birds. Prince Charles, now our King Charles, was happy to reveal that he is a great advocate of talking to plants. They respond. So I am not alone.

The day after the fire I spent the entire day searching among the ash and finally retrieved something that, to this day, is precious to me. Months earlier I had nailed it to one of the fences. It had been part of an art project titled 'Armour' which I had made when I was at the Norwich Art School. On a small copper plaque I had etched these words:

COURAGE, THE CAPACITY TO MOVE
AHEAD IN SPITE OF DESPAIR

Of course, I had to pluck up the courage and call Sky, now living in Australia, and tell him that the entire contents of his shed had been destroyed in the fire. I felt distraught. He had lost everything: surf boards, kites, art folders, fishing kits, tools, diving equipment, bicycles, toys and a lot more. It was heartbreaking when he asked me to try to find bits and bobs for him. It was hard to explain it was all gone. There was nothing left of his shed or its treasured contents. Nothing.

Fire, when uninvited, unintentional, is terrifying. I had witnessed the result of the devastating forest fires in Australia when I had visited Sky: miles and miles of blackened trees, with wildlife burnt alive in the raging furnace. I also had such vivid memories of when I was a child, on the farm at High Barn, how after the harvest we used to burn the stubble. I know this was always done with care, under controlled conditions, when there was little wind and no risk of the fire getting out of control. But it always rather scared me seeing the harvest fields ablaze. This system was banned in 1993.

Considering myself to be a bit of a jack of all trades and a master of none, I have never felt I had the authority to speak about anything much. But after the fire I do feel I can speak about the dangers of using a chiminea in a small enclosed space. Perhaps it was stupid of me. Following the fire I could not look at a flame for months. I was very jumpy. I no longer have a chiminea.

Some years later as I was dancing to what had been one of my favourite songs by Bruce Springsteen, *Dancing in the Dark*, with its line: *'You can't start a fire without a spark'*, that song took on a different meaning. His performance was compelling, but I could not help wincing. I now knew a few other things about sparks and fires. That cautionary tale of Matilda who told such dreadful lies and was burned to death sprang to mind again. But unlike Matilda, all these stories which I am sharing are true. Mercifully neither I nor my house were burned in the fire.

Safe, sound and perfect, on 2 October 2014 dear little Sonny, my first grandchild, was born.

The trauma of the fire took its toll on me for quite a while, but with the diversion and wonderful addition to the family of young Sonny, there was happiness all around and so much to be grateful for. We also had another wonderful event to look forward to: the marriage of Orion to Vanessa. The Apple Farm venue at Freshwater was a perfect setting for the July celebration. Little Sonny, who was not yet two years old, was one of the adorable page boys. And there was another 'bun in the oven'. Ness and Orion were expecting their second child.

Family and friends all mucked in for the wedding, making food, arranging flowers and decorating the various barns. I had been busy making yards of bunting. Ness's mum, the master cake-maker, had baked the most incredible and delicious three-tier wedding cake which she had adorned with edible flowers. I loved her outfit, an elegant white dress with its flowery print matching the cake to perfection.

It was such a joyful interlude. Such a happy day. A day which I was so pleased Rich was able to enjoy. It started with laughter when all the family piled into a pale-green vintage coach and were driven from Gurnard to the venue in West Wight. Rich had generously arranged this for us, to ensure we would all arrive for the wedding on time. Not getting lost, not forgetting anything vital, organisation and punctuality are sometimes a little challenging for our side of the family!

Before 2016 was out dear little Jude Walter arrived on 18 November, a brother for Sonny, another perfect little soul. The family was growing.

For Rich and me, the ensuing months and year was primarily governed by weekly hospital visits and repeated blood tests and scans. We lived constantly with apprehension as to the effectiveness of the treatment which Rich had by now decided to try. His symptoms happened to fit exactly with the very specific criteria required for the latest clinical trials of Ibrutinib and Venetoclax. One of them had dreadful side effects, as is so often the case, and his face blew up like a football so that he could hardly see out of his poor eyes. Both drugs slowed down the progression of the cancer for five years from the date of the original diagnosis, but in the end the cancer won.

Rich never wished to talk about his illness, the inevitability of death or if he feared what was happening to him. Nor did he ever wish to bother the doctors and consultants by asking innumerable questions. I kept tabs on all the appointments and wrote a detailed report following every consultation.

Rich died on 15 November 2017.

I never heard him complain. He insisted he was not in pain, but I never quite knew if this was true. In the latter stages, as his health deteriorated rapidly, we would just sit together holding hands sometimes for hours; his face would crumple up, he would fight back the tears for a few moments and then with his soft husky voice I would hear those familiar words: 'It will all be all right, you see.'

I was so grateful that Orion came over to be with us at the hospital during Rich's final days. I deeply regret that we were unable to transfer him to the hospice but due to complex reasons in the end this was not possible. I know the hospice would have provided a calm and more appropriate environment in which dear Rich might more peacefully have been able to slip away.

'Wonderful' was his final word, as he sucked on a foam swab which I had soaked in his favourite cider. I sat talking to him for quite a while and could clearly hear him answering me.

I named the beautiful olive-skinned gentle nurse who had recently come on duty the 'Italian Angel'. She was so beautiful, Italian, and I do believe she was one of the Earth Angels who had been sent to comfort us all. She helped me wash Rich; together we brushed his beautiful hair and beard. Strangely he looked so well in the end. So good-looking. No different from the day we first met. I laid him out, covered him up in one of my favourite scarves, his shroud, and kissed him goodbye. I couldn't believe he was gone... but he's never far away.

We had promised Rich that we would do everything we could to grant him his wish, to spend his final hours in his own home. But events overtook us and sadly we had not managed this for him either. He did come home for the night before his funeral and I was able to sit with him peacefully, feeling his calm presence in the soft candlelight. Knowing that Rich could not have had long for this world, during those final months when he was sleeping I often walked around Langstone Harbour anticipating the inevitability of his funeral. I had rehearsed the exact wording for his eulogy which I intended to deliver. It was a way of preparing myself for the worst, I suppose. When the day came, I could not find the courage and preferred to take a back seat.

The task of sorting out, dismantling and finally clearing his house was not easy – especially selling off his treasured collection of vintage and classic car books. He loved the old chest in his bedroom in which he kept all his favourite car memorabilia and magazines. He had discarded so many, but liked to keep just a few special ones to flick through when he fancied reminiscing.

We had been sitting in bed one morning and, as he was turning the pages of one of the magazines, he suddenly dug me in the ribs and laughed very loudly. He exclaimed: 'Goodness me, I recognise this girl, don't I? Have you been hiding in my loft for all these years?' It was a picture of a girl standing beside a car outside a petrol station. Wearing a very short miniskirt, sporting long hair and long eyelashes, she was holding the fuel nozzle, filling the car with petrol. Advertising the petrol, the car, the miniskirt, a hair shampoo…? It had to be one of those, but I'm not exactly sure which.

It was indeed a picture of me from my sixties modelling days. On top of this particular magazine which Rich had kept he had carefully placed a piece of newsprint, knowing of course that one day we were likely to find it. It read: 'I always have a very positive attitude to life.'

I cannot think of a more perfect salute to Rich, that wonderful man, than these beautiful words written by his son, Stuart, which he read so courageously at his father's funeral:

He was a gentleman, a gentle man, a gentle man.

A cyclist, a painter,
A mortgage down-payment maker.

A bather, a gazer, a grandfather, a dreamer.
An everyday believer.

A supporter of blue, a family man.
A striker, a lover, a shopper, a husband.

He was a gentleman, a gentle man.

A classic car owner, with a mild-mannered persona,
A joker, a builder, a news-time watcher, a dad.

A sufferer, a smiler, a bus pass holder,
A man with a shed, a father of four.
A man of the law who never swore.

He was a gentleman, a gentle man.

A journey planner, hairdresser to kids,
An off-road biker, a scenic hiker.

A gardener, a traveller, a semi-detached decorator.
A humanitarian with a shower that dripped,
An Isle of Wight hopper and Lidl shopper.

He was a gentleman, a gentle man.

A pillar, a shoulder, a man with a book-keeping folder,
A loss of a son, never gave up,
A loss of a wife still grasped life.

A courageous handyman, an unassuming friend,
A humble mate, never late.

A partner in love, an engineer of all things good,
A hole in our hearts where once he stood.

He was a gentle man.

I had collected some acorns from the woods in which we had camped that summer in Sussex before his diagnosis. I imagine that the six tiny oak trees which I have grown from those acorns, and which we planted in his memory in the corner of the field where our shepherd's hut once stood, will one day stand tall and graciously, just as he did.

I always knew, Rich was 'The bell that rang true'.

Chapter 23

Twilight years

My cottage home. Preparing for an Open Studios event at my house in Gurnard in the summer of 2019. The picture is of High Barn, my childhood home, painted by my sister Anabel

Sky by now was 30 years old and living in Australia, with dual Australian and UK nationality. Before Rich's death he had committed himself to an incredible project.

John had heard that *Zazen*, the catamaran that he had sold, was up for sale – and he had a vague idea that he might like to buy her back. He sent Sky on a flying mission from Perth to check out the boat, which had been left for years in a marina in Sydney. On first sight Sky could see the enormous amount of work that would be needed to renovate the boat and bring her back from the abyss of abandonment. It would be very costly and a painstakingly slow business.

The seacocks and hatches had been left open, so the boat was full of water. The bulkheads had all warped and were partially delaminating, owing to the extreme heat. Sails had been left on the boom uncovered and exposed to the fierce damaging sunlight. The various sea birds had moved in and had used the deck as their convenient toilet. It was a completely indescribable and very sad mess, a deteriorating wreck, and certainly not worth the money that the owner was asking. Sky returned to Perth and told his father all about it. John gave up on the idea of buying her.

Sky told me he was 'completely wired', unable to sleep. He number-crunched for days, realising that the equipment alone on the boat was worth a lot. Winches, radio, navigational aids, sextant, sails, charts, tools, materials, anchors, rope, safety harnesses, buoys, fenders, etc,

etc, etc… Virtually every item the family had sailed with from Cowes Harbour Marina on the Isle of Wight all the way to Australia was still on the boat.

To cut a long story short, after several more visits to assess in more detail the work required in restoring her, and having had lengthy discussions with the owner, Sky realised this was a chance too good to miss – that is, if he could agree on a realistic price for the boat, given the condition that it was in. He had been presented with the opportunity of perhaps having a sailing adventure with *Zazen* after all these years. He would be able to bring back to life the boat which he had stayed on so often when he was a young boy. After a few weeks of negotiations, the boat was his. Having had the experience of building our *Sweet Painted Lady* I had a fairly good understanding of what Sky had taken on.

He was likely to be living with the unmistakable, asphyxiating, sickly and permeating smell of resin. He would be masked up in order to avoid inhaling the fine dust as he sanded the microballoons filler so that the hull would be ultra-smooth and ready for the next stage of painting. He would be living with the unavoidable itching, after preparing the chopped-strand matt glass fibre for doing all the repairs. He might face exhaustion and feel despondent, as making progress was never likely to be as fast as he might have hoped. He would have to face the all-consuming, inescapable hard work day after day if he were ever to complete the project. To all this would be added sleepless nights lying awake planning the schedule of work for the following day.

I think his job was much harder than ours had been. For a start, the boat at forty-five feet was quite a lot larger, and I think it is was easier starting with a clean slate than wrestling to undo and rebuild everything that had fallen into such terrible disrepair. Sky is highly skilled and can turn his hand to anything, so I had no doubts at all that he would make an incredible job of the renovation.

Shortly after Rich had passed away I flew out to see Sky and stayed aboard *Zazen* in Oyster Cove, Port Stephens. I always remained positive and encouraging, and got stuck in helping with all the jobs, cutting glass fibre, painting and sanding, and scrubbing sails. We had shipped out the heavy Read's sewing machine which we had used on board our boat, so I beavered away sewing hatch covers, cockpit seat covers, and mending the spray dodgers. It was all very déjà vu.

Sky's courage and dogged determination, slogging away in Australia's exhausting and searing heat, has been so impressive. He has now been committed to the task for eight years, working intermittently in order to finance the next stage of the restoration. I find it a heartwarming and a heart-breaking story, as I still feel the sadness that we never achieved that dream of cruising with our two children on board *Zazen*. At the same time I knew back then and still know that it does one no good to dwell on what might have been.

I had taken some of Rich's ashes with me to Australia, and we had a little ceremony together, scattering them as we floated candles off across the bay. Rich thought very highly of Sky, and was fond of him, so it felt important to celebrate Rich's life with him, to include him somehow. He had been kind and patient listening to me so often when I used to call him on the phone for a chat when Rich was so ill.

I recall a morning when I was sitting in the cockpit at dawn playing Sky's guitar. I watched as a friend, Tommy was leaving the harbour in his boat. Off on his travels with his dog Bella on board. My mind turned to my own days of cruising when we were so often having to say goodbye to friends. That was never easy. As Tommy and his boat and his dog and his girlfriend drifted out of sight I found myself composing a little ditty:

'Boat people dream the unimaginable,
Boat people dream the fantastical,
Boat people dream up the magical,
And anchor their dreams out at sea.'

During my holiday I had done my best to put on a brave face and to put dark thoughts behind me. Although I found the waves of emotion and days of sorrow exhausting, I also had to accept and try to understand my slight feelings of guilt, and relief that my days would no longer be dictated to by the constant hospital visits, and gratitude that dear Rich was no longer suffering. I felt that there was a kind of alchemy in grief and that in time I would be able to transform it and feel happiness again. This was bound to take a while. I filled my days doing anything to distract myself and keep my mind occupied, often giving unnecessary attention to the smallest of jobs. But having returned home I felt refreshed by my visit, knowing that I had been so lucky to have spent fifteen exciting and very interesting years with Rich. I knew as well that I had been so lucky to have shared that very special time with Sky on board *Zazen* .

Pelicans at Oyster Cove marina. An illustration from my diary when visiting Sky in Australia

I have one son so far away and one so close.

Orion and his family live just around the corner in Gurnard, so it was fun on my return to be able to share all my adventures with them by showing them my sketches. I still always try to keep an illustrated journal when I am off on my travels. It's the only time that I ever seem to come to rest. I find sketching a pleasurable discipline, a kind of meditation. When I look at my funny little penned drawings, all the memories come flooding back to me so vividly as though I was right back there in the very picture itself. I can even smell the day and am able to recall my precise emotions at the time.

It is not at all surprising that both my boys have the sea in their blood, thanks to their father, and having been brought up on the Isle of Wight, known worldwide for its yachting and surrounded by the sea. On my return from seeing Sky I heard all about Orion's exciting latest commission. He is kept on his toes with his flourishing yacht design business or perhaps I should more accurately say he's kept on one of his many boards, bikes or kites. His man cave is jammed with every kind of nautical toy, surf board, plane, kite, wing, drone and bike you can imagine. He works so hard, and I am pleased he takes time out to play hard as well.

I had spent a lot of time wondering what was next in my life, and returned to work running reminiscence sessions. I joined the hospice choir and also joined the team of volunteers at the Isle of Wight Society for the Blind dress agency. I enjoyed helping people choose their wedding outfits and matching them with a 'favourite feathery fascinator', or advising on a floaty number for their next cruise, diplomatically assisting a lady who was trying to squeeze herself into the size-12 dress which she had fallen in love with when what she actually needed was a size 18. I know that feeling of humiliation so well. I am forever wishing I was slimmer, and am still trying to crack a healthy eating plan once and for all. (Perhaps my most recent attempt, the intermittent fasting plan of feast, fast, repeat will work.) But I must give up deluding myself that I am still a young model with that titchy twenty-four-inch waist.

I know that Rich would have been delighted that I was enjoying singing along with the choir, and that my time spent at the dress shop was all in a very good cause. The one thing he always dreaded was losing his sight. Mercifully he did not.

I decided that I would amuse myself by seeing if I could learn one new thing every single day until my time was up. It's never too late to learn something new. My mother took up wood carving at the age of seventy. Goodness… depending on how many more years I have got for this world, would this mean that I might become quite wise? Of course, that would depend on what sort of things I decided I was going to learn. Italian or Mandarin? Play the trumpet? Discover the meaning of life? (I did think I was being quite wise when I tentatively suggested to a friend that with four children it was a mistake to be removing the downstairs lavatory in their house. Just a little thing, but sound advice I thought. The family have moved house now, have more space and, joy oh joy, they are all loving the fact that they now have a downstairs loo. I think only now do they understand my simple obvious logic.)

The other day I had not imagined that when I went off to what I call my 'prance and dance aqua-fit class' at the local fitness centre I would return home so overjoyed to have learnt such a frivolous little thing. But it was something that I had wanted to know for years. As I entered the sports complex, seated at a small table was the rather rotund, jovial lady who books people in to the class and often stacks the shelves in the shop with rather nutritionless-looking, mainly packaged foods. The (I think) newly appointed manager must have had a light-bulb moment and had decided it would be a good idea to display some fresh foods on a table in the hope of tempting the regular gym bunnies. The few bananas, apples, crinkly-skinned oranges and some rather unappetising mushy pears arranged on the table all looked well past their sell-by-date.

There was also a 10 kilo bag of onions beside the table. The jovial lady was removing the crispy reddish-and-honey-coloured outer layers of the onions, preparing them for display on the table. It was obvious that she was taking pride in this new fresh food idea. I admired her thoughtful attention to detail. Out of the blue, the question jumped into my mind, and like a jack-in-the-box the words jumped out of my mouth: 'Do you happen to know how to peel those very tiny little shallot pickling onions?' To which she replied that she did. Her grandmother had shown her (amazing all the things I have heard over the years that grandmothers seem to teach one).

I love pickled onions, and my father did too, but I have always found them impossible to peel. I always thought there must be an easy method, but, being me, I did not have the good sense to consult Mrs Beeton's or be modern and Google it. Anyway, now I know. The kind lady was delighted to describe to me in detail how you need to soak the shallots in brine overnight, strain them, soak them in brine a second time and set aside for another day. Then, with a small paring knife, the skin will effortlessly remove itself. Job done. So in wild excitement and with great relief I rushed off to buy loads of shallot onions so as to get them pickled in time for Christmas. At last, after all these years, now I know, with that little secret up their sleeves, how the women of Stanhoe village prepared all those onions for the Coronation banquet.

So it's never too late to invite in the new. But it's not necessarily always 'cast out the old'. Some things never seem to change, like my rather OCD addiction to making lists, but I love making them. The lists are numerous and various, and they all read a little differently. It's one of the ways I keep tabs on things, and a way of giving myself a good talking to as well.

There's the *Urgent and Important List*. Most of the things on this list never seem to get done because they are usually the boring or less-interesting things. The current list reads something like this: discuss power of attorney with the boys; read hospice advanced care plan; check my will; update celebration of life file and list funeral wishes; see chiropractor; collect medication; see doctor re hernia; check my house and car insurance; learn how to use a computer; buy a new front door to replace the rotten one which you could easily put your foot through this winter without much effort.

Then there is the *Reasonably Important but not Urgent List*, but because of the effort required these things tend to get put on the back burner. Lose weight issue, same old story. Must have a general clutter clearing, which means I will need to be brutal and discerning. I will need to check out what things are of any use, which objects spark joy when I use them or look at them, which are aesthetically pleasing to me, what is of historic interest, which are precious and significant family heirlooms, definitely for keeps. Everything else that I never use, touch, like or even notice will have to go. Work out how to deal with the cobwebs in the inaccessible stairwell. Clean the conservatory roof (but I must get help, it would be stupid at my age to risk scrambling up there spreadeagled across my glass conservatory with a bucket of soapy water and broom in hand). Put Xmas decorations back into the attic (it's now July and I still have not done it, but I don't welcome the annual mission of struggling up the flimsy aluminium ladder, while teetering over the stairwell). I must read the instruction manual for my car, which has been hiding in the glove compartment for over six years. I need to get my head around how to turn the heater and the windscreen wipers on or off. All the various dials, switches and dashboard symbols don't make a lot of sense to me.

On yet another page in my 'To Do' notebook there is the *Fun Positivity List*, my version of a bucket list. It goes on and on, of course, with all the things I can possibly think of that I still want to do in my life. All the interesting and exciting things which you could say are merely self-indulgent. In the words of Abraham Lincoln, 'Most folk are as happy as they make up their minds to be.' I have made up my mind that I am going to prioritise doing things that make me and others happy. I want to remain positive, smile, laugh, feel joyful, have fun, focus on having a purpose too, be useful and be meaningfully occupied. All these, rolled into one, I know will be good for my body, mind, soul and spirit.

First off, I must get back to those Lindy Hop classes. I was hopeless at it, but had never laughed so much. I must add glitter paint to the sea surrounding the large map of the Isle of Wight which I have on my wall. I must eat that delicious mango in the bath. I must find excuses to celebrate anything, have more gatherings at my home so that I can delight in the smiles on my friends' faces when, as they depart, I hand them a 'Surprise Take-Away Party Bag'. I will finish sewing the set of signal flags which I started making four years ago for Sky for his boat. All sewn by hand. A labour of love, but one which I know he will appreciate, a quiet occupation to keep me happy on cold winter's evenings. I must remember to smile when answering the phone, as the caller might detect the smile in my voice and that might make all the difference. Having experienced that recently myself when making a call, I truly found it did make all the difference to the problem I was trying to solve – and in the end that made all the difference to my day.

It's much easier to tick off lots from the *Fun Positivity List*.

The *All the Things I Must Remember List* is a little more thought provoking. I could add some of them to my collection on the walls going up the staircase.

Give 100 percent to everything. Live for today. These twilight years are precious ones, don't waste a moment. Don't just drift through them. Make something wonderful happen, however small. Don't hold resentments against anybody, deal with difficulties if there are any. It's rude not to accept a compliment if I am given one. Remember there are always two sides to a story, mine is not the only one. Other people's business is theirs, not mine.

I don't want to be slapdash with this writing or shoddy with anything I do, but I must guard against the trap of becoming a perfectionist. I must engage brain before speaking, not interrupt people, and listen with more attention. Silence can sometimes be the best answer. I am allowed to say 'No'. In the words of Mahatma Gandhi: 'A "No" uttered from the deepest conviction is better than a "Yes" merely uttered to please, or worse to avoid trouble.' I want to take pride in how I look. When I make a plan I must aim to stick to it. Everyone is interesting, we were all innocent babies once upon a time. Try to get over my technophobia although I am doubtful that I ever will. I must try to tick a few things off the urgent list too, although in all honesty again , I doubt I'll ever get round to it.

Take quiet time out. Don't spend a moment feeling sorry for myself, I know I am very fortunate. Be sensible; if there are problems just tackle one at a time. Quietly question everything. Remember, delight in the little things, spiders' webs, grandchildren's laughter, take in the delicious fragrance as I watch the Evening Primrose petals opening at dusk, pause at the view from my bedroom window. Don't forget to thank my guardian angel every night. No amount of philosophising about things is worth a toss unless I put it into practice. Focus on my purpose. I must never be tempted to agree with the argument which promotes war in the name of peace. I have always loved singing hymns, so I need not feel silly when I am singing along to the early-morning Sunday service when in the bath. And I must keep reminding myself that *Whatever I can do, or dream I can, I must begin it.*

Thinking about 'beginning it', approximately three years after Rich passed away I had been wondering whether to make a brief foray into the minefield of internet dating yet again. I felt daunted having heard so many disastrous accounts, and yet I had also heard of many success stories. I thought nothing ventured nothing gained; I would put my toe in the water before I became too old. I didn't want to leave it too late and miss the boat. After all there might even be a boat leaving port requiring a deck hand. I might even set to sea again, who knows.

It was while I was struggling to write my rather flowery profile for the Classic FM dating site that the name 'Matilda' popped into my head. It had been suggested that until one is confident that the stranger one is hoping to meet is bona fide, it would be wise to adopt a temporary fancy name of some sort. It was a bit ridiculous, but I thought to hell with it: Matilda, that's quite a fun name, and close enough to Miranda, so just for a lark I thought that would do. I would call myself Matilda for the duration.

Negotiating my way around the site was a nightmare; and then trawling through the weird collection of 'possibly available men' was even worse. One never knew if they were actually 'available' or even real, whether they were just amusing themselves fantasising, or what their hidden agendas might be. I learnt very quickly to read between the lines and wised up to some of the less savoury dating site lingo. But I readily admit that in the early days of Covid lockdown it provided brief spells of light-hearted amusement, as I think it did for millions of others. If the truth were known there are probably hundreds of disillusioned folk out there: 'Forbidden fruit Covid relationship disasters' I call them.

Anyway, I stuck with it for a couple of months and agreed to meet a man who had travelled on a Blue Sky coach from the Midlands for a week's holiday on the island. He was staying at the Shangri-La Hotel in Shanklin. When I asked him why he went by the name of 'Moonlight Sonata', he explained that Beethoven was his favourite composer, but also the only classical composer he had ever heard of.

As we wandered along Cowes seafront he recounted his entire life history to me. It was all very tragic and a bit spooky. We downed a coffee at the seafront hotel by which time in the 'extended life story version' I learnt that he had worked out how to hang himself from a beam in his kitchen. I respectfully suggested that if ever he felt suicidal he might find it helpful to call the Samaritans. We wandered back into Cowes and politely bade each other farewell. I did not tell him that my real name was not Matilda.

Then there was the brief encounter with a Cornish builder who in his youth had sheared 300 sheep a day, and as a result had terrible back problems, poor man. I learnt a lot more about sheep, which was interesting. And I learnt quite a lot more about him, too, most of which was not my cup of tea. His somewhat cavalier behaviour didn't float my boat. And I do know a little about boats.

The dog owner who arrived with his dog, having said he would 'not' be bringing the dog, was a disappointment too. A real nutcase. He kept tripping over his untied shoelaces and his dog's lead. He had more conversation with the dog than he had with me. After a laboured lunch at the Folly Inn, the car journey back to the ferry was even more laboured. Teary eyed he starred vacantly into mine and said they shone like moonstones and that he was in love. With me I wondered? Or with another lady? His dog more than likely. But he had got it all worked out. We would go on lots of cruises together, and I would sell my house and we would live together happily ever after in his lovely bungalow somewhere near Reading with easy access to the M25.

Sadly I learnt very quickly that there are a lot of lonely old men out there who seem willing to shack up with anybody willy-nilly or just kill time having little dalliances every other month. I was so relieved when my month's subscription expired. I could let myself off the hook, and draw a firm line under internet dating for ever. It was not for me.

I turned my mind to more curious and interesting issues, like trying to work out how to deal with the slugs which seem to appear at night in my little sitting room and leave their beautiful, silvery artwork trails all over the carpet for me to admire in the morning. This being an old cottage, I guess they live under the floorboards in the damp and sneak up through a tiny crack when I have gone to bed, just to have a change of scene and take a look around.

With many a cold winter evening stretching ahead I had plenty of time to cast my mind back to 1946 when I was born. If my father were alive today he would be 119, and it would be hard to describe to him the world in which we are now living. He would hardly recognise it, let alone believe some of the weird things that are happening nowadays. I wanted to talk to him and imagined he might be able to hear me:

Dad, I just wanted you to know. Much water has passed under the bridge since you died all those years ago. But I have some really exciting news for you. Its the year 2021 now and your twelfth great grandchild, my third grandson, dear little Max James was born on 12 February. A third son for Orion and Ness. He is an absolute treasure. And I wanted to say I am so sorry I did not return that day when I drove off to London. I wished I had stopped and talked to you. Thank you for all that you were. And all that you could not possibly have been. You were bold, brave, a genius, and I loved it that you enjoyed playing those magic tricks on us with your pretend plastic chocolates, hiding the odd one for a joke amid a box of real Black Magic when we had Granny and Aunty Bessie over for tea on a Sunday. I have such a vivid image of you hopping down to the water's edge at Brancaster on your one leg for a high tide evening splash around. I was so lucky to have you as my father for nineteen years, but it was not long enough. We never had the chance to get to know each other. I feel sad that you have not had the chance to meet your six grandchildren and twelve great grandchildren. I imagine you would have loved that Great Grandad role. I wish you were here tonight sitting by my cosy woodburning stove. I have always jokingly said that I would rather have my dear little woodburner than a useless boyfriend any day. But of course I would much rather have you here with me tonight, than a useless boyfriend or the woodburner. Sending you all my love.

It is a very different world now, one which I barely recognise myself.

I feel I can't keep up, and I sometimes think that there are aspects of it which I don't even want to engage with, particularly the techy side of things. I don't understand it. It all frightens me because I do not have that kind of a brain. Mine is not wired the techy way. I have a lot of admiration for those older folk who are mastering the art.

I am of course grateful, because through some dint of miraculous technical wizardry these words that I am writing are whizzing off to somewhere and will apparently be stored safe and sound on a tiny little 'stick' no bigger than a postage stamp. Simultaneously they will reappear somehow on another little screen and my various helpers, having checked them on their magical devices, will then whizz them back to me for rechecking. They will then vanish and reinvent themselves, turn themselves into a book which you are now holding in your very own hand right now. And I will be sighing a big sigh of relief… and God only knows how any of this happens. Or, to put it more respectfully, only God knows how any of this works.

I prefer to imagine that there are heavenly hosts of golden angels floating around above me, spiriting my words away and busily working their magic. When they sense they are dealing with a traumatised customer who is having a drama queen moment, believing she has lost half of what she has just written (pressed the wrong button or something), they recruit a few glittery-winged empathic fairies as assistants who flit around her waving their delicate sparkly wands and she is able to calmly carry on with her writing.

So to all you techy geniuses out there who understand how all this works – you who have perhaps envisaged, designed and created such an ingenious method of communication – I hope you can hear that I am grateful. Even if you are a Humanoid Android Artificially Intelligent Something or Other, and although the thought of you scares me, and the world does wonder if you are a good idea, I still try to trust that this is all in the name of progress and that somebody or something out there actually knows what's going on and is in control. I keep the faith and believe that it must all be for the good. God is Good.

Do I sound like an ignorant little Luddite? Probably. Someone refusing to worship or be seduced by all the social media. Instagram, Twitter, TikTok, Facebook, Snapchat, Linkedin, and Blogs. I feel more in tune with Frogs, Kit-Kats, Knapsacks, Tuk-Tuks and those delicious little Tic Tacs useful for sweetening the breath after having indulged in an overdose of garlic. I have just about mastered WhatsApp. Although I am always wondering What's That? I have often been told that I am stubborn. But stubborness is one of the most commonly known personality traits of my Taurean star sign, so along with some other rather more complimentary traits I pacify myself and just accept that my stubbornness is excusable.

You see, I can remember attending the Pitman College for typing in Oxford Street in London. I owned a cute little Olivetti typewriter. I loved it. It was bright yellow. My mother said she thought it was really boring that I was trying to learn how to type, but I thought it was a good idea, just another string to my bow. That typewriter is regarded as an antique now I expect. I bashed and clattered away on it night after night in a typing frenzy, the sound ricocheting around the walls of my tiny bedsit in Earl's Court. Despite my efforts I never achieved the required speeds that would warrant me being awarded a Certificate of Excellence. I dealt with paper and envelopes and stamps and cheques and pennies and remember all those old-fashioned things and ways.

Never mind. I must not bash on about the olden days. But amid the numerous seemingly micro managed little children of today I do hope there will be a revival of the art of conversation and of good 'old-fashioned' manners. They never go amiss.

I want to bask in my happy memories of those days gone by, let go of the sadder ones, live in the present in my way, anticipating the very best for each day. When I feel concerned about the future I remember Rich's comforting words which I found written in his handwriting on a scrap of paper in that same old bedside chest: *'May each sunset linger, reflecting a fulfilling day of achievements made, of blessings given, and of faith renewed.'*

I am not going to dwell on or even mention all the controversial issues that concern me and all of us. There are so many, too many. Most recently having ridden the wave of the Covid pandemic, hopefully over time it will be possible to heal from the aftermath of this historically disturbing period of lockdown.

If I allow my mind to ramble off and envisage a snapshot of the future, who knows what it might look like? Will it be compulsory to wear flip-flops all day and all night? Will we never question why, never look back, because as a result we discover that when we get out of bed in the morning it's always on the right side and we smile our way through every day without ever complaining about a thing? Will little Alexa get the flu, but she won't be contagious? And on hot midsummer nights when an occasional bout of anxiety hits and we can't get to sleep, provided we ask her politely, Alexa will put us to sleep. But we'll wake up on the right side of the bed the following morning, because we were polite to her, toed the line and wore our flip-flops to bed. Fair is fair. You get back what you give out .

Perhaps it will be a punishable offence to hold a mobile phone; marriages on Mars will be commonplace, and all birds will fly backwards. A cathedral built out of defunct white goods will win an architectural award in Helsinki, and church congregations will swell. We will gaze at the rainbow-coloured moon, and even the scientists will be unable to explain why stars are now purple. The previously perfectly content little sperm will come out in protest against the latest 'immobilising contraceptive pill' and a queen bee will become prime minister. Christmas will be known as *'Samtsrich'*, and joint celebrations of all faiths will unite as one. We will lay down our arms, give up the fight, hold hands and respectfully and peacefully share our unique historic rituals. Us oldies may think it convenient that all we will need to do is blink at the knob on the cooker and it will ignite, but there may be no need even to do that, because we will be able to live on fresh air; we won't need any of our pills, ailments will be a thing of the past.

Back to reality. The harsh truth is that these twilight years are advancing, and the joy of collapsing after lunch for that afternoon rest becomes a delightful habit. It is reassuring that research scientists have established without any doubt that having a nap is the most effective way of retaining one's youthfulness and a way of keeping the grey matter charging on all cylinders. So that's an extra-special advantage of getting older. We can conveniently use napping as a valid excuse when we feel the need to recline on our sofa having had a boozy lunch. The other plus is qualifying for a bus pass. Riding on a bus is such fun. One of my favourite occupations. It's surprising what interesting things ones can spot when riding on the top of the bus going from or to somewhere (provided of course you have still got your eyes open, and have not fallen asleep after that lunch), but the back seat on the top makes a really comfortable day bed when journeying home, if that's what you feel in need of.

Of course, unfortunately and inevitably lurking in the background, the odds are that one day there may be the need for some kind of an operation. We are lucky if we escape it. So far, so good. To date I seem to be holding out quite well, although my hernia plays up from time to time, but I just tend to ignore it and mumble 'never mind', and the dull pain usually disappears.

But it's an unavoidable fact that our poor old, tired physical bodies are beginning to wear out and seize up. There are the hip replacements, the knee replacements, the teeth replacements, and the risk of having a fall which usually sets one back dramatically. There are the endless debilitating back problems, sciatica, failing eyesight and deafness, and the embarrassment of flatulence and, 'Tena Lady' here I come, that dreaded incontinence.

I sometimes think that deafness or 'selective hearing' could be a convenient way of managing one's exhaustion when one is trying to make polite chitchat at some gathering or other. One can be a bit sneaky and just pretend you have not heard what's going on. Just sit back quietly in the corner, gaze into space and not bother with conversation any more – perhaps that feels less stressful. I am fortunate. My hearing seems fine at the moment.

But I have to say that my heart sometimes flutters in ways I wish it would not, unlike the way it used to in the incurably romantic days of my youth, when I fell in love with the bus driver whose face was magically reflected in the wing mirror of the coach in which we were travelling on that holiday to see the châteaux of the Loire Valley in France. Now the ever-faithful old heart might be in need of some more serious attention, even as dramatic as a triple bypass operation, in order to make sure it keeps ticking along. Gall bladders might be playing up, redundant and need to be disposed of, and feet or even legs might need to be removed due to diabetes.

All of these ailments of course don't bear thinking about. They are no fun at all. When a surgical intervention does become necessary, having recovered from the butchery of an operation at least we must be grateful that hopefully we no longer have to endure agonising pain.

I dare not think of the devastating effect that the diagnosis of a terminal illness would have, knowing as a result I would then have to face the prospect of weeks and months of tiring tests and treatment, relentless hospital appointments, and of the consultant's kind words raising my hopes in his effort to sweeten the pill. Or I might have to make the difficult decision whether or not to be a guinea pig and agree to engaging in trials of new drugs. Many are lucky having done so, some not so lucky. In some cases, life is prolonged perhaps; but often, in truth, with very little quality of life.

Having lived with this situation on a daily basis while Rich survived his five years of treatment I certainly gained insight into the extraordinary tenacity of the human spirit. On those days when keeping up the fight felt too exhausting, not worth the effort, and the struggle and feelings of pointlessness consumed him, I found I was lost for words. There was no way of pacifying poor Rich.

There are many people who are not ill, just old, frail, and weakening, living out their twilight years in semi-isolation in old folk's homes. From the outside looking in, 'God's waiting rooms' seem isolating and lonely places.

During my reminiscence work in the care homes, more than a handful of people have asked me why they have been forgotten about. And more than a few have pleaded with me to put them out of their misery and make sure they did not wake the following morning. Finding myself faced with this predicament it makes me wonder about the ethical issue of the Hippocratic Oath. Doctors around the world face this question on a daily basis. Would it not be kinder to listen to those who are suffering and honour their request? Many lie in a semi-comatose state under thin sheets, hardly present, just existing. Some, with their failing energy, can perhaps just manage a monosyllabic exchange with a rushed and weary care assistant. It is this harsh reality of old age that leads to the ethical question of euthanasia and whether assisted dying should be more easily accessible, accepted as every human being's right to choose.

But we who are still forging on have work to do. We are fortunate, we must not complain. I constantly have to remind myself that I must guard against those tell-tale signs of the 'mutton dressed up as lamb' look. As my hair is beginning to fall out in unwelcome handfuls and my skin is becoming blotchy, and none of the expensive cosmetics I used to rely on for an instant transformation in my youth seem to have the desired effect any more, I just have to tell myself it does not matter. Vanity is a thing of the past. It is my sanity that is important, and I must guard against imagining the worst. That fear of dementia. One day, might I not remember my name?

I rattle around with my pill boxes always at the ready. And when I have finally managed to make a doctor's appointment, which everyone knows nowadays is nigh impossible, I do feel exasperated when I am told I am only allowed to discuss two of my ailments. I probably have at least five or six niggling ones that I am only slightly curious about anyway, but I still feel the need to be reassured that there is nothing major wrong with me. I feel despondent when I am then prescribed more pills and am advised that I may well need to take yet even more to counteract the side effects of the ones first prescribed.

Cutting my fingers on the sharp edges of the hermetically sealed, silver-packaged medication is a risk, a wrestling match that creates stress I could well do without. I must make an appointment with the chiropodist, but she will need strong nail clippers, ones more suitable for trimming a pony's hooves than my once-dainty toenails. My unsightly nails have toughened with old age, my tired feet ache. I don't have any bunions or corns as yet, thank goodness, but my toes seem twisted – probably due to the ridiculous pair of blue-and-white, high-heeled shoes, several sizes too small, which I was hell-bent on forcing my feet into having bought them from the smart Galeries Lafayette store when we were in Paris. I suppose I thought I looked a really chic teenager when I paraded in them for the bus driver with whom I had fallen in love on that same holiday to the Loire.

Yes, growing older means the buffer or bumping post is coming up. In train language it's the stop block, the device that prevents a carriage going past the end of a particular section of track. The old steam locomotives eventually wore out and were beyond repair, needing constant inspection and daily maintenance. They were outdated, inefficient and costly. As we age we are no different, really. But whereas the old steam trains lay abandoned in a siding, our family, the noble doctors, nurses and carers, do their best to keep us up and running, even if stoking us up doesn't really work any more. When we have gone beyond the point of no return we may puff, puff, puff, and chuff, chuff, chuff along for a while, but eventually our fire will extinguish itself. I seem to have been to the crematorium way too many times recently to bid farewell to friends and colleagues. Their time was up.

Every morning when I rise I will myself to say: 'Thoughts create reality – I am getting younger every day.' I will not allow all this 'getting older stuff' to get the better of me. No. Not for one moment. I must not stumble and shuffle and shamble along. I will keep dashing, skipping and striding out there regardless.

Chapter 24

Just for today

Party time. My three grandchildren Sonny, Jude and Max keeping an eye on things from an upstairs window at my 77th birthday party on April 29th 2023. Photography by Jane Burton

I have sailed, struggled and slept, jogged, juggled and leapt along through life. A daughter, a sister, an aunt, a young woman and twice a wife. A mother, a daughter-in-law, an ex-wife and a single parent. A partner, a mother-in-law, a grandmother and a friend. I have worn many hats, played many different roles. Each with its particular emphasis either on behaviour, expectations, duty or rights has served me at the different stages in my life. I have been the people-pleaser, the provider, the follower, the leader. The victim, the rescuer, the carer… and, as a child, I loved to dress up, perform and 'play the fool'. I have always made plans, set myself goals and finally, after all these years, it is peace of mind that matters more than anything. So I have realised that living for today is the best way of achieving that.

Today I jumped out of bed, earlier than usual, checking my '*Urgent and Important To-Do*' list but knowing full well that I would not get round to ticking much of it. I had such a busy day ahead: a contemplative walk up and down the garden to say 'good morning' to it, followed by a quick coffee and toast. I realised the cherry tree may well be in blossom for my birthday on 29 April, which will be lovely. It is so pretty. It is white, but as it fills out the blossom takes on a very subtle light green tinge. I call it my 'bride' tree.

Off to work. As yet I have not drawn a line under it, and I am a lot older than several of the people whom I visit in the residential homes. But I don't let this bother me, as I still feel only a little older than forty-five. It's all about how one feels, not what the number is. I am fortunate to have been blessed, it seems, with copious amounts of energy, so I keep trucking on. Sometimes I worry that there is something wrong with me. I often find myself saying this and apologising too, which is ridiculous if you think of it. Why should I think that there is something wrong with me just because I still feel relatively youthful, inspired and enthusiastic at seventy-seven? Surely I should be feeling very fortunate.

I have to say I can feel a little daunted sometimes when I arrive at a residential home and I find most of the residents dead to the world. In the morning perhaps they are not yet awake, and would prefer to be left quiet and just drift through till lunchtime. If I am delivering an afternoon session they have just had their lunch and it is definitely time for a snooze. I often have to let go of my grand plan for the session, not coerce people in any way. Whoever joins in… that's just as it should be.

This morning I was working at a home in West Wight. There were ten folk in the sitting room, not a very cheery room but it is at least quite spacious and it does overlook the garden. It smelt fresh with several vases of bright daffodils on the tables. The TV is usually on, which it was today, so I politely asked if it was okay to turn it off.

A rather odd selection of pictures were adorning the walls. I am always tempted to go and straighten them. It's one of my obsessions, pictures hanging crookedly on walls. The other is seeing price labels on flowerpots, with the white barcode and price standing out stark against the black plastic pot. I know the staff are always so busy and have not the time for attention to such detail, but being into the aesthetics of things I think simple adjustments can make all the difference to an environment and atmosphere. It's probably me being too much of a fanatical fusspot, but it still bothers me. So this morning I did straighten a picture or two, and turned two rather tired-looking pot plants round so as to obscure the tell-tale £2.99 price label.

Having introduced myself I realised one lady was troubled, continually trying to throw her Zimmer frame into the middle of the room. The carers tried to pacify her. A very frail-looking gentleman was brought through in a wheelchair by two Indian carers and rather awkwardly transferred to an upright chair. He looked very uncomfortable, so I found a cushion for his back, fetched him a footstool, and placed his cup of tea on a table so as he could reach it.

Another little sparrow-like lady was almost disappearing beneath the cushions which were propping her up, and was clearly very sleepy. I sat and held her hand for a moment, but she remained vacant, living in her own world somewhere, and it seemed there was really nobody at home. She squeezed my hand in recognition of something. Pushing her head forward she stroked my hair, and through her pale misty watering eyes she gazed into mine . . . I told her she looked very beautiful. I wondered if she was too shy to smile having heard my words. She seemed to be wondering and then clearly fatigued she slumped back beneath her cushions.

Moving on there was a smartly dressed gentleman sitting at a table at the end of the room reading the newspaper. His half-eaten breakfast cereal was still beside him. Having wiped his nose on the newspaper, he declined my invitation to join the group and said he wanted to read.

After my usual brief introduction and sharing a little about myself I told those gathered round how I'd love to hear about their lives. I suggested that they might like to share their thoughts and memories about their hobbies, pastimes and passions. I often use a prompt by showing photographs, using 'tell me a story' cards, scents and aromas, or interesting memorabilia; but on this occasion I simply focused on the theme of 'our passions in life'.

I am frequently met by a bit of a blank, brick wall. Not one of resistance exactly, but one of suspicion that I am testing them to see what, if anything, they are able to recall about their lives. With the inevitable weariness of their advancing years the residents often seem doubtful and say that even if they could remember it would not be interesting. It would be dull, it would be sad, because now that they are old they can't do or say anything interesting any more. I regularly hear from those who have given up all hope that they know they have been forgotten. Those who are still hanging on in there with a little more positivity often ask if they have been forgotten. They are still wondering *if* that is so.

These very real and natural doubts, fears, and worries are often voiced, and this is the first hurdle we have to get over together. I have to bridge this gap. I reiterate that I want to hear the details of their rich, colourful and fascinating lives. I am confident, more often than not, that when they are prompted and listened to with proper care and attention, all sorts of memories and stories do come to mind and that sharing them will be a positive, affirming experience, so we carry on.

This morning, rather reminiscent of the nursery rhyme, *Tinker, Tailor…*, the diversity of their interests and stories captivated me. Having spent many years doing this work in varied settings, using different techniques and approaches, I found this session an extra-special one that I shall remember for ever.

Among us we had a gentleman who had left school at thirteen, and shortly after that he had joined the army. He said he did not want to talk about that, because you don't talk about the war. When he retired he took up fishing. Not sea fishing – he liked to go to the fishing lakes. It was peaceful. He would sit on a sunny afternoon by the still water. His wife always went with him, and while she read her book he would often fall asleep. But it didn't matter, because as well as reading she was able to keep an eye on his fishing rod. She was clever that way, he proudly told us. She would tap him on the shoulder to wake him up and then ply him with a warm cup of tea from their flask. When he had eventually succeeded in catching a fish, usually a carp, he would throw it back into the water. He was never happier. Fishing taught him about patience. He loved his wife, she had always been patient with him, and he loved it that she loved to go fishing with him.

Then there was a lady who adored knitting. She was wearing one of her own home-knits, a cardigan, pale lavender, with brown leather buttons. I asked her if I could feel it. It looked so lovely and soft. She had found knitting a very therapeutic pastime, but she could never knit socks. She said she was not intelligent enough. They were too complicated – four needles and all that. She could no longer knit because of her arthritic fingers.

Years ago she had been a seamstress. Her grandmother had shown her how to sew on a button properly so that it would not fall off. She had learnt some things at school too, but not a lot that she considered of much use to her in life. It was her grandmother who had been the most influential and had taught her all the practical things that she reckoned she needed to know. She told us that one of the things her grandmother used to say to her was: 'Never say you are "going" to do something. Say that you "hope" to do whatever that something is, because you never know. You can never be sure of what might befall you.'

She thought that had been a sound piece of advice. She was not so sure about her mother's suggestion, when she went to a tea dance wearing her mother's old fur coat, that she must sew into the hem of her petticoat cotton-wool balls soaked in the delightful combination of Dettol and Eau de Cologne in an attempt to disguise the coat's odour of mothballs. The young men might not appreciate the unusual fragrance of mothballs. Laughing, she said she was not sure which they might prefer.

Another gentleman loved sailing. He had owned many boats. He thought it was a wonderful pastime in which all the family could become involved, which they were. And it was outdoors in the fresh air, and physically beneficial too. He was sad that all he had now were his memories. He knew he had to work hard with his mind so as not to fall into a melancholic state. He had his family, and they were what mattered now. He wanted me to know his age, which he was not sure of; but with a series of dates and calculations we managed to work out that he was ninety-two. He was thrilled, not only because he had thought he was around ninety-seven and so he had instantaneously regained five years, but also because he found he could still do maths, which he had enjoyed at school.

Then there was the lady who truly was an expert on growing fuchsias. She had so much information and knew that there were well over 100 species and countless varieties. It was fascinating. She had over the years taken numerous cuttings. With a glint in her eye, she admitted that she had cheekily stolen quite a few from other people's gardens, and had sold over twenty varieties. She loved drawing the flowers, as they were so intricate. Her particular favourite was the one which grows wild in the hedgerows in Cornwall. Having lived there myself I was able to share my limited knowledge about them. She had decided it was good to keep looking cheerful and always wear bright colours. I agreed wholeheartedly with her. She admired my pink jumper, but as I was leaving she said did not like my black coat. I apologised and said I promised to wear my cheery red coat the next time I visited.

Another lady insisted she was boring, but of course she was far from that. She had been in management and said she was a people person. If there was an upset in her office she always managed to sort it out and she invariably got people together. She built bridges and didn't let people get away with any nonsense. She had become fed up with all the red tape, thought it was a waste of time and a waste of the government's resources. She had never wanted to go into politics, but thought she might have made a better job of it than some of the prime ministers who had been in office during her lifetime.

Again we did the maths and realised she had known of seventeen prime ministers. We could not quite remember all their names, but I assured her that next time I visited I would bring her a list of them all. She liked that idea. She loved typing and still had her wonky old Remington. It was in her daughter's attic. She described how you had to replace the tape or ribbon which had the ink on it, and how you had to press a lever down if you wanted to write the £ sign in red. 'More red tape,' she said, laughing. Reflecting, quietly, she said she thought it was a good idea to think of all the things she had done, all the things she had not done and all the things she still might do. What a beautiful and positive soul she was.

With the imminent coronation of King Charles, one lady said that her passion has always been following the Royal Family. She had all the dates at her fingertips: the births, deaths and marriages, divorces and scandals. She knew all the stories inside out. When I asked if she had been present at the coronation of Queen Elizabeth, she was eager to tell her story. She had wanted to go to London to wave her flag. She stayed with her Auntie Rose and Uncle George. One of their goldfishes had died and her Auntie Rose flushed it down the lavatory. That was all she remembered about the coronation. Coronation goldfish on the menu from now on then. We laughed together.

This funny story prompted the 'home-knit lady' to tell her experience of the 1953 coronation. She had been given a day off from work, and her cousin had asked her if she would mind perming her hair. She hadn't really wanted to do that. She wanted to watch the TV but finally agreed and said she would. They had a tiny black-and-white television set bought especially so as to be able to watch the crowning of the Queen. She had struggled to watch it while perming the hair with that terrible smelly stuff. The upshot of it was that her father was none too pleased. In fact he was furious because for weeks afterwards the whole house stank of ammonia.

Finally came the Lady of the Quorn foxhunt. A rather grand lady, serene, she sat upright in her chair. Though she was very hard of hearing, it was clear that she was not about to give up and feel excluded just because she could not hear. I made sure she got the gist of everything that the others were saying. Her passion had always been horses. From the age of three, when she remembered sitting on a pony for the first time, she had never wanted to do anything other than ride a horse. She was so proud that she had ridden with the Quorn, founded in 1696, the oldest and most well-known pack in England.

We ended with a song. As I tapped out on the side table the rhythm of 'My Old Man Said Follow the Van', one of the ladies started tapping along with her feet and spontaneously taught me the sequence of moves for tap dancing which she used to teach. I wanted to hear all about it, but sadly had to tear myself away and get to my next session.

What a fascinating morning. It was as though having drawn back the curtains of these people's homes I was peering in through their windows, taking a peep into their lives. More importantly I felt they had rediscovered themselves and had also discovered each other. Often I find that some of these ladies and gentlemen have not even spoken to each other. This had been a successful session, a positive and uplifting interlude in what might otherwise have been a rather uneventful, lonely day.

I prefer to call these sessions 'Making Memories Matter'. We can never be denied our memories. Structured reminiscing can be a catalyst enabling people to recall details about their lives and bringing back a little joy. It can help people believe that, although perhaps sadly no longer comforted by the familiarity of their own home and by the presence of their loved ones, they are not just alienated lone ships in the night passing each other by.

Don't we all, whatever our ages, want to know that we are at least still being noticed, appreciated and loved? I certainly would not want to think that I had been completely forgotten about. I always hope to be able to reassure all these dear people that they have not been.

After I'd got back home I found that I too was reminiscing. I was remembering going with my parents to a meeting with the bank manager in King's Lynn. I must have been around twelve years old or maybe a little younger, eight, Sonny's age. I have no memory of what the meeting was about, but the visit itself for some reason made a lasting impression on me.

We were all seated around a highly polished, oval mahogany table in the bank manager's inner sanctum, and I remember being impressed but a little intimidated by the floor-to-ceiling, imposing mahogany bookshelves. Finding reading so difficult, I wondered what on earth all the files and books could possibly be about, and how anybody would ever have the time to read them all.

There was a knock at the door and a very neatly dressed lady entered, bearing a heavily laden silver tray. She proceeded to serve us tea from an ornately engraved silver teapot, pouring the tea into fine bone-china tea cups. The milk had already been poured from a matching milk jug into the cups, the old-fashioned way to make a proper cup of tea. The lady then handed round the sugar lumps and tongs – no rude grabbing of a sugar lump in those days, or packeted sugar in an impenetrable little paper phial. This was a fine-dining tea party with the bank manager.

Nowadays every other bank seems to be closing down. Bank managers must exist, I suppose, but one never expects to be able speak to them – let alone meet them in the flesh, be invited to their offices and be served tea from a silver teapot. Some things in life go full circle, but I doubt that such gentility is ever likely to return.

Chapter 25

Romance returns

Lower Bay. A favourite beach in Bequia, a sketch from my holiday journal of February 2023

I scampered off to a book signing by Hunter Davies in Cowes the other day, having been invited by a girlfriend. I did not expect, as a result of a fortuitous meeting on that very evening, the seed would be sown and I would contemplate writing about my life. And how could I ever have anticipated that I would meet such an interesting gentleman? One who at his 'ripe young age' does not cling to his past, but with his great zest for life has chosen to create a happy future for himself. He appears to be daunted by nothing, forever looking on the bright side, amusing others and himself, witty, stimulating, and one who makes me and many others laugh.

He was signing his most recent book, one of many over his long journalistic career. After I'd bought a copy, with its intriguing title *Love in Old Age*, he signed it for me, and I was mildly amused by the flirtatious chat-up lines which he had hidden up his sleeve.

I had not been out on a date, if you can call it that, for years, so a little nervously I accepted his invitation to an informal dinner and found myself having a takeaway pizza with him and his friend. The interrogation continued over the meal: the 'formal interview' for the 'vacant post' provided entertainment for his Seaview friend as we busily munched our pizzas. A pen hung permanently around his neck on a rather tatty piece of string, and with it in hand he jotted down notes on a paper napkin. I appeared to be ticking most of his essential boxes as the three of us chuckled our way through the evening. There was a frisson – sparks were flying on that serendipitous evening.

Who would have dreamed it? I certainly didn't.

I was too embarrassed to disclose the fact that I had tried internet dating when he asked me that question. I managed to be expedient with the truth. He, on the other hand, proudly regaled me and his friend with endless stories and intriguing details of his various rendezvous with all sorts of ladies. Entertaining them, often three per week, for lunch at his favourite Hampstead Heath bistro must have provided endless amusement for the waiters and waitresses.

He seemed to have difficulty remembering my name. He insisted on calling me Amanda, which I am seriously not fond of, then Matilda, then Amanda, then Matilda. I wondered if he had simply not heard my name in the first place when we were in the shop at his book signing, or was he completely deaf, or was this a short-term memory problem? I sincerely hoped not. Obviously I didn't like to ask. Several times I politely corrected him. 'By the way, my name is not Matilda.' As he nervously raised his eyebrows, I realised he hadn't got a clue what my name was. So rather abruptly I helped him out. 'I have told you that my name is actually Miranda.' More raising of eyebrows, more giggles and laughter… And he still gets it wrong even today.

We know that laughter is the very best of medicines, so I am considering chucking out my collection of pills (which supposedly keep my blood pressure under control, thin my blood and do a few other things) and just rely on his company to keep me in fine fettle as I get older and younger. I am sure that this will be a more effective treatment.

How strange though, since I had never told him that while having that brief dalliance with the internet dating scene I went by the name of Matilda. According to him: 'It was all written in the stars, pet.'

Hunter has implied on more than one occasion that I am just a tad 'away with the fairies', but that's OK, I don't mind. Perhaps I am. He is completely out of the box, a one-off himself, so perhaps in some respects we are two of a kind. He is a generous, vibrant, positive, polite, energetic, childlike and clever man. And I am discovering he can be rude, frenetic, impatient, contrary and very bossy, especially when he is not getting what he wants precisely when he wants it. He happily admits his shortcomings. We all have them. I have them in bucket loads but at our age, now so well set in our ways, it's too late to change, so it's best just to try to ignore any irritations and get on and enjoy what little time we have left for this world.

Hunter is a rare gem and a kind man who says 'yes' to pretty well everything. Without his initial suggestion and continued encouragement, patience, constructive criticism, knowledge, support and love I would never have attempted trying to string so many words together. I feel fortunate to have collided with him and to have him as a best friend, buddy and companion. He is ten years older than me, and

A memorable sunny day trip. I organised a surprise boat trip to the Needles on the Isle of Wight for Hunter in August 2023

we enjoy chatting about many of our memories from the golden olden days. I find it interesting and comforting.

Although I had been dreaming of having a hot holiday, I had not entertained the idea that my dream would ever come true, so when I was invited by Hunter to join him on a holiday to Bequia, the largest island in the Grenadines, it was all hard to believe.

I have got a bit of a thing about when I go off on holiday. I always think I must have some nice new underwear. I don't know where that thinking comes from, but it's always been a treat to go and buy a new bra and some pants, especially if I am heading off into the sun. The downside is that I have always found that having a bra fitting is such a hurdle to jump over; it seems such a hoo-ha, finding a shop in the first place that does such a thing nowadays. Standing for hours shivering while endless measurements are taken. Can I face it?

This dilemma made me think about my beautiful mother.

One of the things that seemed to irk her somewhat was the matter of her droopy breasts. She went to bed every night wearing a bra, which was quite strange since usually one takes one's bra off when one goes to bed. But she didn't. Her boobs, I remember, seemed to be rather like two elongated lobes, a bit like overripe, wizened papaya fruit, and they had no hope of recovery. I wonder what underwear she was forced to wear when she was a child…

When we were children, before our breasts had developed, we wore liberty bodices. They were rather uninteresting, shapeless, sleeveless bodices made out of a warm fleecy fabric and they had tiny linen-covered buttons down the front which were awkward to do up and often used to break. These garments were more than just vests, and so were intended to keep us cosy and warm, which I suppose they did to some extent. I always thought what a strange name this was, since the garment didn't seem to me to be very liberating. The thick, fleecy material rather robbed one of any sense of femininity.

But if one looks back to the early 1900s, when the universal fashion was a very restrictive boned corset – tightly laced at the front to flatten the chest and drawn in even more tightly to accentuate the waistline – then the progression to the liberty bodice makes sense. Women were being liberated from these days of such tight-laced fashion.

Anyway, I remember feeling incredibly excited when the day came. I think I was about thirteen (they develop much earlier these days though), and my mother had decided it might be about time for me to start wearing a bra. My half-risen little cupcake bosoms were going to be nurtured and gently supported in some kind of a little pouch. As I grew up, so of course did they. I measured a 34B and thought, as I did not understand these things, that I would be that size for ever. Bras were completely devoid of any lace or prettiness or colour in those days, just boring white Playtex. But, nevertheless, a bit of an improvement on the liberty bodice.

Well, I did after much deliberation decide that before the pending holiday to Bequia I had better have a fitting for a new bra. Luckily, I happened upon a shop, 'Exclusive underwear for discerning ladies'. That'll do. A very helpful lady logged me immediately. Recognising my anxiety, measuring me with her very cold hands, she gave me all sorts of advice. I had decided that underwired bras were not for me. I had read that they can distort your rib cage or some such nonsense, but the idea of the wire digging into me was not fun. I just wanted to be comfortable, feel as though I was not really wearing anything. Her nod indicated that she understood.

'What size are you usually?'

'Ah, I don't know.'

'When were you last measured?

'Um, well when I was about thirteen, I think. I am a 34B.'

She now seemed a little lost. What can she have thought? I was now a woman of seventy-seven, and I had never been measured since I was thirteen! She patiently measured me again, apologising this time for her cold hands. She checked, and double checked, triple checked and checked again, and finally informed me that I was now a 38DD.

'Oh, good!' Well, now I know.

After all that I decided I would go and have a cup of tea. I was too tired to start trying on double-Ds.

I did risk an experiment with a sports bra once. Yet another kind lady in the sports shop told me this bra would give me Ultra Max Support when I was leaping about doing my energetic gym sessions. It was a highly engineered, efficiently structured and state-of-the-art piece of kit. I thought it was just a bra. But, oh no, it was of course very costly too. I fell under the spell of her sweet-talking gym-bra patter and bought it.

What a disaster. Apart from the money, which I could ill afford, its colour almost blinded me. It was vibrant, eye-catching electric pink with a bright azure blue stripe dancing diagonally across it – and, of course, some logo which I couldn't have cared less about. Had I wanted to attract attention to myself at the gym I think I might have done so wearing this number. I had to torment and contort myself for about fifteen minutes every day trying to get in and then out of this ridiculous sports bra. More like a straitjacket. Never again

So, fast forward, and I'm off to Bequia. The well-planned holiday had been organised, booked, cancelled, rebooked. Oops – so can I be bothered to go through this all over again, check that my bra size is still the same? But, yes, I must have some nice new, fresh clean undies, so off I trotted the day before we flew off and told myself not to fret, be patient and it would all be OK. I decided it would boost my morale and be forgivable to indulge myself in a little prettiness, comfort and style.

Well informed, well armed, I braved the M&S bra-fitting department. I braced myself as the familiar cold hands of the kind lady measured me this way and that and then she announced that I'm now a 36D apparently, surprise, surprise. It's all a mystery to me. I seem to have shrunk. Two hours later I left the shop, having splashed out and treated myself to five new bras: Black, Nude, Plum, Misty Blue and Bright Green. Correct size, perfect fit, pretty, lacey, fun and each with a pair of colour-coordinated pants.

We went off on a magical holiday and, I presume, so long as I stay the same size all will be well. There will be no need to struggle with the nightmare of buying a new bra ever again in my life. Joy, oh joy. Thank goodness for that. All's well that ends well.

But how will this story end? How does one ever draw a story to its conclusion? I have fretted, as this concern has hovered nervously around me since day one. Sometimes, when the words were flowing along effortlessly or rushing at me instantaneously like metal filings to a magnet, I thought, well, there won't be an end because I am still here, still going strong. On tough days when words presented themselves in a discombobulated jumble I felt as though I were battling against my fury, caught out in an unexpected storm. I trawled for memories from way back, and having retrieved them I did not want to let them slip through the net of my weary mind.

Then, suddenly inspired again, I found that words flashed up as though they were a leading light guiding me into a safe harbour, and I felt desperate not to let them vanish over the horizon back into the dark night. Sometimes when my mind was blank I felt a drogue anchor was dragging me backwards, slowing me down. I felt I was dredging a river and heaving up a heavy anchor from the depths. My ship was sinking and I was going down with it. I might drown.

When it was not going according to plan and I was dogged by scrutinising my every word, I wanted to ditch the whole silly idea; but to wilfully cast myself adrift felt like failure, which I was not prepared to give in to. When I sent out an SOS, the many kind words from encouraging friends felt like the essential 'all hands on deck' that I needed. They were right there for me in those moments of self doubt. Having been salvaged and on an even keel again, back at the helm I have sailed on.

I have enjoyed observing myself when writing. It has not been a chore. It has been an unexpected, completely new experience. I have found the process a very different one to that of producing an artwork. It has been much more challenging, intense, direct, explicit, time consuming and emotionally demanding. While reviewing my life I have been living through all the experiences as an observer and have been surprised about some of the things I have remembered. Not only have I learnt a lot about myself and others, I also feel that when writing about other people, and situations, from that one-step-removed position, I have been able to have some rather more reflective insights.

When writing I have sometimes had to pinch myself and say: 'Was that me? Was I really there? Did I do that? Why on earth didn't I do something different ? That was a strange choice to have made.' But no matter where you go, there you are and here I am.

From beginning to end I feel as though I have been on a very testing year long solo voyage. I threw life lines out to you. Having done so I have imagined all along that I have had you, the reader, on board as company. Thank you for coming to the rescue. You have stuck with me. Not abandoned me. You have helped see me through. So, whether you were actually there or not, you were in my mind, I needed you as crew on board my ship. I am glad you joined me on my single-handed voyage of self-discovery.

Just like the many changing moods of the wind and sea, so have been my thoughts, moods and my emotions. As I have been recalling and trying to describe some of the most mundane moments, some poignant ones and the ramifications of some of the more distressing ones, I have had to forgo my niggling concerns about sounding politically incorrect, ageist, racist, sexist, judgemental, unsubtle or demeaning. I have had to ditch my 'hitch-hiking saboteur' who jumped into my mind many a time and tried to convince me that this book is a whole load of 'gobbledygooking waffle' which nobody would ever want to read. I have had to fight off my demons. I have kept going, telling my story up to the present day.

It is autumn 2023 now and Hunter and the family are coming for a meal today. In my tiny house, the space has to be organised in order to accommodate them all. I have spent the past hour rearranging all the furniture in the conservatory so that all seven of us can fit round the table.

That gate-leg oak table is a historic family heirloom. It's the one my mother had when she was young, and we have a picture of her sitting at it, writing. The Victorian chaise longue, a perfect place to recline after a meal, was bought in Norfolk, for sixpence at the auction on Burnham Market's village green. Hopefully these beautiful pieces of old-world furniture will become fashionable again one day.

The table is set for dinner now with flowers, candles and the Lazy Susan. The boys love this. When they last came for a meal, young Jude said they were so lucky to have two grandmas: one with a large house and a huge long table with things all down the middle and another one (that's me, Granmanda) with a small house with a round table with this twirly thing in the middle. 'It's got all the different dishes on, and we can twizzle it round and round and choose what we want.'

So here I am now with my Granmanda hat on. I love being a grandmother. I have several friends my age who are sad as they would like to be one too, but are doubtful that they will ever become one. From time to time I feel a little sadness that I have not been able to share the joys and amusement of grandparenting with their grandfather.

Happy Granmanda. Story time in the snug with my first two grandchildren

But I don't want to dwell in the past. It is not good. I want to live in the present and enjoy the golden moments of being a granny and have fun being useful.

Once, when we were all enjoying a game of clock golf at one of the boys' birthday outings, it was fun keeping an eye on the three little ones, all under seven at the time. I was doing simple but useful things like finding a rubbish bin for their empty crisp packets and picking up the numerous items of clothing which kept falling off the overloaded pram. I could not stop laughing as 'Daddy', who was supposed to be in charge of the complicated scoring system, was busy designing a boat on the back of the score card.

At another gathering in a local community field, to which twenty little children had been invited for fun and games and a birthday tea, I had gathered up a bucketful of dog mess. Not very pleasant, but essential, I thought. When I informed Orion that in the early hours that morning I had been on a 'dog poo clearing mission', his words: 'Where did we find you, Mum?' made me smile. I felt that I had been truly appreciated that day.

But now, just for today, I must not get distracted. I must get busy with the next job in hand, arrange all the little dishes and fill them with the grandchildren's favourite goodies: pine nuts, carrot sticks, cucumber slices, potato rings, blueberries, parmesan cheese, pistachios, pomegranate seeds, strawberries, and not forgetting the … whatever it is I have forgotten. There is bound to be something.

Rattle, rattle, rattle at the letterbox. This is what they always do when they arrive. Then they call through, 'Granmanda, Granmanda,' just to let me know they are really here, in case I have not heard. And here they are. They have all tumbled in through the door: Sonny, Jude and Max, Mummy Ness, Daddy Orion and Hunter.

'Shall we have a celebratory drink before we eat? And I want to apologise, too.'

I am feeling excited and a little nervous. Are they all wondering what we are about to celebrate? Are they thinking, we had her birthday back in April so she won't need to celebrate that again? And she can't be expecting a baby! And what on earth does she need to apologise for? I never quite know what anybody is ever truly thinking or perhaps wanting to tell you. Thoughts can be private, and we have every right to keep them to ourselves. If I feel it's best to remain quietly polite and not ask people what they are thinking, I can at least tell them whatever I want myself. Today is one of those days. So I go ahead.

Spanning the ages, Hunter and Max.
Two of the loves in my life hand-in-hand.

'Well, you know they say that things often come in threes. I want to celebrate you all. My dear grandchildren. You three precious little gemstones, Sonny, Jude and Max. I am so lucky. I love you all so much. And you probably won't understand this, but you three are my greatest teachers. You are so enthusiastic, full of curiosity and innocence. Full of vibrant energy and such fun. I must always remind myself to take that leaf out of your childhood book.

'And I wanted to say that after all these years of working in the old folk's home, today I have just had one of my best-ever sessions. It was so wonderful. Worth celebrating.

'I want to apologise for having been so preoccupied this last year. I have been writing my book as you know and I have had to be very disciplined or it would never have got written. But today I have been writing this. It's almost the last paragraph of the final chapter, so that was the third thing I thought was definitely worth a celebration.

'I want to thank John. I will always be grateful for the gift he gave me, the voyage we shared. It was an incredible experience to have built *Sweet Painted Lady*, and then to have sailed together on the high seas.

'Right now, today, I have you, Hunter, by my side. Often while I was preoccupied, doubting my capacity to eventually get this done, you never ceased believing in me. Thank you. My arms are around you. We will be best friends for ever.

'Among all the things on my bucket list, one of which is to visit every cathedral in Britain. Oh! There is just one more thing which is very, very important.

'Sonny, do you remember last year when you were seven and I was seventy-six we went for our day trip on the bus to Ventnor? You said you wanted to take me to see the famous Glitter Rocks. The wonderful sparkling granite rocks piled up on the seafront as part of the sea defence. We walked along from the town towards Bonchurch. We scrambled out over the rocks and sat there for a while. I went and bought a cup of coffee from the café, and when I came back you were gazing up into the sky. I asked if you minded me asking what you were thinking about. You said you imagined you were sitting up among the stars looking down at the Glitter Rocks.

'I asked you if you would come with me when you were twenty-one, I would be ninety by then, to sit on the beautiful Glitter Rocks again. You promised you would. I am really looking forward to that outing, but there are several years to go before you will be twenty-one and I will be ninety.'

I wonder what other surprises and adventures might be out there for us all. I feel sure there will be many more.

That's part of the magical mystery of life. We just don't know what is round the corner. It's a bit like being out at sea. At break of day never knowing what ships might appear on the horizon….

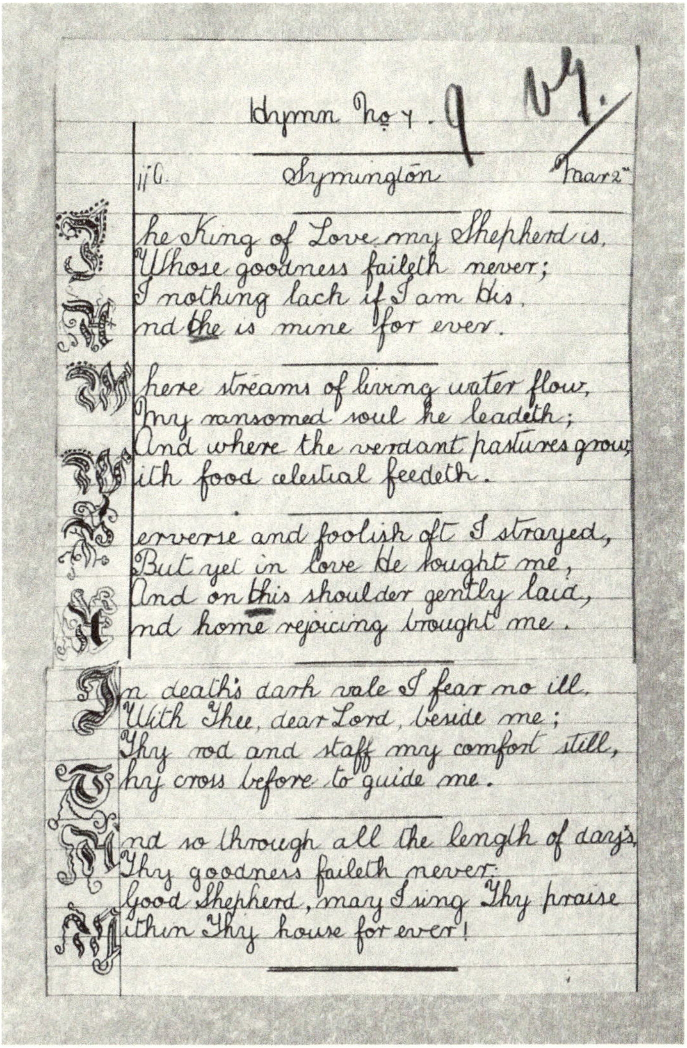
Hymn No. 7. 9 VG.

1/6. Symington Mar 2nd

The King of Love my Shepherd is,
Whose goodness faileth never;
I nothing lack if I am His,
And He is mine for ever.

Where streams of living water flow,
My ransomed soul he leadeth;
And where the verdant pastures grow,
With food celestial feedeth.

Perverse and foolish oft I strayed,
But yet in love He sought me,
And on His shoulder gently laid,
And home rejoicing brought me.

In death's dark vale I fear no ill,
With Thee, dear Lord, beside me;
Thy rod and staff my comfort still,
Thy cross before to guide me.

And so through all the length of days,
Thy goodness faileth never:
Good Shepherd, may I sing Thy praise
Within Thy house for ever!

The King of Love My Shepherd Is

I found this gem amongst all the treasures in the old oak family chest. Unfortunately I do not know my father's age when he copied out this hymn. But what beautiful handwriting, so carefully done. I can feel how hard he was trying, no doubt in the hope of satisfying the critical eye of his teacher

Acknowledgements

I have valued the support of my family and of so many very special friends who encouraged me to keep going when I was in doubt.

The enthusiastic team in the Media Department of the Isle of Wight College, led by Louise Downer, put their heads together and came up with ideas for the layout. My particular thanks to Karen Smithies, who patiently assisted me with the initial typing, Mandy Meadows for her help with the layout and Chloe House for her design for the front cover.

To Ros Whistance who so wisely advised me not to touch anything technical that might stress me out and who kindly put me in touch with Brian David who has skillfully edited my manuscript. To Paul Clark, such a brilliant teacher who came to the rescue on so many occasions when I was floundering around not understanding the vagaries of my lap top. To David and Ros Whistance who magically appeared out of the blue and finally pulled the whole book into shape. Their familiarity with the InDesign programme and calm approach as they navigated their way through the Amazon jungle was just what I needed.

To Hunter Davies who sowed the seed of the idea that I should tell my story for my grandchildren. I had never contemplated writing an actual book, and without his unwavering patience, inspirational enthusiasm, professional advice, time and generosity of spirit I doubt that I would ever have completed it.

Thank you all from the bottom of my heart.

I have published this book myself, making it as professional as possible, with the help of some dear friends. I knew that at the age of 77 and writing my first book and not having been a celebrity chef, a TV weather girl or having any claims to fame, that there was no chance of a real publisher being interested. So I went ahead and did it on my own.

But after it was finished my friend Hunter sent a couple of chapters – the first, and the one about crossing the Atlantic – to a distinguished publisher, Alan Samson at Penguin Books, to see what he might think.

To my surprise and delight he kindly gave me his comments.

I thought I would like to share them with you.

Nothing came of it, as sales and marketing could not see the audience for the memoirs of an elderly unknown woman, but I was pleased to read his reactions. It made me feel I had not been totally wasting my time. I did have a tale to tell. And now you have read it. And I hope enjoyed it.

Thanks, Miranda

Dear Hunter

Miranda is a natural writer. The introductory chapter, recounting the different ways people decorate their lavatories, draws in the reader with its warm, humorous and self-deprecating tone.

The sample Chapter 18 ('Starry, starry night') displays Miranda's keen observational eye. I liked the notion of an immersive voyage experience being created in a spare room, Huku Ulu wobble-board and all, since it is the closest that I shall get to an ocean-going voyage myself.

It is a staggering achievement, navigating those 3,032 miles at an estimated rate of 135 miles per day. The 4-hour watches; the doldrums and horse latitudes where the boat is motionless; the squally weather when there are 850 miles to go; the perils of a super-tanker looming nearby. No wonder the mood-swings match those of the changing weather. Miranda vividly describes all of this, and I greatly admire her eye for detail – her descriptions of the tuna, the sea slug and the mysterious remora fish are very good.

I also like the human element she captures – the depressed crew they encounter who have also departed from Las Palmas with their inappropriate catamaran design, the pleasure at picking up local radio stations as they come to the end of their voyage, and the welcoming and incredulous French families when Miranda and John finally reach land in the Caribbean. In this chapter we get no real sense of John himself, but I presume that this is covered in one or two of the previous chapters.

It is excellent material. At our weekly Acquisitions Meeting, one question is going to be: 'What is Miranda's platform? Many successful writers avoid social media, but it will be the first question that is asked of any new one.

Let me think further on how best to help the book secure publication, which is what it manifestly deserves.

All best wishes

Alan

Alan Samson
Publisher, Non-Fiction
Penguin Michael Joseph

Made in United States
North Haven, CT
29 August 2024

56701472R00243